Apprenticeship Companion

Learning and Development Practitioner Level 3:

Tim Webb
PGCE, FBII, FInstLM

The Choir Press

Titles in the Apprenticeship Companion series

Level 3: Business Administrator
Level 3: Customer Service Specialist
Level 3: Team Leader/Supervisor
Level 5: Operations / Departmental Manager
Learning and Development Practitioner Level 3

First published in the United Kingdom in 2023 by
The Choir Press

ISBN 978-1-78963-391-7

For Freya

Foreword

Having already written a number books, you might think the endless hours of writing, researching and proof reading would deter any attempt to repeat the process. Given that this is now the fifth book in the Companion series, that clearly hasn't happened! This time the challenge has been a little easier. The benefit of 20:20 hindsight and a great deal of the research done previously, whilst it has been no walk in the park, it has certainly been very rewarding!

The time, effort and endeavour spent working in the early morning and late at night, will all be worth it, if just one of today's Learning and Development Practitioners finds it a beneficial and effective support resource as they complete their studies and carry out their work.

I have taken the materials and resources I have used and developed over the years I have taught and recompiled it into a format which, I hope, will be of benefit to all who have the stamina to wade through the detail it contains. I have tried hard to steer clear of the traditional, drab, textbook style and have striven to lighten what can be a rather mundane subject being so entrenched in theory.

It is no coincidence the book follows the Standard for the Level 3 Learning and Development Practitioner Apprenticeship and has been designed to provide the reader with support through each module of the programme.

I hope that everyone who delves into this document finds something of interest and reward, and for those who use it to support their efforts to develop themselves and their career, I wish you every success.

Remember – you only get out, what you put in!

Contents

Chapter 1: Personal and Professional Development

Personal and Professional Development

There was a time when personal and professional development was provided and managed by the employer. You went on a few courses chosen by your employer, said yes when you were offered the chance to take on a new project and waited until the time was right to move up, or move on. But it is not like that anymore.

These days, **you** are responsible for your personal and professional development and **you** need to identify and look for your own opportunities. In order to achieve this, you need to know what needs to be changed and what needs to be developed. The only way to do this is to take a deep and thorough look at yourself, not just at work, but personally too. How can you manage and direct others if you do not have knowledge of your own weaknesses and inadequacies?

Professional Development

Can be defined as:

> *"the process of improving and increasing the skills and capabilities of employees by providing education and training or through watching others perform the job."*

Professional Development is focused on gaining new capabilities and experience and improving the knowledge and skills that improve potential in the work environment. These skills make staff more efficient and effective at their job. It is also suggested that it helps build and maintain the morale of employees and is thought to attract higher quality staff to an organisation.

> *"professional development is either related to a current role or a role you want to do in the future"*

With changes happening in our working lives every day, it is important to develop one's skillset to remain effective in a career.

For professional development to be truly effective, the knowledge and understanding of the subject area must always be at the highest possible level. The acquisition of such skills and knowledge is primarily for career advancement, however, it inevitably includes an element of personal development as well.

Broadly speaking, it may include formal types of vocational education or training that leads to a career related qualification. It may also include more informal training and development, which may be delivered whilst working on the job in order to develop and enhance professional skills.

Some examples of professional development are:

- *IT training*
- *Health and Safety*
- *Accountancy or budgeting*
- *Legal knowledge or expertise*

Benefits of Professional Development

Investing in employees is beneficial to the whole organisation and can boost the bottom line. Listed below are some of the organisational benefits which can be expected because of effective professional development training initiatives:

Increase the collective knowledge of the team.

Encouraging employees to train in relevant subjects and applications — an advanced course in a software package they use daily, can have an immediate effect on productivity. Professional development can also help raise overall staff expertise when employees with vastly different backgrounds and levels of experience are required to work together such as on projects.

Boost employees' job satisfaction

When employees can do their jobs more effectively, they become more confident. This leads to greater job satisfaction and improved employee retention. There are countless professional development and training options available, including mentorships, job shadowing and cross training.

Make the organisation more appealing.

When providing training and development opportunities, it builds a positive reputation as an employer that cares about its workforce and wants to employ only the best. Customers and clients will benefit too, from the high level of efficient service they receive. Employees are your brand ambassadors. When they attend conferences and seminars, they represent and reflect all that is good about the organisation.

Attract the right kind of job applicants

Organisations want to attract the most highly driven and career-focused candidates when they advertise a job. By offering them an enticing picture of how they can grow professionally or expand the career avenues available to them if they come to work for you is an attractive add on to an attractive salary.

Helps retain staff

Employees need to feel they are appreciated and making a difference. But they also want to feel like they are developing expertise and becoming more well-rounded. If employees do not feel challenged, or they sense their careers have stalled, they will look for opportunities elsewhere.

Lifelong learning exposes employees to new experiences and stimulates motivation and improves engagement in work. Professional development not only helps to build and maintain motivation, but it also develops loyalty.

Make succession planning easier.
Professional development programs are tools for developing future leaders for the organisation. The ability to promote existing staff to managerial positions in the future using targeted training now, can help ensure the best and brightest are readied to move up.

Personal Development

"the process of self-improvement through activities such as developing employment skills, increasing consciousness and building wealth."

Personal development is about improving talents and potential, both in and out of the workplace.

Personal development sits alongside professional growth —to progress in a career, personal; development will be needed first. It helps with handling fears, taking on more responsibility, and succeeding with greater challenges.

Personal Development requires broadening of knowledge, improvement and development of skills and develop and refinement of behaviours to ensure performance with the utmost professionalism.

You may have experienced something like this:

There are two people in a team, both of whom are skilled at managing budgets. They are both accurate, detail-oriented and deliver the results needed. One of them is a real people person, their interpersonal and communication skills are fantastic and they have no problem getting the information they require quickly from colleagues at any level. The other person does not have this skill and often encounters conflict with other colleagues.

Which of these people needs personal development?

Both can do their jobs. Both have the skills required on a professional level to deliver results, however, with the benefit of excellent relationship building skills one of them will always be one step ahead.

Some examples of personal development are:

- *Leadership training*
- *Management training*
- *Time management*
- *Handling difficult situations and conflict management*
- *Communication skills*

Personal development relates to life skills. These are what is needed to achieve life goals. It focuses on helping to improve talents, whether they are related to work or not.

Personal and professional development courses can improve motivation and help to develop excellence in your domain.

Benefits of Personal Development

Personal development offers many different benefits.

- *Boosting self-awareness*
- *Increasing self-knowledge*
- *Developing your existing skills or learning new ones*
- *Renewing or building your self-esteem or identity*
- *Developing pre-existing talents or strengths*
- *Enhancing your employability*
- *Improve the quality of your life.*
- *Positively affecting your social status and wealth*

All these activities can help make a major difference in life. When feeling helpless, these are skill sets which can help turn the odds in your favour. By focusing on personal development, it ensures the right skill sets are available.

The difference between Personal and Professional Development

It is clear from the definition that professional development relates to enhancing the workforce and/or an individual within that workforce. The objectives will usually be specific to the organisation and its goals at a specific time and the skills that would be required to deliver the products/services.

The definition of personal development suggests it is used when individuals, seek to update their own knowledge and learn skills that they would like to have. This means the activities are more unique to the individual and their personal objectives.

Personal and Professional Development

When contrasting personal development against professional development, it is easier to see that there is a connection rather than trying to identify differences.

Both professional and personal development are similar in that they both represent a drive towards improvement, greater understanding and increased effectivity (either an individual or a group).

Both require effort, time and resources (often money) to get involved in and both regularly reoccur for all individuals and not just professionals.

Whilst personal development might seem to be separate from the professional life, it could be a great way to achieve career objectives. It is not just what is learnt that could help at work; making a commitment to personal development clear to an employer, will demonstrate dedication and the ability to learn and grow.

The key to managing personal development is knowing one's strengths and areas for improvement. Knowing these can help you to develop your weaknesses and turn them into strengths.

Finally, neither Personal nor Professional development can be completed satisfactorily without a depth of self-awareness which is far greater than that currently held. Only by developing a thorough understanding of what is needed and how to achieve it, can the skills be developed to achieve the goal.

Activities suitable for Personal and Professional Development

Personal Development	*Professional Development*
Emotional Wellbeing	*Management Training*
Health and fitness	*Skill-based training*
Communication	*Internal Assessment*
Motivation	*Conflict Resolution*
Spirituality	*Online Education*
Self-belief	*Networking*
Journaling	*Research*

Personal development makes a difference in life on a daily basis. At almost every stage of life, something new will be learnt which will help development as a person.

Key Stages in Development Planning

There are several stages to go through to plan personal and professional development. These can be defined as:

- ***analyse current skills, knowledge and experience*** – *to identify skills gaps and where we are now.*
- ***identify development needs and set objectives*** – *to focus on where we need to be.*
- ***identify learning styles.***
- ***arrange resources and support mechanisms to meet the objectives*** – *the basis of how we are going to achieve our goals.*
- ***monitor and review progress and overcome barriers to learning*** – *to make sure we are still going the right way.*

At the heart of the process, there are three questions:

Where am I now?
To answer this question, we need to have a look at our current, personal, situation – e.g., our skills, knowledge and experience; qualifications; job description and tasks; salary package; grade or position at work.

Where do I want or need to be?
Where we would like to be in the future. This can be six months ahead, a year, five years or a period that fits into our future plans. We need to consider our goals, the things we want or need to achieve – e.g., a higher salary; promotion; increased knowledge and skills in specific areas at work; greater job satisfaction; improved job security; improve employability prospects.

How will I get there?
The route achieving this is what will be recorded in our Personal Development plan. We need to identify the steps we need to take to begin to work towards our goals.

This may include qualifications, a career review, do voluntary work to gain specific experience, ask to broaden experience within current work role, shadow colleagues to learn from them, consider the best learning options for you personally.

Remember! This is about focussing on your personal goals and set targets that are specific to you and your needs.

Self-Awareness

Where are we now?

The first step in the process of planning both personal and professional development is to know where we are now. This is known as self-awareness.

Self-awareness is the ability to recognise our own emotions and the effect they may have on us and others. Without being aware of, and understanding, our own behaviour and emotions, it will be difficult for us to plan development successfully.

Self-awareness is the conscious knowledge of ourselves – our character, desires, beliefs, qualities, motives and feelings. Having a good sense of these aspects of ourselves can help us in the workplace, and in our private lives.

We can assess our personal growth and understanding through self-awareness by, for example:

- *being aware of how people and things around us influence us*
- *learning about how we can influence and interact with others*

Developing self-awareness, and understanding our own psychology, is a skill that is part of our personal and professional development. Self-awareness can be applied in our working lives to help us to, for example:

- *understand emotions more clearly* – *ours and other people's*
- *improve our communication skills* – *and interact with others in the workplace and resolve conflict more effectively*
- *improve leadership skills* – *and our general operational performance*
- *improve job satisfaction* – *by focusing on job roles and tasks that truly motivate us*
- *maximise career development opportunities*

When you look in a mirror – what do you see? Do you see the person you are? The person you want to be or the person you think other people see?

The very first step on the road to self-development is to recognise that the image we see is simply a reflection of the packaging we come in! That packaging is about as relevant as the cardboard box your breakfast cereals are delivered in!! – You do not eat the box – it is what is inside the box that matters!!

We seldom look inside the packaging because we are afraid of what we might find, but without absolute honesty, you will never recognise what is really inside.

We are disinclined to spend time on self-reflection. Even when personal feedback is presented to us, we are not always open to it, because honest feedback is not always flattering.

Self-awareness is being aware of oneself including one's traits, feelings and behaviours.

As we grow up, we base many of our actions, responses and attitudes on things that we have learned and been told along the way. We might base our initial education and career choices on what our family members did. However, these choices might not suit our real desires, beliefs or character, and we need to develop our self-awareness to discover more options.

It is quite difficult today to even find time to think about who we are, what our strengths and weaknesses are, our personalities, our habits and values. Consequently, many of us have a low level of self-awareness. Despite this, developing self-awareness is an essential first step toward maximising management skills. It can improve judgment and help identify opportunities for professional development and personal growth.

Self-awareness is also associated with soft skills – There are thought to be five elements to this – Personality, Values, Habits, Needs and Emotions.

These are considered below:

Personality: *– Personalities cannot be changed, but values and needs are based on what we learn about ourselves. Understanding our own personality can help us find in what environment we can be successful. Awareness of our personality helps us analyse such a decision.*

Values: *– It is important that we know and focus on our personal values. When we focus on our values, we are more likely to accomplish what we consider most important.*

Habits: *– Our habits are the behaviours that we repeat daily and often automatically. Although we would like to possess the habits that help us interact effectively with and manage others, we can probably all identify at least one of our habits that decrease our effectiveness.*

Needs: *– Maslow and other scholars have identified a variety of psychological needs that drive our behaviours such as needs for esteem, affection, belonging, achievement, self-actualisation, power and control.*

Emotions: *–Understanding your own feelings, what causes them, and how they impact our thoughts and actions is emotional self-awareness. Persons with high emotional self-awareness understand the internal process associated with emotional experiences and, therefore, has greater control over them*

The first step on the road to personal development, is to take a long hard look at ourselves and be brutally honest about our true targets and expectations in life.

If you cannot be totally honest with yourself – you will never be honest with anyone.

There are many tests and techniques available that help us to identify and understand ourselves in greater depth. They look at our character, qualities, motivation, feelings and so on, so that we can access information about ourselves that is often hidden or undiscovered.

Self-Reflection

Self-reflection facilitates the development of skills and reviews their effectiveness. It is about challenging in a positive way, what one does, why it is done and how it is done. It is then straightforward to assess whether there is a better, or more efficient, way of doing it if repeated in the future.

In any role, whether at home or at work, reflection is an important part of learning. You would not use a recipe a second time around if the dish did not work the first time. You would either adjust the recipe or find a new and, hopefully, better one. When we do our job, we can become stuck in a routine that may not be working effectively. Thinking about your own skills can help you identify changes you might need to make.

Reflective questions to ask yourself:

Strengths – *What are my strengths? For example, am I well organised? Do I remember things?*
Weaknesses – *What are my weaknesses? For example, am I easily distracted? Do I need more practise with a particular skill?*
Skills – *What skills do I have and what am I good at?*
Problems – *What problems are there at work/home that may affect me? For example, responsibilities or distractions that may impact on study or work.*
Achievements – *What have I achieved?*
Happiness – *Are there things I am unhappy with or disappointed about? What makes me happy?*
Solutions – *What could I do to improve in these areas?*

Although self-reflection can seem difficult at first, or even selfish or embarrassing, as it does not come naturally, you will find it becomes easier with practise and the end result could be a happier and more efficient you.

Self-Reflection tools

Self-reflection is often used as a management or coaching tool and the process focuses strongly on self-awareness.

Keeping a journal can be a useful tool. Going through the process of writing down our thoughts, experiences and feelings on a regular basis can help us to understand more about ourselves, especially when we review entries at a later date.

Listening to our inner voice can reveal things that we may not have realised previously. Just writing down some of the thoughts as they pass through our mind can be revealing, then reviewing them once a week can add to our self-awareness.

Practising mindfulness helps us to be aware of things going on in our minds, concentrate on the moment and allow unnecessary thoughts to pass through. There are many resources online, some of which are free, that help us to understand and train the mind, to improve concentration and aid stress management.

Psychometric tests

There are many psychometric tests available and it is easy to find them online. They are designed to show someone's personality, mental ability, opinions, strengths, weaknesses and preferences.

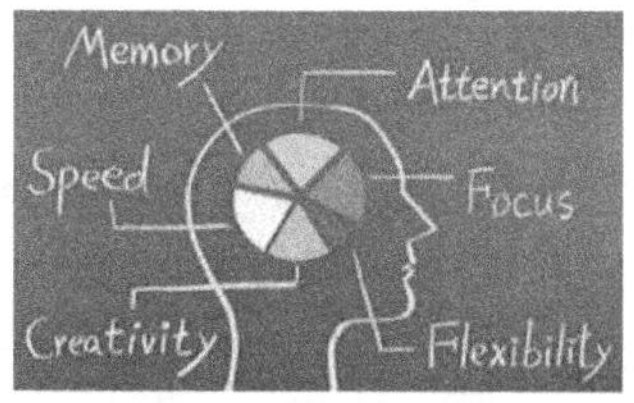

They are often used by employers, or prospective employers, to see how an individual's own mix of natural skills and attributes will fit into what the organisation wants.

They can be used as a recruitment selection tool by employers, but they are also useful when developing self-awareness skills. They help to unmask our hidden qualities and habits and focus on our natural abilities and preferences.

Types of Psychometric Testing

There are two main types: personality tests and aptitude tests.

> ***Personality tests*** *explore your interests, values and motivations, analysing how your character fits with the role and organisation. They analyse your emotions, behaviours and relationships in a variety of situations.*
>
> ***Aptitude tests*** *assess your reasoning or cognitive ability, determining whether you have got the right skillset for a role. Usually administered under exam conditions, you will often be given one minute to answer each multiple-choice question. Your intelligence levels are compared to a standard, meaning that you must achieve a certain score to pass.*

Myers-Briggs Type Indicator

Have you ever heard someone describe themselves as an INTJ or an ESTP and wondered what those cryptic-sounding letters could mean? What these people are referring to is their personality type based on the Myers-Briggs Type Indicator (MBTI).

The Myers-Briggs Personality Type Indicator is a self-assessment questionnaire designed to identify a personality type, strengths, and preferences. The questionnaire was developed by Isabel Myers and her mother Katherine Briggs based on their work with Carl Jung's theory of personality types. Today, the MBTI inventory is one of the most widely used psychological instruments in the world.

Based on the answers in the questionnaire, people are identified as having one of 16 personality types. The goal of the MBTI is to allow people to further explore and understand their own personalities including their likes, dislikes, strengths, weaknesses, possible career preferences, and compatibility with other people.

When answering the questions, the outcomes are not easy to predict and we end up with an in-depth and revealing description of our personality.

No one personality type is "best" or "better" than another. It is not a tool designed to look for dysfunction or abnormality. Instead, its goal is simply to help you learn more about yourself. The questionnaire itself is made up of four different scales which create the 16 personality types.

Extraversion (E) – Introversion (I)

The extraversion-introversion dichotomy was first explored by Jung in his theory of personality to describe how people respond and interact with the world around them. While these terms are familiar to most people, the way in which they are used in the MBTI differs somewhat from their popular usage.

Extraverts are "outward-turning" and tend to be action-oriented, enjoy more frequent social interaction, and feel energised after spending time with other people. Introverts are "inward-turning" and tend to be thought-oriented, enjoy deep and meaningful social interactions, and feel recharged after spending time alone.

Everyone exhibits extraversion and introversion to some degree, but most tend to have an overall preference for one or the other.

Sensing (S) – Intuition (N)

This scale involves looking at how people gather information from the world around them. Just like with extraversion and introversion, all people spend some time sensing and intuiting depending on the situation. According to the MBTI, people tend to be dominant in one area or the other.

People who prefer sensing tend to pay a great deal of attention to reality, particularly to what they can learn from their own senses. They tend to focus on facts and details and enjoy getting hands-on experience. Those who prefer intuition pay more attention to things like patterns and impressions. They enjoy thinking about possibilities, imagining the future, and abstract theories.

Thinking (T) – Feeling (F)

This scale focuses on how people make decisions based on the information that they gathered from their sensing or intuition functions. People who prefer thinking place a greater emphasis on facts and objective data.

They tend to be consistent, logical, and impersonal when weighing a decision. Those who prefer feeling are more likely to consider people and emotions when arriving at a conclusion.

Judging (J) – Perceiving (P)

The final scale involves how people tend to deal with the outside world. Those who lean toward judging prefer structure and firm decisions. People who lean toward perceiving are more open, flexible, and adaptable. These two tendencies interact with the other scales.

Remember, all people at least spend some time extroverting. The judging-perceiving scale helps describe whether you extravert when you are taking in new information (sensing and intuiting) or when you are making decisions (thinking and feeling).

The MBTI Types

Depending on where you are on the scale will depend on which letter you are assigned in each category, to create the four-digit code. The resulting personality type can then be checked by the code formed.

Code		*Personality Type*
ISTJ	=	*The Inspector*
ISTP	=	*The Crafter*
ISFJ	=	*The Protector*
ISFP	=	*The Artist*
INFJ	=	*The Advocate*
INFP	=	*The Mediator*
INTJ	=	*The Architect*
INTP	=	*The Thinker*
ESTP	=	*The Persuader*
ESTJ	=	*The Director*
ESFP	=	*The Performer*
ESFJ	=	*The Caregiver*
ENFP	=	*The Champion*
ENFJ	=	*The Giver*
ENTP	=	*The Debater*
ENTJ	=	*The Commander*

The characteristics for each personality type are substantial and there is no reason to include them here. The test can be completed online, and the results will be presented after the test for the personality type identified.

How MBTI differs from other personality tests

First, the MBTI is not really a "test." There are no right or wrong answers, and one type is not better than any other type. The purpose of the indicator is not to evaluate mental health or offer any type of diagnosis.

Unlike many other types of psychological evaluation, the results are not compared against any norms. Instead of looking at a score in comparison to the results of other people, the goal of the instrument is to simply offer further information about your own unique personality.

While there are many versions of the MBTI available online, it should be noted that any of the informal questionnaires that you may find on the Internet are only approximations of the real thing.

The real MBTI must be administered by a trained and qualified practitioner that includes a follow-up of the results.

The current version of the Myers-Briggs Type Indicator includes 93 forced-choice questions in the North American version and 88 forced-choice questions in the European version. For each question, there are two different options from which the respondent must choose.

The 4 C's of Mental Toughness - Lyons (2015)

Mental Toughness is a personality trait that improves performance and wellbeing meaning that you are more likely to be successful in your personal and professional life.

Mental Toughness is defined as Resilience - the ability to bounce back from setbacks and failures- and Confidence -the ability to spot and seize opportunities. Mentally tough people are more outcome focused and better at making things happen without being distracted by their own or other peoples' emotions.

Mental Toughness can be measured using the MTQ48 psychometric tool, which was constructed by Professor Peter Clough of Manchester Metropolitan University.

It is scientifically valid and reliable and based on a 4C's framework, which measures key components of mental toughness - Control, Commitment, Challenge and Confidence.

Control

Control is your self-esteem - your life's purpose and your sense of control over your life and emotions.

Control is the extent to which you feel you are in control of your life and that you can make a difference and change things.

If you are high on Control, you have a good sense of who you are and what you stand for and are "comfortable in your own skin." You are also better able to control your emotions meaning you can keep your anxieties in check and are less likely to be distracted by the emotions of others or reveal your emotional state to other people.

Alternatively, if you are at the other end of the scale –and low on control –you will feel that events happen to you and are outside your personal control or influence.

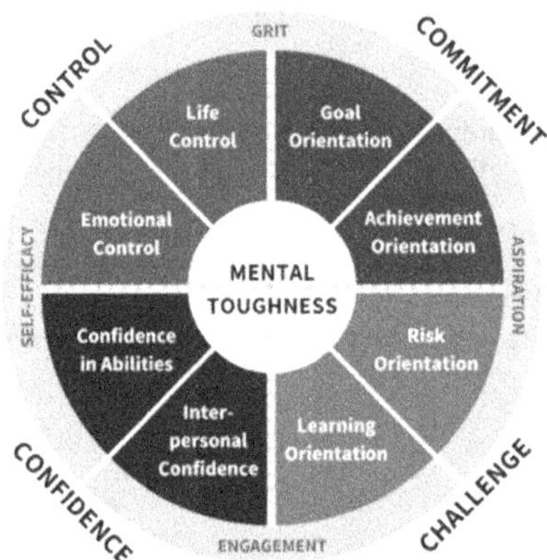

Commitment

Commitment is your focus and reliability and being high on commitment means that you can effectively set goals and targets and reliably and consistently achieve them without being distracted. You are strong at establishing routines and habits that enable you to be successful.

Alternatively, if you are at the other end of the scale – and low on commitment – you will sometimes fail or find it difficult to set goals and targets and then prioritise them. You may also find it difficult to focus and be easily distracted by other people and competing priorities. You rarely adopt routines or habits to make you successful.

The Control and Commitment scales together represent the Resilience part of the Mental Toughness definition, namely the ability to bounce back from setbacks and opportunities. This intuitively, as well as scientifically, makes sense because if you face a setback or failure your momentum slows or stops altogether, and you naturally question yourself and revisit your self-identity.

You then need to re-affirm and reassess who you are and then develop some momentum to enable you to bounce back. You can do this by setting and achieving a series of goals and targets, often small and simple at first, to rebuild your confidence and return to your chosen path.

Challenge

Challenge is your drive and adaptability and being high on challenge means that you are driven to be as good as you can be and to achieve your personal best. You see challenges, change, adversity and variety as opportunities rather than threats. You are likely to be adaptable and agile.

Alternatively, if you are at the other end of the scale –and low on challenge –you view change as a threat and so avoid new and challenging situations for fear of failure or wishing not to expend what you perceive will be a wasted effort.

Confidence

Confidence is your self-belief and influence and describes to what extent you believe you can perform productively and proficiently and the ability to influence others.

Being high on confidence means that you have the self-belief to successfully complete on tasks that other individuals with similar ability, but lower confidence would think beyond them. In practice if you are high on Confidence, you will take setbacks, whether internally or externally generated, in your stride. You will keep your head, maintain your routine and often stiffen your resolve.

However, if you are low on confidence, you can easily be unsettled by the setback and feel undermined. Your head could drop. Your internal voice's positive commentary is vital here to counteract this loss of confidence and negativity.

The Challenge and Confidence scales together represent the Confidence part of the Mental Toughness definition, namely your ability to spot and seize an opportunity. This intuitively, as well as scientifically, makes sense because if you are a risk taker you see more situations more clearly as opportunities and are willing to embrace and explore them. If you are confident in your abilities and you easily engage with others, you are also much more likely to convert the potential opportunity of these situations into successful outcomes.

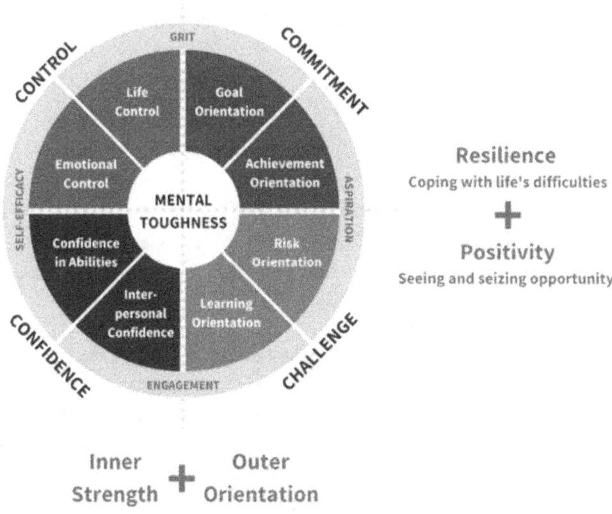

Measuring mental toughness

The MTQ48 is both popular and versatile used globally across all sectors and in culture, leadership organisational change career transition and stress management situations. It is an ideal measure for those professionals who enjoy and endure high stress public facing roles, comprising uncertainty, pace and rapidly changing priorities. It gives them a profile which they can use as a starting point to reflect and then work on developing their mental toughness using a toolbox of traditional interventions such as visualisation, positive thinking and attentional control and others.

Management Tools

Many of the tools that we use in management can be useful to use when developing self-awareness. For example, we can learn from:

- ***formal feedback from others*** – *e.g., formal reviews with a line manager*
- ***informal feedback*** – *e.g., passing comments from colleagues or customers*
- ***360-degree appraisals*** – *e.g., a formal review that takes comments from senior managers, customer and colleagues*
- ***learning activities*** – *e.g., courses on management or career development*
- ***development activities*** – *e.g., working in a different department or role; taking on voluntary work*
- ***attending counselling or mentoring sessions*** – *e.g., to focus on personal development*

By finding out about how others view us, in a professional and controlled way, we can learn more about ourselves and the impacts we have on other people.

Feedback Mechanisms

We all need feedback to find out how well we are doing, which is a very important element when developing self-awareness. When feedback is good, it gives us positive reinforcement and gives us the confidence to carry on and develop our strengths further. The negative aspects of feedback are just as useful, if not even more valuable, because they show us where we need to make changes.

When working to improve performance, feedback needs to be collected over time to allow time for objectives to be achieved or to take effect. If the period is too short, there may not be enough data available to be able to measure progress. If too long, energy and motivation to achieve objectives may decrease, and opportunities to improve may be missed.

If we do not give and receive feedback, we have no way of knowing how we are doing from an objective point of view. Our efforts need to be measured against outside standards and opinions to reflect a realistic, three-dimensional picture of our performance in the workplace.

Different feedback mechanisms

We all like to feel valued and that our opinions matter. We cannot force people to give us feedback, although we can make sure that we pursue our organisation's policies and procedures for giving and receiving feedback. As managers going through a process of developing self-awareness, we can actively seek out feedback from useful sources that will help us review our progress.

Understanding different feedback mechanisms helps to give insight into:

- *how to maximise the effectiveness of feedback we receive*
- *how to give effective feedback to others – particularly team members*

When giving feedback it is important to consider the person receiving the feedback. If the feedback is positive, it is a good opportunity to give praise and encouragement. This empowers and motivates the team member to continue doing well and not lose focus. They feel valued and respected and will benefit from feeling appreciated and recognised.

When we are asked to give feedback about someone else, it can be a good idea to only say things that we would say to that person's face. This helps us to keep our comments objective, fair, valid and useful.

When delivered tactfully, constructive criticism and genuine praise are both valuable and welcome.

There are many different mechanisms for giving feedback, including, for example:

Formal reviews

These provide valuable, organised and focused opportunities for the individual to have detailed conversations with their line manager. Formal reviews usually start with a performance appraisal form that shows objectives, comments and maybe a rating system. The form is then discussed during a meeting when the individual and their line manager can:

- *give and receive feedback*
- *review progress so far*
- *discuss current strengths and issues*
- *set goals and targets for the next stage*

Informal feedback during work activities
Informal feedback can be given at any time – e.g., on completion of a project, at the end of a shift, or when something good or bad happens at work. Opportunities to give informal feedback are usually unplanned and can just be a quick chat, a passing comment, or a spontaneous note or email.

Feedback from peers
Individuals can ask their peers to give them feedback. It can be useful to have feedback from people we work with who can, for example:

- *understand the work environment and requirements*
- *understand how to do the tasks being discussed*
- *give valuable and appropriate information that can be used to make future improvements*

Formal feedback from customers, suppliers or other stakeholders
This can occur when an organisation asks customers, suppliers or other people outside the organisation to give feedback. The information is usually collected on questionnaires, forms or in surveys.

Informal feedback from customers, suppliers or other stakeholders
Customers, suppliers and other people outside the organisation can decide to give spontaneous, informal feedback, verbally or in writing. This could be praise from a customer after a meal, or complaints from a supplier about late payments.

Sandwich technique for delivering negative points

If some of the feedback is negative, this needs to be delivered carefully and objectively. The best way can be to use a sandwich technique, where negative news is put between two bits of positive news, for example:

- *praise the individual for a good aspect of their performance*
- *mention and explain areas that need to be improved, and give guidance and support about how to improve*
- *finish on a high note about positive aspects, plans and hopes for future developments and improvements*

360-Degree Feedback

You will have identified some aspects of your performance, impact and behaviour which have been identified through your self-evaluation which you might wish to gather feedback about.

Add a small number of other elements specific to your role and context to ensure the feedback is relevant and sufficiently comprehensive. Then consider your main stakeholders, internally and externally. What 3-5 things about you and your performance have the most critical impact on meeting their needs?

Some organisations use a 360-degree model for formal appraisal, where performance feedback is given from a full circle of people at work – senior managers, line managers, colleagues, team members, customers and the person being appraised.

The idea is to give a rounded view of performance from many angles that gives more valuable and detailed feedback than might be gained from just one-line manager. It considers the importance of a wider circle of work relationships.

This mechanism is particularly useful when evaluating skills, experience and knowledge connected with self-awareness. To maximise its effectiveness, it can be beneficial to compare self-appraisal with comments from other people to gain a more objective view.

By gathering feedback from different sources, as happens in the 360-degree appraisal, it can:

- ***provide access to a three-dimensional picture of ourselves from other people's perspectives***
- ***give access to reliable feedback from certain sources*** *–gaining useful, valid insight and information*
- ***see how some feedback is unreliable*** *– and should not be taken too seriously or personally*

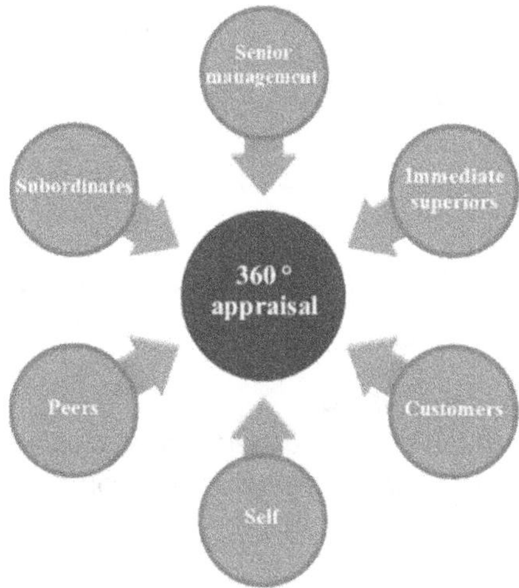

Gathering feedback

Feedback should be gathered from the right sources. It needs to come from those who have a valid opinion because they know you and are affected by your work and because they are an unbiased source. The feedback will not help if it is vague, distorted or misleading. Compile a list of people who are potential sources of feedback and seek their agreement to participating. Ensure the list of those who agree gives sufficiently comprehensive coverage and is representative of all 360°. If not, find some others.

Analyse the feedback to identify trends, contradictions and clues for your future development. Remember that the perceptions of others are their 'truth.' Whether you agree is irrelevant; this is what they see and how they feel, so take it seriously.

What is the feedback telling you about your behaviour, attitude, approach, impact and performance? What does it say about your style as a leader and manager?

To further underpin your analysis of the latter you may wish to research and consider theories on leadership practice e.g., Adair's 'Action Centred Leadership, McGregor's Theory X & Y as well team theories such as Belbin's 'Team Roles.'

There are many sources of feedback and it can be collected from, for example:

- ***line managers*** – *e.g., in formal appraisals or informal chats*
- ***customers*** – *e.g., in surveys, comments or complaints*
- ***team members and other colleagues*** – *e.g., during appraisals or informal discussions*
- ***training providers*** – *e.g., in reports and debriefing sessions after completing a unit of a training course or following an observation session*
- ***coaches and mentors*** – *e.g., as part of a question-and-answer session after a learning activity or discussion*

It is important to look at the feedback in detail and be objective about the comments. Some feedback will be reliable, useful and easily interpreted. For example, structured and informed feedback from a line manager, coach or training provider will be valuable as they have the skills to give useful and constructive criticism.

Good Quality Feedback

Good-quality feedback is likely to be based on good knowledge about, for example:

- *the individual*
- *the workplace environment*
- *observations of the situation and task being reviewed*
- *the organisation's standards and requirements*

This means that the results can be interpreted as being valid and truthful. This gives the individual an honest view of themselves and they can:

- ***be positive about the feedback*** *– positive feedback is great for confidence and morale, and negative feedback is useful*
- ***learn from the issues that need to be improved*** *– and appreciate the opportunity to learn something about their performance they might not have seen before*
- ***enjoy and accept praise***
- ***take confidence from positive comments*** *– they are a guide that things are going well and need to continue to the same high standard*

Poor quality feedback

Some feedback is not reliable, however, due to the inexperience of some of those taking part. There may be emotional and over-critical comments from some people due to personal reasons, which may not be honest, valid or useful. For example, customers sometimes leave feedback that is biased, emotional and subjective. When this happens, it is important to interpret the feedback in context, check facts very carefully and look for useful and valid information that can be used as a guide for improving performance.

By gathering feedback from different sources, as happens in the 360-degree appraisal, we can:

- ***have access to a three-dimensional picture of ourselves from other people's perspectives***
- ***have access to reliable feedback from certain sources*** *– so that we can gain useful and valid insight and information*
- ***see how some feedback is unreliable*** *– and should not be taken too seriously or personally*

Coaching tools

Johari Window

The Johari Window is another tool that can be used to coach the development of self-awareness. It was designed in 1955 by American psychologists, Ingham and Luft.

The idea is that we examine information about ourselves and enter it into the relevant 'pane of the window.' The exercise of entering details can be revealing in itself, but we can work to change the sizes of the windowpanes as a focus for further analysis and personal development planning.

The Johari Window model is a simple and useful tool for illustrating and improving self-awareness. Today the Johari Window model is especially relevant due to modern emphasis on, and the influence of, 'soft' skills, behaviour, empathy, cooperation, inter-group development and interpersonal development.

The four Johari Window perspectives are called 'regions' or 'areas' or 'quadrants. Each of these regions contains and represents the information - feelings, motivation, etc - known about the person, in terms of whether the information is known or unknown by the person, and whether the information is known or unknown by others.

A simple version of a Johari Window would be as follows:

1. Open/free area	*2. Blind area*
Known by the person *Known by others* *Information about the person – e.g., skills, knowledge, experience, behaviour, attitude, feelings*	*Not known by the person* *Known by others* *Things that others know about the person that they do not know or realise themselves – e.g., issues that are deliberately withheld from the person*
3. Hidden area	***4. Unknown area***
Known by the person *Not known by others* *Information that is withheld from others – e.g., feelings, fears, worries, manipulative intentions, secrets*	*Not known to the person* *Not known by others* *Information that has not been recognised or revealed – e.g., a young person's undiscovered talents and attributes that need to be revealed*

The idea is to enlarge the open/free area by:

- ***reducing the blind area*** – *usually achieved through giving and receiving feedback*
- ***reducing the hidden area*** – *through the process of disclosure*

The four regions, (aka areas, quadrants, or perspectives) are as follows, showing the quadrant numbers and commonly used names:

Quadrant 1 - 'Open self/area' or 'free area' or 'public area', or 'arena'

Region 1 is also known as the 'area of free activity'. This is the information about the person - behaviour, attitude, feelings, emotion, knowledge, experience, skills, views, etc - known by the person.

Established employees logically tend to have larger open areas than new employees. New employees start with relatively small open areas because relatively little knowledge about them is shared. The size of the open area can be expanded horizontally into the blind space, by seeking and actively listening to feedback from other employees This process is known as 'feedback solicitation'. Also, other employees can help a new employee expand their open area by offering feedback, sensitively of course.

The size of the open area can also be expanded vertically downwards into the hidden or avoided space by the person's disclosure of information, feelings, etc about him/herself to others. Also, colleagues can help a person expand their open area into the hidden area by asking the person about him/herself.

Managers and team leaders can play an important role in facilitating feedback and disclosure amongst employees, and in directly giving feedback to individuals about their own blind areas. Leaders also have a big responsibility to promote a culture and expectation for open, honest, positive, helpful, constructive, sensitive communications, and the sharing of knowledge throughout their organisation.

Top performing groups, departments, companies and organisations always tend to have a culture of open positive communication, so encouraging the positive development of the 'open area' or 'open self' for everyone is a simple yet fundamental aspect of effective leadership.

Quadrant 2 - 'Blind self' or 'blind area' or 'blind spot'

Region 2 is what is known about a person by others but is unknown by the person him/herself. By seeking or soliciting feedback from others, the aim should be to reduce this area and thereby to increase the open area, i.e., to increase self-awareness. This blind area is not an effective or productive space.

This blind area could also be referred to as ignorance about oneself, or issues in which one is deluded. A blind area could also include issues that others are deliberately withholding from a person. We all know how difficult it is to work well when kept in the dark. No-one works well when subject to 'mushroom management'. People who are 'thick-skinned' tend to have a large 'blind area'.

Colleagues and managers can take some responsibility for helping an individual to reduce their blind area - in turn increasing the open area - by giving sensitive feedback and encouraging disclosure.

Managers should promote a climate of non-judgemental feedback, and colleague response to individual disclosure, which reduces fear and therefore encourages both processes to happen. The extent to which an individual seeks feedback, and the issues on which feedback is sought, must always be at the individual's own discretion.

Some people are more resilient than others - care needs to be taken to avoid causing emotional upset. The process of soliciting serious and deep feedback relates to the process of 'self-actualisation' described in Maslow's Hierarchy of Needs development and motivation model.

Quadrant 3 - 'Hidden self' or 'hidden area' or 'avoided self/area' or 'facade'

Region 3 is what is known to oneself but kept hidden from, and therefore unknown, to others. This hidden or avoided self represents information, feelings, etc, anything that a person knows about him/self, but which is not revealed or is kept hidden from others.

The hidden area could also include sensitivities, fears, hidden agendas, manipulative intentions, secrets - anything that a person knows but does not reveal, for whatever reason. It is natural for very personal and private information and feelings to remain hidden, indeed, certain information, feelings and experiences have no bearing on work, and so can and should remain hidden. However, typically, a lot of hidden information is not very personal, it is work- or performance-related, and so is better positioned in the open area.

Relevant hidden information and feelings, etc, should be moved into the open area through the process of 'disclosure'. The aim should be to disclose and expose relevant information and feelings - hence the Johari Window terminology 'self-disclosure' and 'exposure process', thereby increasing the open area. By telling others how we feel and other information about ourselves we reduce the hidden area, and increase the open area, which enables better understanding, cooperation, trust, team-working effectiveness and productivity. Reducing hidden areas also reduces the potential for confusion, misunderstanding, poor communication, etc, which all distract from and undermine team effectiveness.
Organisational culture and working atmosphere have a major influence on group members' preparedness to disclose their hidden selves. Most people fear judgement or vulnerability and therefore hold back hidden information and feelings, which, if moved into the open area, i.e., known by others as well, would enhance mutual understanding, and thereby improve group awareness, enabling better individual performance and group effectiveness.

The extent to which an individual discloses personal feelings and information, and the issues which are disclosed, and to whom, must always be at the individual's own discretion. Some people are more keen and able than others to disclose. People should disclose at a pace and depth that they find personally comfortable. As with feedback, some people are more resilient than others - care needs to be taken to avoid causing emotional upset. Also, as with soliciting feedback, the process of serious disclosure relates to the process of 'self-actualisation' described in Maslow's Hierarchy of Needs development and motivation model.

Quadrant 4 - 'Unknown self' or 'area of unknown activity' or 'unknown area'
Region 4 contains information, feelings, latent abilities, aptitudes, experiences etc, that are unknown to the person him/herself and unknown to others in the group. These unknown issues take a variety of forms: they can be feelings, behaviours, attitudes, capabilities, aptitudes, which can be quite close to the surface, and which can be positive and useful, or they can be deeper aspects of a person's personality, influencing his/her behaviour to various degrees. Large unknown areas would typically be expected in younger people, and people who lack experience or self-belief.

Examples of unknown factors are as follows, and the first example is particularly relevant and common, especially in typical organisations and teams:

- *an ability that is under-estimated or un-tried through lack of opportunity, encouragement, confidence or training*
- *a natural ability or aptitude that a person does not realise they possess*
- *a fear or aversion that a person does not know they have*
- *an unknown illness*
- *repressed or subconscious feelings*
- *conditioned behaviour or attitudes from childhood*

The processes by which this information and knowledge can be uncovered are various and can be prompted through self-discovery or observation by others, or in certain situations through collective or mutual discovery, of the sort of discovery experienced on outward bound courses or other deep or intensive group work. Counselling can also uncover unknown issues, but this would then be known to the person and by one other, rather than by a group.

Whether unknown 'discovered' knowledge moves into the hidden, blind or open area depends on who discovers it and what they do with the knowledge, notably whether it is then given as feedback, or disclosed. As with the processes of soliciting feedback and disclosure, striving to discover information and feelings in the unknown relates to the process of 'self-actualisation' described in Maslow's Hierarchy of Needs development and motivation model.

Again, as with disclosure and soliciting feedback, the process of self-discovery is a sensitive one. The extent and depth to which an individual can seek out and discover their unknown feelings must always be at the individual's own discretion. Some people are more keen and able than others to do this.

Uncovering 'hidden talents' - that is unknown aptitudes and skills, not to be confused with developing the Johari 'hidden area' - is another aspect of developing the unknown area and is not so sensitive as unknown feelings. Providing people with the opportunity to try new things, with no great pressure to succeed, is often a useful way to discover unknown abilities, and thereby reduce the unknown area.

Managers and leaders can help by creating an environment that encourages self-discovery, and to promote the processes of self-discovery, constructive observation and feedback among team members. It is a widely accepted fact that most staff in any organisation are at any time working well within their potential.

Creating a culture, climate and expectation for self-discovery helps people to fulfil more of their potential and thereby achieve more and contribute more to organisational performance.

One note of caution about Johari region 4: The unknown area could also include repressed or subconscious feelings rooted in formative events and traumatic past experiences, which can stay unknown for a lifetime. In a work or organisational context, the Johari Window should not be used to address issues of a clinical nature.

The Wheel of Life

The Wheel of Life Exercise is a popular coaching assessment tool because it is a simple yet powerful diagnostic tool.

The Wheel of Life is based on the notion that there are specific categories - or *areas of focus* - that form the cornerstone of your overall life experience.

The Wheel of Life categories can include:

Health: *Your physical health and well-being (can also include your emotional health).*
Relationships: *Includes your primary intimate relationship, family, and friends.*
Social: *Includes religious/spiritual communities and other group activities.*
Financial: *Your ability to manage your money effectively, save, budget, and invest.*
Professional/Business: *This is your work category, which can break out into a Wheel of Business.*
Personal Growth: *Although not everyone might have an area of focus for personal development, anyone interested in Self-development does.*
Spirituality: *This can be its own category or simply the driving force behind all your areas of focus.*

These are the basic categories of most people's Wheel of Life.

Additional Wheel of Life categories might include:

Mental State
Attitude
Creativity
Contribution
Lifestyle
Recreation
……… Or anything else that might play a dominant role in your life.

How to select your wheel of life categories

The key is to determine the areas that are most important to ***you***. We all tend to focus on certain areas at the expense of other areas. So, your areas of focus should include both your strengths AND your weaknesses. The reason why all the key areas are important is that many of them hit on basic human needs. Maslow suggests that, when we do not address these basic needs, our lives fall out of balance (that is, we exhibit neurotic behaviour).

Challenge Your Beliefs

Generally, the reason why we fail to grow in particular areas of our lives is due to subconscious limiting beliefs and a fixed mindset.

Before you go through this process, it is important to address your mindset about your intelligence, your skills, your abilities, and your personality.

Before your start, the Wheel of Life Exercise, the reason why many people fail to get to grips with these types of coaching exercises is that they start off with lots of preconceived notions. They answer questions based on what they think they "should" answer as opposed to what is true for them. The key to overcoming this tendency is to clear your mind before you do this exercise.

Assess your current level of fulfilment

After you have identified the major categories for your Wheel of Life, place them into a chart as if they are the pieces of a pie.

The entire circle represents your overall life, and each piece represents a different area of focus. It might look something like this:

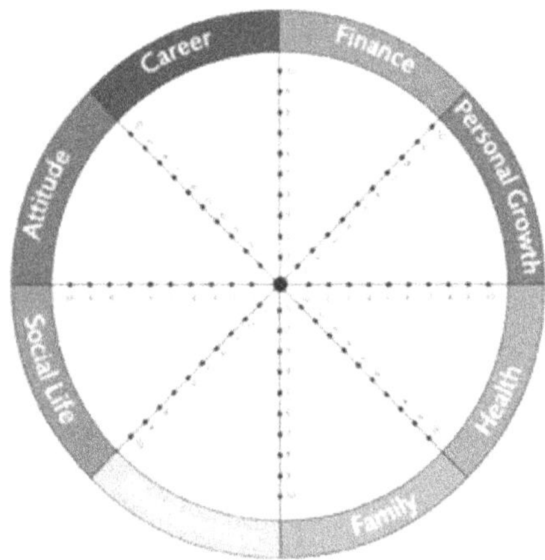

We all tend to have certain areas we are more proficient in and we all tend to spend time in these areas, neglecting our areas of weakness.

You may, for example, do an excellent job eating properly, exercising, and staying active (your Health category), but you are terrible at living within your means, paying off your credit cards, saving for the future, and finding more ways to add value (your financial category).

The Wheel of Life exercise brings these discrepancies to your conscious mind.

Emotional Intelligence

The first building block of emotional intelligence is self-awareness.

Emotional intelligence is the capacity to be aware of, control and express our emotions, and use them effectively in interpersonal relationships. It is the ability to step into someone else's shoes' and see things from their point of view.

It was developed as a psychological theory by Peter Salovey and John Mayer in 1997:

"Emotional intelligence is the ability to perceive emotions, to access and generate emotions so as to assist thought, to understand emotions and emotional knowledge, and to reflectively regulate emotions so as to promote emotional and intellectual growth."

The ability to understand how people feel and react can be extremely useful when managing and leading others, and can be applied on two levels:

personal – *understanding our own feelings or reactions*
interpersonal – *understanding other people's feelings and reactions*

As managers and leaders, we often must work as a team or develop relationships with colleagues, customers and other stakeholders. A reasonable degree of emotional intelligence can help managers be, for example:

empathetic – *e.g., able to put themselves in other people's shoes*
sensitive to others – *e.g., able to sense and respond to their needs, problems and feelings*
understanding and sympathetic – *e.g., able to understand the complexities of life and make allowances when things go wrong*
good at reading other people's emotions correctly – *e.g., able to identify the less obvious causes for emotional outbursts*

These skills give leaders a great advantage, especially when they are involved with functions that rely on relationship management. Leaders with good emotional intelligence skills instinctively know how to manipulate situations, inspire and motivate people, and get the best out of them.

Salovey and Mayer's Emotional Intelligence Theory

According to their definition, emotional intelligence is the ability to process information about your own emotions and other people's. It is also the ability to use this information to guide your thoughts and behaviour.

Thus, emotionally intelligent people pay attention to, use, understand and manage their emotions.

According to these two authors, for a person to be categorised as emotionally intelligent, they must have four basic abilities:

- ***Ability to perceive and correctly express their emotions and other people's.***
- ***The ability to use emotions in a way that facilitates thought.***
- ***Capacity to understand emotions, emotional language, and emotional signals.***
- ***The ability to manage their emotions to achieve goals.***

In this particular emotional intelligence theory, each ability has four different stages. However, this process does not necessarily happen spontaneously. On the contrary, it usually requires a conscious effort.

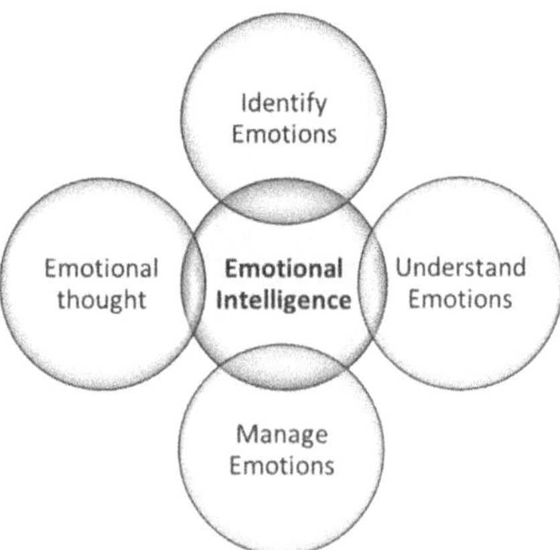

1. Emotional perception and expression

The first emotional intelligence skill is identifying your own emotions and other people's. First, you should be able to understand what you are feeling. This includes your thoughts as well as your emotions.

In the second stage, you acquire the ability to do the same with the way other people think and feel. For example, you can understand other people's feelings, or the feelings expressed by a piece of artwork.

In the third stage, you acquire the ability to correctly express your emotions. Not only that, but you learn to communicate your needs.

In the fourth and last stage, you gain the ability to distinguish between correct and incorrect emotional expressions.

2. Emotional thought

In the first stage, emotions help you direct your thoughts to the most important information. In this stage, you are not yet able to take your own emotions into account.

During the second stage, your emotions start to intensify so you can identify them. As a result, you can use them to help you make decisions.

According to Salovey and Meyer, your emotions affect your mood in the third stage. Consequently, you can consider different points of view on a particular subject.

Lastly, in the fourth stage, your emotions help you make good decisions and think more creatively.

3. Understanding emotions

First, you acquire the ability to distinguish between basic emotions and learn to use the right words to describe them. Then, this ability takes you a step further to be able to place the emotion in your emotional state.

In the third stage, you can interpret complex emotions. Lastly, you acquire the ability to detect the transitions between emotions. For example, the transition from anger to shame or surprise to joy.

4. Emotional regulation for intellectual and emotional growth

To begin, this ability requires your willingness not to limit the important role that your emotions have. This is much easier to achieve with positive emotions than negative emotions. During this step, you will let yourself choose which emotions you want to identify with according to whether they are useful or not.

In the previous step, you acquire the ability to study emotions. This would happen according to how influential, reasonable, or clear the emotions are. Lastly, you would be able to regulate your emotions and other people's, moderating the negative ones and increasing the positive ones.

Goleman's Theory of Emotional Intelligence

One model that explains emotional intelligence was developed by Daniel Goleman, a psychologist and science journalist, following on from Salovey and Mayer's theory. The theory identifies four components:

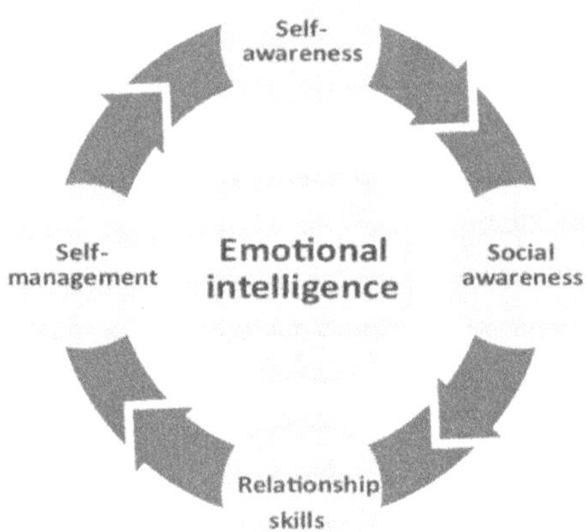

Self-awareness *– the conscious knowledge of our character, beliefs, emotions, qualities and desires*
Self-management and motivation *– the ability to stay calm under pressure and stay motivated to achieve goals*
Social awareness *– the ability to have empathy and understand other people's emotions and feelings*
Relationship skills *– the ability to influence, negotiate, communicate, build rapport and develop networks*

As the diagram shows, the focus for emotional intelligence is relationship management. Emotional development can be achieved through, for example:

team-building exercises
coaching
training in negotiation and communication skills

In leadership roles, emotional intelligence can provide an extra insight into which approach will be most effective when guiding and inspiring the team to follow. By using emotional intelligence, leaders can:

read other people's feelings and reactions more accurately
adapt their approach
employ appropriate skills

According to Goleman, the higher someone goes in an organisation, the more the emotional skills matter.

Senior managers and directors can hire people with the skills and knowledge that the organisation needs, but they need to be very competent in emotional intelligence themselves. Good relationship capabilities become more critical as careers progress.

Qualities of those with high Emotional Intelligence scores

1. They're not perfectionists.

Being a perfectionist can get in the way of completing tasks and achieving goals since it can lead to having trouble getting started, procrastinating, and looking for the right answer when there is not one. Therefore, people with EI are not perfectionists. They realise that perfection does not exist and push forward. If they make a mistake, they will adjust and learn from it.

2. They know how to balance work and play.

Working 24/7 and not taking care of yourself adds unnecessary stress and health problems to your life. Because of this, people with EI know when it is time to work and when to play. For example, if they need to disconnect from the world for a couple of hours, or even an entire weekend, they will because they need the time to unplug to reduce the stress levels.

3. They embrace change.

Instead of dreading change, emotionally intelligent people realise that change is a part of life. Being afraid of change hinders success, so they adapt to the changes around them and always have a plan in place should any sort of change occur.

4. They do not get easily distracted.

People with high EI can pay attention to the task at hand and are not easily distracted by their surroundings, such as text or random thought.

5. They're empathetic.

Being able to relate to others, show compassion, and take the time to help someone are all crucial components of EI. Additionally, being empathic makes people with EI curious about other people and leads them to ask lots of questions whenever they meet someone new.

6. They know their strengths and weaknesses.

Emotionally intelligent people know what they are good at and what they are not so great at. They have not just accepted their strengths and weaknesses; they also know how to leverage their strengths and weaknesses by working with the right people in the right situation.

7. They're self-motivated.

Were you that ambitious and hard-working kid who was motivated to achieve a goal--and not just because there was a reward at the end? Being a real go-getter, even at a young age, is another quality possessed by people with EI.

8. They do not dwell in the past.

People with high EI do not have the time to dwell in the past because they are too busy contemplating the possibilities that tomorrow will bring. They do not let past mistakes consume them with negativity. They do not hold grudges. Both add stress and prevent us from moving forward.

9. They focus on the positive.

Emotionally intelligent people would rather devote their time and energy to solving a problem. Instead of harping on the negative, they look at the positive and what they have control over. Furthermore, they also spend their time with other positive people and not the people who constantly complain.

10. They set boundaries

While people with high EI may seem like pushovers because of their politeness and compassion, they have the power to establish boundaries. For example, they know how to say no to others. The reason? It prevents them from getting overwhelmed, burned out, and stressed because they have too many commitments. Instead, they are aware that saying no frees them up from completing previous commitments.

Conclusion

Having learned what emotional intelligence is, how it is measured, and why it is important to success. Whether new to the study of emotional intelligence or a seasoned veteran, everyone has the ability and choice to continue to increase their Emotional intelligence.

Inclusivity and Unconscious Bias

Unconscious Bias is related to equality and diversity and is therefore linked directly to inclusivity.

When we look at self-awareness, we need to examine our unconscious bias as it can affect all aspects of the work environment – e.g., management of individuals, recruitment, training, promotion opportunities, performance management or customer service.

Definitions of Inclusivity and Unconscious Bias

Being aware of the need for inclusivity in the workplace is important, as is an awareness that we need to avoid unconscious bias when making decisions that affect the workforce, customers and other stakeholders. But what do these terms mean?

Unconscious bias

"the unintended inclination or prejudice for or against an individual or a group"

Everyone has unconscious bias. It is a natural and unintended influence on how we make decisions, based on unconscious preferences rather than careful, conscious consideration. We naturally favour others who are like us or share the same values – e.g., in looks, attitudes, education, accent, colour, ethnicity, beliefs or work ethic.

Information that influences us can come from many sources – e.g., our own experiences and upbringing; what we read, hear or see around us or in the media; other people we meet; our education and family background; what we have seen and learned in the workplace. Our brains react to information all the time, and they use unconscious shortcuts to speed up decision making processes.

Although unconscious bias can be useful in a dangerous situation, where we must make a split-second decision about survival, it is not a useful attribute when making decisions in the workplace. We need to overcome any instinctive judgements and make conscious, well-rounded and well considered decisions, especially when dealing with colleagues, customers and others.

Inclusivity

"the intention or policy of including people who might otherwise be excluded"

We often here about how something is exclusive, and this is seen as something positive and desirable. It implies that it is a special privilege to be part of a select group that will only allow a few, carefully chosen people to join or be associated with it. However, this attitude is not helpful or desirable in the workplace. It leads to discrimination, which is illegal on certain grounds and has very negative impacts on the organisation and its stakeholders – anyone who has anything to do with it.

Instead, organisations need to be inclusive. They need to have policies of including people who might otherwise be left out.
An organisation that embraces inclusivity can have many benefits including, for example:

a more diverse workforce *– e.g., people from many different backgrounds with a wide variety of attributes, experience, skills, knowledge and culture*
being able to tap into a wide of range human resources *– that may not seem obvious at first*
the ability to offer a diverse range of products and services *– to a diverse range of customers and service users*
more diverse opportunities to expand and stabilise its position in the market *– creating opportunities that a less inclusive organisation would miss*
being able to offer more secure employment *– due to its wide appeal to a broad range of customers*

How Unconscious Bias can impact on Inclusion

When considering our own self-awareness, we need to make sure that our words and actions support inclusivity and make sure that everyone feels valued and included – e.g., minority groups generally; people with disabilities; people from different cultures, ethnic groups or religions; people with unusual skills; people who have a great deal to offer but may not mix easily.

Whilst emotional intelligence can give valuable insight into working relationships, we need to make sure that we do not apply too much of ourselves, and our experiences, when making decisions. This is particularly true when dealing with, for example:

- ***recruitment of staff***
- ***promotion and career development of team members***
- ***evaluating team members and recognising their strengths and weaknesses***

For example, a manager who went to university may favour job candidates who also went to university, even though other candidates are just as suitable for the job. The manager unconsciously remembers how their own university experience shaped and helped them in their career, and they assume that a degree is essential, even if it is not a mandatory requirement in the job description. This is called affinity bias, where the manager feels an affinity with people who have the same life experiences.

The university experience can be a harmless link that makes for easier communication when getting to know someone. However, if that manager fails to think consciously about all the candidates and just favours the graduates, when there is no operational reason to do so, their action would be discriminatory and potentially liable for legal action. They need to include all suitable candidates in their shortlist, not just the graduates.

Another form of unconscious bias is known as the halo effect, where a positive trait is transferred to someone without any evidence. For example, a team member who speaks with a 'posh' accent, uses body language very effectively and wears designer clothes may be considered as having better skills, knowledge and experience than they have. If selected for an unsuitable role, the manager and organisation could suffer, for example:

complaints – *e.g., from dissatisfied colleagues or customers when the candidate proves unsuitable*
increased costs – *e.g., from additional training or recruitment costs*
a bad reputation – *e.g., from showing poor judgement*

Where unconscious bias is against a protected characteristic under the Equality Act 2010, it can be discriminatory and possibly lead to legal action.

The nine protected characteristics are:

age
disability or impairment
gender
gender reassignment
marriage or civil partnership
race
religion or beliefs
sexual orientation
pregnancy or maternity

Discrimination based on these characteristics is illegal, and complaints and legal action could be the serious consequences of forgetting about inclusivity and allowing unconscious bias to affect judgement.

Unconscious thoughts can be based on stereotypes and prejudices, and unconscious bias when selecting people for promotion or recruitment can lead to, for example:

- ***discrimination in the workplace*** *– e.g., from allowing prejudices to affect judgement when selecting team members for promotion*
- ***possible legal action being taken*** *– e.g., if a team member is discriminated against on the grounds of a protected characteristic*
- ***a less diverse workforce*** *– e.g., if people of particular race are overlooked for promotion or recruitment*
- ***some people's talents being overstated*** *– e.g., if their image does not reflect the truth about their skills and attributes*
- ***some people's talents going unrecognised*** *– e.g., if they are awkward, shy and unable to 'sell' their considerable talents well*
- ***an inability to adapt to change*** *– e.g., from holding onto outdated, unhelpful and stereotypical ideas about people and their actions*
- ***an inability to exploit and develop new markets with diverse customers*** **–** *which restricts the chances of stability, success and sustainability for the organisation*

Some of these effects apply to the organisation as a whole, but they can all be influenced by unconscious bias on a more personal level. A manager who is unaware of the impact of their own unconscious bias, and how it affects their ability to be inclusive in their outlook, will have an effect on their team members, other teams and the organisation as a whole. Their inability to see how their instinctive prejudices affect people around them can easily lead to resentment, lack of respect and potentially serious consequences for all concerned.

Identifying Development Needs

Skills Audits

The normal process for analysing current skills, knowledge and experience is to use a skills audit. This is a simple process which identifies what you are good at what you are not so good at as well as things you may not have done before.

An audit is:

a simple process to identify your strengths and weaknesses.

The skills audit will help analyse the current position – where I am I now? – and reveal areas that are strong and those that need attention. These can be entered onto a Personal Development Plan, so that strengths and skills gaps can be identified and then start to decide what and how to consolidate or improve.

Skills audits can be used to list the skills that are relevant to a role, then assess own ability using a scoring system. The skills tested can be for a current role, to see where improvement is needed, or a role for the future.

In the example below, an experienced departmental manager in a supermarket wants to apply for promotion to deputy store manager.

The skills audit below is based on the skills and attributes shown in the organisation's job description for the deputy manager position. This helps identify skills gaps that will need to be addressed if the application is to be successful.

The current skill level in each area is rated as 1 = poor and 5 = excellent

Skills and attributes	*Current ability*					*Action to be taken*
	1	**2**	**3**	**4**	**5**	
Experience of all departments within the store			✓			*Need to work in other store areas – see line manager*
Evaluating competitors' stores and managing advantage			✓			*OK for fresh produce, useful to try other areas competitive*
Leadership skills				✓		*OK*
General staff management skills				✓		*OK*
Communication skills			✓			*Usually very good, but need more at senior management level – ask line manager*
Training and coaching skills					✓	*One of my strengths*
Purchasing and negotiating delivery and discounts	✓					*Do not have to do this in current role – Ask procurement team if I can shadow them for a day/week?*
Ability to promote and generate sales – *demonstrations, displays*					✓	*One of my strengths*
Customer service skills					✓	*One of my strengths*
Budgeting/finance skills			✓			*Only have to do a bit – need to shadow someone*
Working to the organisation's and industry's standards					✓	*OK*
Maintaining health and safety -e.g., fire evacuation, first-aid cover, risk awareness, minimising hazards,			✓			*OK in my area, do not really need to worry about chemicals here – find out a bit more for rest of store*

Preparing a Skills Audit

A definitive and comprehensive list is made of the skills that are relevant to the role, covering all the relevant criteria.

When deciding what skills are necessary to audit, the details can be taken from a variety of sources – the job description and person specification should go some way to providing most of the criteria for this, but can be supplemented by criteria from the organisation's own policies, procedures and standards. The national occupational standards, professional bodies' standards, etc. can also be sources of information.

The final list should be checked by all parties concerned or involved.

The existing skill set is then compared to the list and a simple rating system applied which shows the level of skill for each criterion.

The rating can be from self-evaluation or be done with someone else, such as the line manager.

Below are just two samples of skills audits:

Personal Skills Audit						
		1	2	3	4	5
1	*Lack confidence in expressing my needs*		✓			
2	*Manage time effectively*			✓		
3	*I am competent to lead*		✓			
4	*I cope with stress well*				✓	
5	*I do not have the confidence to give presentations*			✓		
6	*I am patient when teaching and coaching others*		✓			
7	*I can handle a number of tasks*		✓			
8	*I do not have the confidence to influence others*			✓		
9	*I can motivate others*			✓		
10	*I do not make people do tasks*			✓		

Professional Skills Audit		
Skills required	*Rating (1–5)*	*Action to be taken*
Computing skills	**4**	*Undertake short courses (if possible) to enhance computing skills*
Leadership skills	**4**	*Get more involved in communities/societies*
Numeracy skills	**4**	*Discuss with lecturers and fellow students on ways to improve*
Revision and exam techniques	**3**	*Learn from lecturers and fellow students on techniques to revise and answer exam questions.*
Time-management and organisation skills	**2**	*Jot down all activities that need to be done accordingly in a diary*
Oral presentation skills	**4**	*Learn to fully utilise and use other presentation aids that are available besides PowerPoint*
Critical analysis and logical argument skills	**3**	*Get more involved in group discussions*
Selecting and prioritising information when reading	**3**	*Listen to lectures and identify which are the important points*
Referencing skills	**3**	*Write more essays and get used to the Harvard referencing style*
Summarising skills	**4**	*Need to fully understand the topic*
Developing appropriate writing style	**3**	*Read more articles and journals to get used to the writing style so that it can be implemented*
Search skills (library and e-resources)	**3**	*Fully utilise the library's 'resources and support' section*
Utilising and comprehension	**5**	*Listen more to the way people converse with each other and try and pick up whatever necessary*
Proofreading and editing	**3**	*Take another look at the work*

SWOT Analysis

As well as doing a skills audit and reflecting on your choices, you can also do a **SWOT** analysis to focus your attention on your strengths and weaknesses. These are the things which you are good at and things you are not so good at or need additional support or training to achieve a higher level of competence.

SWOT stands for Strengths, Weaknesses, Opportunities, and Threats.

The strengths and weaknesses are factors which affect you personally. Strengths are things you are good at, things you can do without support or help. This could include literacy or numeracy. It could include being well organised, etc.

Weaknesses are things you need help or support to achieve. It may be that you can happily read a newspaper, but a textbook may be more challenging. You can maybe deal with personal finance including paying bills and managing credit cards, but departmental budgets and cost management you find difficult and need help with. It may also be that you are simply disorganised! These are your strengths and weaknesses!

Opportunities and threats are not about you personally, but about society in general. Opportunities are the things that help you to achieve your targets such as free training courses, help with childcare whilst studying, work shadowing opportunities, etc. Threats are the things which may prevent you from achieving your targets such as the economic climate, lack of opportunities, etc. Both opportunities and threats are matters outside of your control, but you should be aware of these issues.

S *Strengths*
W *Weaknesses*
O *Opportunities for improvement*
T *Threats to such progress* – *things that may stop progress.*

The next stage is to prepare a SWOT analysis to identify development needs in more detail. This shows what is needed to be able to develop skills, experience and knowledge to be in a good position to apply for promotion or a new role.

Strengths	*Weaknesses*
Personal finance Paying bills Managing credit cards	Departmental budgets Cost management Disorganised
Free training courses Help with childcare. Work shadowing Inflation	Economic climate Lack of opportunities Inflation
Opportunities	*Threats*

Self-Reflection

Self-reflection helps to develop skills and review their effectiveness, rather than just carry-on doing things as you have always done them. It is then straightforward to assess whether there is a better, or more efficient, way of performing the task again, if repeated in the future.

In any role, whether at home or at work, reflection is an important part of learning. You would not use a recipe a second time around if the dish did not work the first time! You would either adjust the recipe or find a new one.

When we do our job, we can become stuck in a routine that may not be working effectively. Thinking about your own skills can help you identify changes you might need to make.

Reflective questions to ask yourself:

- ***Strengths –*** *What are my strengths? Am I well organised? Do I remember things?*
- ***Weaknesses*** – *What are my weaknesses? Am I easily distracted? Do I need more practise with a particular skill?*
- ***Skills*** – *What skills do I have? What am I good at?*
- ***Problems*** – *What problems are there at work/home that may affect me? For example, responsibilities or distractions that may impact on study or work.*
- ***Achievements*** – *What have I achieved?*

- ***Happiness*** – *Are there things I am dissatisfied with or disappointed about? What makes me happy?*
- ***Solutions*** **–** *What could I do to improve in these areas?*

Although self-reflection can seem difficult at first, or even selfish or embarrassing, as it does not come naturally, you will find it becomes easier with practise and the end result could be a happier and more efficient you.

Setting Objectives

Having analysed where you are now and where you want to be. It is time to work out the steps on the route to get there and then set personal objectives to plan how to reach that destination.

When setting personal work objectives, it is important to have a realistic number of goals. If overloaded, people feel overwhelmed and are more likely to fail, give up and lose confidence. Honesty about achievements and expectations is important.

It can be useful to support this process with personal reflection and discussions with senior colleagues, maybe during the appraisal process. Once you have established your needs, you can set objectives that support your strengths, address your weaknesses and help you to improve your performance.

SMART Objectives

By having goals and objectives clearly in mind, there is a much greater chance of success. One good way to set goals is to use SMART objectives:

SMART is an acronym used to guide your goal setting.

To ensure the goals set are clear and attainable, each one should be:

Specific *(simple, sensible, significant).*
Measurable *(meaningful, motivating).*
Achievable *(agreed, attainable).*
Relevant *(reasonable, realistic and resourced, results-based).*
Time bound *(time-based, time limited, time-sensitive).*

Some authors have expanded it to include extra focus areas.

SMARTER, for example, includes Evaluated and Reviewed.

S	*Specific*	*What are the details of the learning activity, task or training course that I want to do? What qualifications do I need for that promotion? Which job am I aiming for?*
M	*Measurable*	*Is there a certificate or report that can show my progress? Can I count the number of units I am covering so that I can see my progress?*
A	*Achievable*	*Can I do it? What support do I need to find to make sure that I can achieve these goals?*
R	*Realistic*	*Is it realistic to do the training or tasks in the time that is allowed? Is it realistic to work full time and do all of this study quickly, or do I need to study over a longer period of time?*
T	*Time-bound*	*What are the deadlines? Do I need to have completed this task before my tutor comes next time, or in time for my annual review?*

How to Use SMART objectives

1. Specific

The goal should be clear and specific, or it will not be possible to focus endeavour or feel motivated to achieve it. When writing the goal, try to answer the five "W" questions:

- *What do I want to accomplish?*
- *Why is this goal important?*
- *Who is involved?*
- *Where is it located?*
- *Which resources or limits are involved?*

Example:
Imagine that you are currently a marketing executive, and you would like to become head of marketing. A specific goal could be, "I want to gain the skills and experience necessary to become head of marketing within my organisation, so that I can build my career and lead a successful team."

2. Measurable

It is important to have metrics for goals, so progress can be tracked and motivation maintained. Being able to assess progress helps maintain focus, meet deadlines, and feel the excitement of getting closer to achieving the goal.

- *A measurable goal should address questions such as:*
- *How much?*

- *How many?*
- *How will I know when it is accomplished?*

Example:
You might measure your goal of acquiring the skills to become head of marketing by determining that you will have completed the necessary training courses and gained the relevant experience within five years' time.

3. Achievable

Goals need to be realistic. In other words, it should stretch ability but remain possible. When an achievable goal is set, it is likely that past opportunities or additional resources success closer.

An achievable goal will usually answer questions such as:

- *How can I accomplish this goal?*
- *How realistically attainable is the goal, based on other likely constraints, such as budgets, time, human resources?*

Example:
You might need to ask yourself whether developing the skills required to become head of marketing is realistic, based on your existing experience and qualifications. For example, do you have the time to complete the required training effectively? Are the necessary resources available to you? Can you afford to do it?

4. Relevant

It is important that the goal matters both personally and that it aligns with other relevant goals. Everyone will need support and assistance to achieve goals, but it is important to retain control over them. Ensure that plans drive everyone forward, but that responsibility for own goals is retained.

A relevant goal can answer "yes" to these questions:

- *Does this seem worthwhile?*
- *Is this the right time?*
- *Does this match our other efforts/needs?*
- *Am I the right person to reach this goal?*
- *Is it applicable in the current socio-economic environment?*

Example:
You might want to gain the skills to become head of marketing within your organisation, but is it the right time to undertake the required training, or work toward additional qualifications? Are you sure that you are the right person for the head of marketing role? Have you considered your spouse's goals? For example, if you want to start a family, would completing training in your free time make this more difficult?

5. Time-bound

A goal without a deadline has no target. By setting a completion date, there is a target to work towards and this can help prevent routine tasks from taking priority over the longer-term goals.

A time-bound goal will usually answer these questions:

- *When?*
- *What can I do six months from now?*
- *What can I do six weeks from now?*
- *What can I do today?*

Example:

Gaining the skills to become head of marketing may require additional training or experience. How long will it take to acquire these skills? Will further training be needed to give eligibility for certain exams or qualifications? It is important to set a realistic time frame for accomplishing the lesser goals necessary to achieve the final objective.

Advantages and Disadvantages of SMART Objectives

SMART is a powerful tool which ensures clarity, focus and motivation necessary to achieve goals. Objectives or goals set using SMART goals are easily used by anyone, anywhere, without the need for specialist tools or training.

When using SMART, it creates clear, attainable and meaningful goals, and develops the motivation, action plan, and support needed to achieve them.

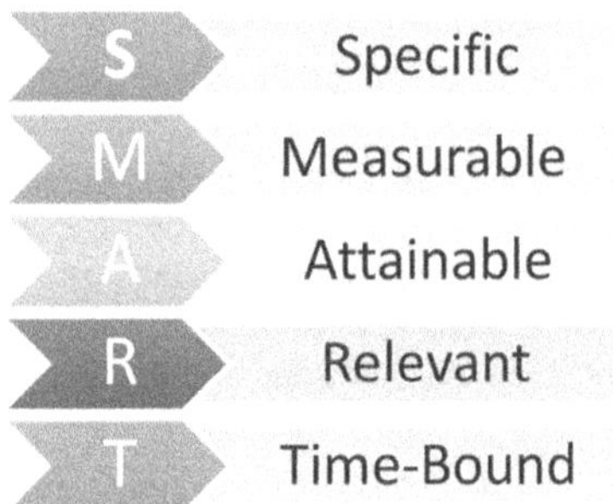

Personal Development Plan (PDP)

A PDP is a document that is based on awareness, values, reflection, goal setting and planning for personal development. This can be at work, in education or in the context of self-improvement.

Employees who are taking part in personal, professional, development are typically asked to record their development by completing a PDP.

A Personal Development Plan is a written summary of self-reflection used to identify ways to achieve the academic, personal, or career-based goals identified as a result. This then forms an action plan of how those goals can be achieved.

Objectives are put in place, based on the areas you would like to improve, and the plan consists of your own personalised actions that will help you to achieve them.

A PDP is simply a plan, just like any other plan. The only difference is that it relates specifically to you.

When you first start thinking about personal development, it can seem as if you know nothing, and have no skills. You may find this point rather overwhelming! But it is important to bear two things in mind:

You do have skills. You have been learning and developing all your life, and you already have many, many skills.

You do not have to improve everything all at once. In fact, you are much better off not trying to do that.

Focus on just one or two areas at a time, and you will see much larger improvements, and also feel less overwhelmed.

There is a reason why personal development is sometimes called 'lifelong learning': there is no time limit on it!

An effective Personal and Professional Development Plan will include:

A clear vision of where you want to be and why.

It is really helpful to think about where you want to be and what you want to do. It can be useful to think in terms of different lengths of time: for example, one month, six months, one year, five years.

The vision should be as detailed as possible, across all spheres of life:

- *career*
- *where you want to live*
- *hobbies*
- *even relationships*

The more detail included, right down to how you will feel about it, the easier it will be to hold onto your vision when times are hard.

Knowledge of the skills needing development in order to achieve the vision

The next step to your personal development plan is to think about what skills you need to develop, and why this is important to achieving your vision.
For example:

- *Do you need certain skills to get a particular job, or to advance in your chosen career?*
- *Are you planning to live abroad, and therefore need to develop your language skills?*
- *Are you struggling to manage a particular situation, and need new skills to help?*
- *Have you been told that you lack particular skills and need to develop them to work effectively with others, or on your own?*

It is important to ensure the skills being targeted are clearly linked to a purpose, which is in turn linked to the vision. Without this level of clarity, any personal development efforts may fail. It is vital to concentrate on the right skills and be fully aware of timescales involved.

A clear idea of the expected standard and how current performance differs from that.

The difference between current performance and desired performance, details the scale of the task. It also affects the duration and the effort needed to complete it.

If you are planning to move abroad in a year's time, or go travelling, you may need to develop your language skills. But, if you have already lived in that country for a period and speak the language well, you may not need to do more than keep your language skills up via listening to foreign radio.

If, however, you have never learnt the language, and you are starting from scratch, you may need some intensive language tuition, or even an immersion course, to ensure that your skills develop quickly enough.

A level of priority for each area
You cannot do everything at once.

Instead, you need to prioritise. One very good way to do this is to list all your areas for development, then ask yourself two questions about each one, answering on a scale of one to five:

- *How important is this to me?*
- *How essential is it to develop it now?*

Combine the scores for the two questions for each area and it will indicate which areas to focus on first, because they are either more important, or they are more time critical.

Leave the other areas for a later date: next year, or even a few years' time.

A detailed idea of how to get from where you are now for each goal, to where you want to be
It sounds straightforward, however, you need to know how you are going to get from (a) to (b): where you are now, to where you want to be? Are you going to enrol on a course? Learn online, go to college or attend an evening class?

Just as with your vision, it can be helpful to break this down by time: in a month/six months/a year, what will you have done on the way to your ultimate goals? This makes it easier to check your progress and keep yourself on track.

Planning and Preparing a Development Plan

Planning and delivering your personal development can be thought of as personal strategic thinking and planning – where do you want to be, and how will you get there?

1. Why are you trying to develop?
It is important to understand why you are trying to develop.

The answers to all the questions about 'what' and 'where' (what should I do? Should I address my weaknesses, or build my strengths? Where should I begin?) all become clearer once you identify why you want to change. It is important to be clear about this purpose, so that you can assess whether your learning and development activities are moving you closer to your goals. It is also easier to get motivated when you have a clear picture of where you want to be at the end of the process.

2. Planning your development

Planning and documenting personal development will help make it more realistic.

There is something about writing things down that makes the overambitious look ridiculous, and the unrealistic stand out like a sore thumb.

Planning for your personal development, which includes time limits and stages of development, will force you to be realistic about what you can achieve by when.

A written plan provides a way of keeping tabs on goals, even formally altering them if necessary.

I may not have gone where I intended to go, but I think I have ended up where I needed to be. *Douglas Adams*

3. Documenting your plans

Writing down your plans and activities enables you to review your progress.

By documenting personal development plans and activities, it will not only enable progress to be reviewed, but also provides a record of your thinking over time.

It is incredibly easy to forget how you felt about things at different stages, and even why you thought a particular goal was important. Carefully documenting your thinking will help to show you what works best, what you have enjoyed and disliked, and quite probably point you towards more suitable activities or areas for development.

4. What works for you?

It is important to establish which development methods work best for you.

There are an enormous range of development activities available, from formal training sessions, through online training to experiential learning, reading and discussing ideas with others. As with anything, it is important to find out what works best for you—as in, what you enjoy most and also what helps you to learn and develop quickly and effectively.

5. Focus

What is really important in your personal development?

Use your vision to identify what really matters now — what you have to do first to achieve your vision — and concentrate on that. Only once you have achieved that, or at least made reasonable progress, should you move on. ‘

6. Grasp new opportunities
Do not be afraid to take opportunities that you had not considered before.

Not everything in life, or personal development, is predictable. Sometimes you may be offered an amazing opportunity to do something that does not fit with your immediate priorities, but which sounds too good to miss. It is worth considering whether taking this opportunity will slow down your progress towards your ultimate goal and, if so, whether that matters. It is not worth turning something down simply because you have never thought of doing it, and therefore it does not feature in your 'life plans.'

Ultimately, being offered this kind of opportunity probably helps you to define your goals better: if it sounds very exciting and you really want to do it, then do. If it changes your goal and vision, so be it.

Our biggest regrets are not for the things we have done but for the things we have not done. *Chad Michael Murray*

7. Let personal development evolve
Your priorities will change — and that is OK

Few, if any, of us would say that we were exactly the same person at 35 that we were at 15, or even 25. As you grow and change, taking on new responsibilities in work or at home, so your priorities and goals will change.

The key is to recognise that this is fine.

Regular review and revision of your personal development activities and plans will ensure that they change with your priorities and remain relevant.

Continuing Professional Development Log (CPD)

Continuing Professional Development (CPD) is the term used to describe the learning activities professionals engage in to develop and enhance their abilities. It enables learning to become conscious and proactive, rather than passive and reactive. It may include life-long learning, maintaining the currency of skills and knowledge, developing occupational effectiveness, impact and achievement.

CPD is the commitment of professionals to the enhancement of their personal and professional knowledge, skills and proficiency throughout their careers.

A CPD log combines and records the different methodologies undertaken for learning, such as training workshops, conferences and events, e-learning programs, best practice techniques and ideas sharing, completed by an individual over a period of time.

Development recorded in the PDP is transferred to the CPD Log when it has been satisfactorily completed.
By undertaking CPD, academic and practical qualifications do not become obsolete, allowing individuals to continually 'up skill' or 're-skill' themselves, regardless of occupation, age or educational level, thereby maintaining their occupational competence.

Benefits of CPD.

For Individuals

CPD helps individuals focus on how they can become a more competent and effective professional. Training and learning increase confidence and overall capability, and underpin career progression.

CPD enables employees to adapt to changes in work/industry requirements.

Recording CPD provides evidence of professional development (this can be useful for supervision and appraisals).

A CPD log evidences commitment to self-development and professionalism.

For Organisations

Providing learning benefits the organisation by promoting a healthy learning culture leading to a more fulfilled workforce and retaining valuable staff.

Employees may have an obligation to undertake CPD as a member of a professional body.

Allocating Time for CPD

Most professional bodies generally define Continuing Professional Development requirements as a minimum number of hours each year. CPD hours can also be converted to points, units or credits. Most institutions allow members to choose subjects of relevance to them as individuals, a minority also require their members to seek CPD on a range of core subjects.

Recording CPD

An individual must record their annual Continuing Professional Development using a CPD log and must ensure it is correct, maintained and meets the requirements of their professional body or association.

The Cost of Personal and Professional Development

Anything which is beneficial in our lives almost always comes at a cost and that is also true of Development. There can be a personal cost as well as a cost for the organisation. It is, however, true to say that the cost of development is often far outweighed by the benefits it brings.

The costs of development can include any or all of the following:

- *Financial cost of the training*
- *Time spent on training.*
- *Expenses involved in attending the training.*
- *The cost of providing mentors and coaches.*
- *Loss of production whilst training.*
- *Cost of replacement staff.*

There may also be additional cost regarding resources. It maybe that new software or machinery needs to be purchased to facilitate the development. It may be that structural alterations may be needed to facilitate this or additional resources such as PPE may need to be purchased. It may require that other staff need to be trained first to bring them to a standard whereby they can perform the task being left vacant by another staff member taking up their development.

Chapter 2: The Organisation, Business and Commerce

Business Sectors

There are three principal sectors within business. These are:

- *Private Sector*
- *Public Sector*
- *Voluntary / Third Sector*

The private sectors include all the businesses who are in Private ownership and exist to generate a profit. At its most simple, we have the self-employed which could be a one-man band, to a partnership of two or more individuals who work together to make money. Such organisations are usually privately owned and the people who operate it keep all the profits and divide it between themselves in a previously agreed manner.

The next type of organisation is a Private Company. A company is essentially a legal entity in its own right. It may or may not be limited. The term limited refers to whether or not the liability of the company is limited to the value of its shares and assets or whether the directors have absolute liability for all debts. There are tax benefits depending on the structure of the company.

The next type of company is a Public Limited Company. This indicates the company is owned by shareholders and those shares are available for purchase by anyone on the stock market. People will buy the shares in order to receive a dividend. The divided is paid once or twice a year and the amount paid will depend on the success or otherwise of the company.

Organisations are legally required to take care of their financial obligations. They need to keep records that can be used to show relevant stakeholders that operations are being run properly and in accordance with legislation, regulations and rules.

Depending on the type of organisation, the internal and external stakeholders that need to be satisfied about financial issues will vary.

Internal Stakeholders

Internal stakeholders who need to be satisfied about how an organisation looks after its financial procedures could include, for example:

- ***business owners*** – *e.g., sole proprietors or partners who need to know the levels of profit and cash flow*
- ***shareholders*** – *e.g., employees or others who own shares in a company who need to keep an eye on their investment*
- ***employees*** – *e.g., who rely on the organisation to operate payroll and bonus systems*

External Stakeholders

External stakeholders could include, for example:

- ***banks and other lenders*** – *e.g., who provide business loans to the organisation*
- ***national and local government agencies*** – *e.g., who collect taxes and provide grants*
- ***external customers*** – *e.g., individuals and companies who buy and use the organisation's products and services*
- ***charity commission*** – *e.g., who examine accounts and regulate registered charities*

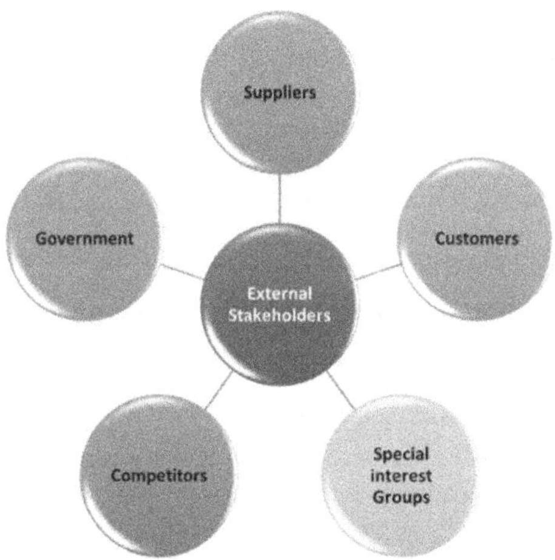

Government departments and agencies are also external stakeholders and are responsible for applying finance-related legislation and regulations and the collection of duties and taxes including:

- ***HM Revenue and Customs (HMRC)*** – *e.g., for VAT, tax and national insurance; money laundering regulations*
- ***Companies House*** – *where accounts and reports are held for limited companies as public records*
- ***the Financial Conduct Authority (FCA)*** – *for the financial services industry*
- ***the Prudential Regulation Authority (PRA)*** – *for banks and other financial institutions*
- ***the Pensions Regulator*** – *for workplace pensions*

Some finance-related legislation is covered by criminal law, such as the Bribery Act 2010. It is important to consider finance-related governance and compliance that organisations need to follow in order to carry out their activities legally and correctly. These include:

- *the purpose of governance and compliance in finance*
- *governance and compliance processes*
- *implications of unresolved governance and compliance issues*

Business Principles

Business Principles are often referred to as the values to of the organisation or its guiding ethics. A better explanation is that they are the foundation statements which are adopted by an organisation, department or team, to guide future decisions.

An organisation may publish its principles to the public and a team may publish its principles to its organisation. At the organisational level principles may address things such as professional conduct, sustainability and fairness to people. At a team level, principles become more specific to the types of decision faced by the team.

There are three levels of Business Principles. The first level is actually a set of fundamental benchmarks or tenets for business. These tenets are applicable to every business, every transaction and every decision made by the management team.

Tenets are universal and unbreakable.

The second level reflects fundamentals of business. These rules, guidance and thoughts are not necessarily true and applicable to every business sector and every organisation within that sector. In effect, common business fundamentals are not universal, whereas tenets are.

The third level are the standards set by the organisation and are typically driven by legislation, industry regulation and practice and the historical culture of the industry. Standards exist for systems, production, sales and financial results. Around two thirds of all business rules are really standards.

The entire spectrum of business principle starts with a few universally acceptable tenets, hundreds of fundamentals and tens of thousands of standards.

Basic Principles

Irrespective of the nature of the business, the sector in which it operates or its structure or size, there are basic principles upon which every organisation must be built. These include:

Integrity

Every organisation must conduct its business with integrity. This means doing the right thing all the time.

Skill, care and diligence
An organisation must conduct its business with all stakeholders with due skill, care and diligence.

Management and control
An organisation must take reasonable care to organise and control its affairs responsibly and effectively, with risk management systems which are adequate, appropriate and effective.

Financial prudence
An organisation must maintain adequate financial resources.

Market conduct
An organisation must observe proper standards of market conduct and behaviour.

Customers' interests
An organisation must pay due regard to the interests of its customers and treat them fairly.

Communications with clients
An organisation must satisfy the information needs of its clients and communicate information to them in a manner which is clear, fair and not misleading.

Conflicts of interest
An organisation must manage conflicts of interest fairly, both between itself and its customers and between other stakeholders.

Relationships of trust
An organisation must take reasonable care to ensure the suitability and accuracy of its advice and discretionary decisions for any customer who is entitled to rely upon its judgment.

Relations with regulators
An organisation must deal with its regulators in an open and cooperative way and disclose anything relating to the organisation of which a regulator would reasonably expect notice.

Organisational Structure

An organisational structure is a visual diagram of a company that describes what employees do, who they report to, and how decisions are made across the business.

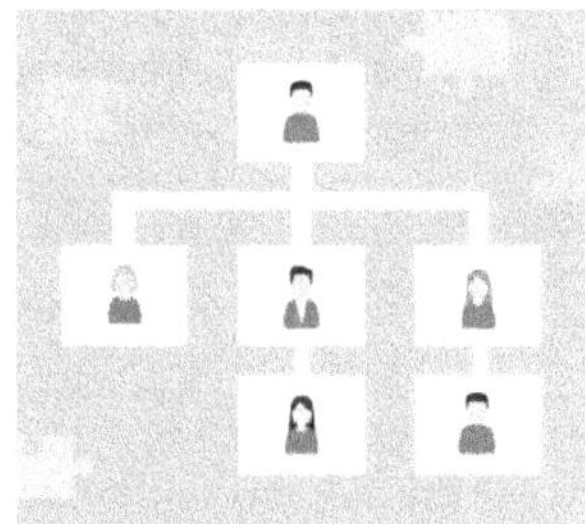

It is a system that outlines how certain activities are directed to achieve the goals of an organisation. These activities can include rules, roles and responsibilities.

The organisational structure also determines how information flows between levels within the company.

In a centralised structure, decisions flow from the top down, while in a decentralised structure, responsibility for decision-making is distributed among various levels of the organisation.

Having an organisational structure in place allows companies to remain efficient and focused.

The organisational structure also identifies where an individual sits within the organisation and indicates the people who report to them and to whom they report.

Understanding Organisational Structures

Businesses of all shapes and sizes use organisational structures. They define the hierarchy within an organisation. A successful organisational structure defines each employee's job and how it fits within the overall system. At its simplest level, the organisational structure lays out who does what in order that the company can meet its objectives.

This structuring provides a company with a visual representation of how it is shaped and how it can best move forward in achieving its goals. Organisational structures are normally illustrated in some sort of chart or diagram like a pyramid, where the most powerful members of the organisation sit at the top, while those with the least amount of power are at the bottom.

Not having a formal structure in place may prove difficult for certain organisations. For instance, employees may have difficulty knowing who they should report to. That can lead to uncertainty as to who is responsible for what in the organisation.

Having a structure in place can help with efficiency and provide clarity for everyone at every level. That also means departments can be more productive, as they are likely to be more focused on energy and time.

Mechanistic vs. Organic Organisational Structures

Organisational structures lie on a scale, with "mechanistic" at one end and "organic" at the other.

The mechanistic structure represents the traditional, top-down approach to organisational structure, whereas the organic structure represents a more collaborative, flexible approach.

Mechanistic Structure

Mechanistic structures, also called bureaucratic structures, are known for having narrow spans of control, as well as high centralisation, specialisation, and formalisation. They are also quite rigid in what specific departments are designed and permitted to do for the company.

This organisational structure is much more formal than an organic structure, using specific standards and practices to govern every decision the business makes. While this model does hold staff more accountable for their work, it can become a hindrance to the creativity and agility the organisation needs to keep up with random changes in its market.

As daunting and inflexible as mechanistic structure sounds, the chain of command, whether long or short, is always clear under this model. As a company grows, it needs to make sure everyone (and every team) knows what is expected of them. An informal structure where Teams are collaborating with others might help get a business off the ground in its early stages but sustaining that growth -- with more people and projects to keep track of will eventually require some policymaking and formalisation. It is therefore advisable to keep plans for a mechanistic structure in reserve as you never know when you will need it.

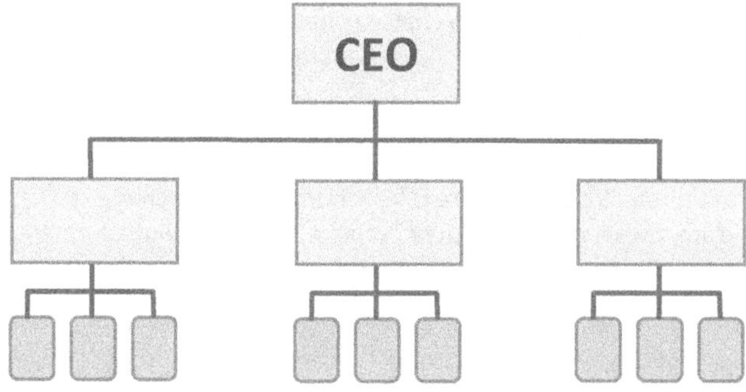

Organic Structure

Organic structures (also known as "flat" structures) are known for their wide spans of control, decentralisation, low specialisation, and loose departmentalisation. This model may have multiple teams answering to one person and taking on projects based on their importance and what the team is capable of -- rather than what the team is designed to do.

This organisational structure is much less formal than a mechanistic structure and takes a bit of an ad-hoc approach to business needs. This can sometimes make the chain of command, whether long or short, difficult to decipher. As a result, leaders might give certain projects the green light more quickly but cause confusion in a project's division of labour.

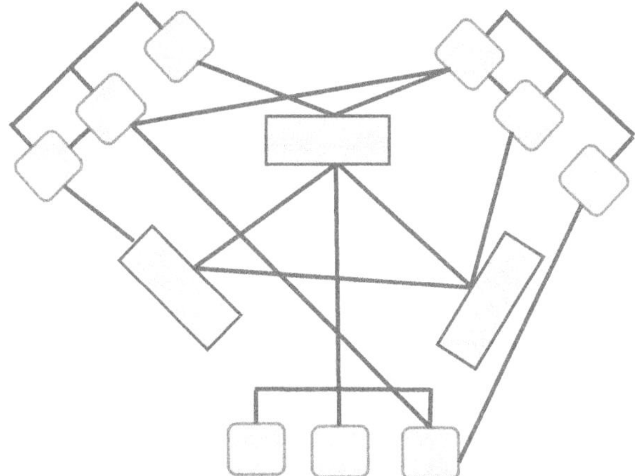

Nonetheless, the flexibility that an organic structure allows for can be extremely helpful to a business that is navigating a fast-moving industry, or simply trying to stabilise itself after a difficult period. It also empowers employees to try new things and develop as professionals, making the organisation's workforce more powerful in the long run.

Start-ups are often perfect for organic structures as they usually comprise only a few employees at the outset and as new staff join the haphazard organic structure is formed. Whilst the organisation remains small, there is little justification for changing the structure but as more people are engaged the diversity of roles will increase and a formal structure will begin to form naturally at which point a formal structure should be implemented.

Alternative types of Organisational Structure

In between the Mechanistic and organic structures on the spectrum discussed above, there are a range of different structures which impose differing degrees of control. Some of these are considered below.

Functional Structure

The choice of structure for each organisation is dependent very much on what they do and the activities they undertake. The Technology industry works under a very different organisational structure to that of the manufacturing industry of fifty years ago. The most common is a functional structure. This is also referred to as a bureaucratic or mechanistic organisational structure and breaks up a company based on the specialisation of its workforce.

A functional organisational structure is based on each job's duties.

Most small-to-medium-sized businesses implement a functional structure. Dividing the firm into departments consisting of marketing, sales, and operations is the act of using a bureaucratic or mechanistic organisational structure.

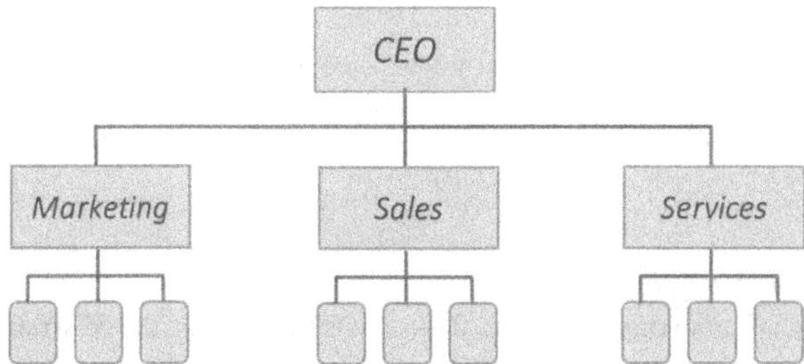

Advantages

The functional structure allows for a high degree of specialisation for employees and is easily scalable should the organisation grow. Also, this structure is mechanistic in nature -- which has the potential to inhibit an employee's growth -- putting staff in skill-based departments can still allow them to delve deep into their field and find out what they are good at.

Disadvantages

A Functional structure also has the potential to create barriers between different functions -- and it can be inefficient if the organisation has a variety of different products or target markets. The barriers created between departments can also limit peoples' knowledge of and communication with other departments, especially those that depend on other departments to succeed.

Division or Multi-division Structure

Divisional structures are common among large companies with many business operations. A company that uses this method, structures its leadership team based on the products, projects, or subsidiaries they operate. A good example of this structure is Johnson & Johnson. With thousands of products and lines of business, the company structures itself, so each business unit operates as its own company with its own president.

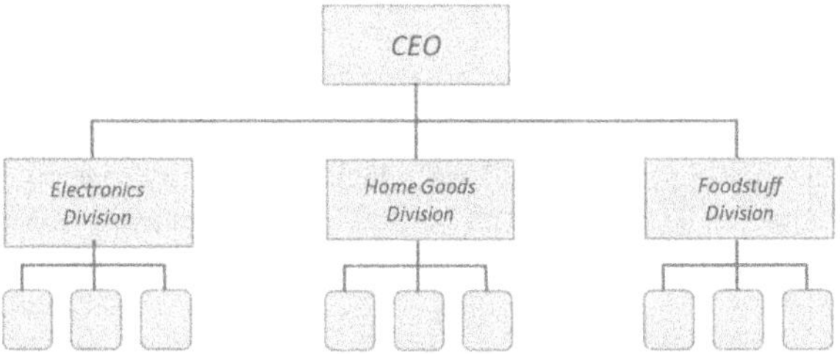

Advantages

This type of structure is ideal for organisations with multiple products and can help shorten product development cycles. This allows small businesses to go to market with new offerings fast.

Disadvantages

It can be difficult to scale under a product-based divisional structure, and the organisation could end up with duplicate resources as different divisions strive to develop new offerings.

Market-Based Structure

A variant of the divisional organisational structure is the market-based structure, where the divisions of an organisation are based around markets, industries, or customer types.

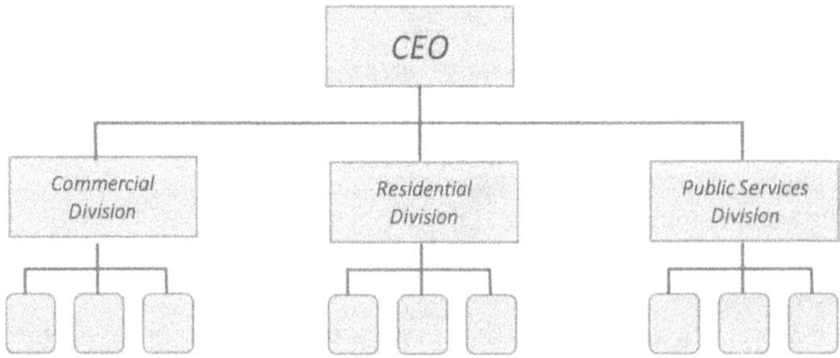

Advantages
The market-based structure is ideal for an organisation that has products or services that are unique to specific market segments and is particularly effective if that organisation has advanced knowledge of those segments. This organisational structure also keeps the business constantly aware of demand changes among its different audience segments.

Disadvantages
Too much autonomy within each market-based team can lead to divisions resulting in systems that are incompatible with one another. Divisions might also end up inadvertently duplicating activities and resources that other divisions are already handling.

Geographic Structure
The geographical organisational structure establishes its divisions based on location. More specifically, the divisions of a geographical structure can include territories, regions, or districts.

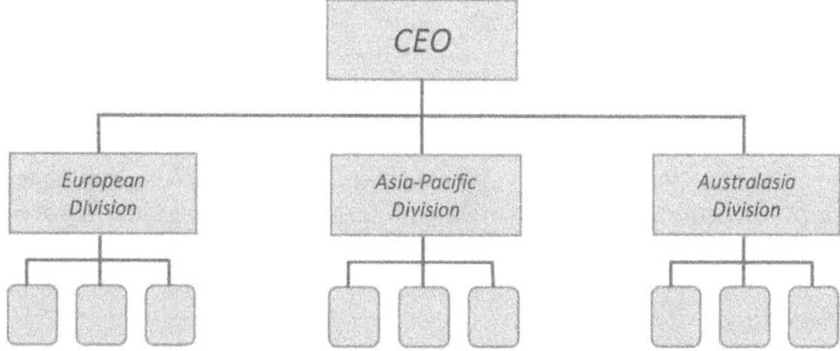

Advantages
This type of structure is best suited to organisations that need to be near sources of supply and/or
customers (e.g., for deliveries or for on-site support). It also brings together many forms of business expertise, allowing each geographical division to make decisions from more diverse points of view.

Disadvantages
The main downside of a geographical organisational structure is that it can be easy for decision making to become decentralised, because the geographic divisions (which can be hundreds, if not thousands of miles away from corporate headquarters) often have a great deal of autonomy and independence. Likewise, when you have a marketing department for each region, you run the risk of creating campaigns that compete with (and weaken) other divisions across your digital channels.

Flat Structure

While a more traditional organisational structure might look more like a pyramid -- with multiple tiers of supervisors, managers and directors between staff and senior management, the flat structure limits the levels of management, so all staff are only a few steps away from leadership. It also might not always take the form or a pyramid, or any shape for that matter. As we mentioned earlier, it is also a form of the "Organic Structure" identified above.

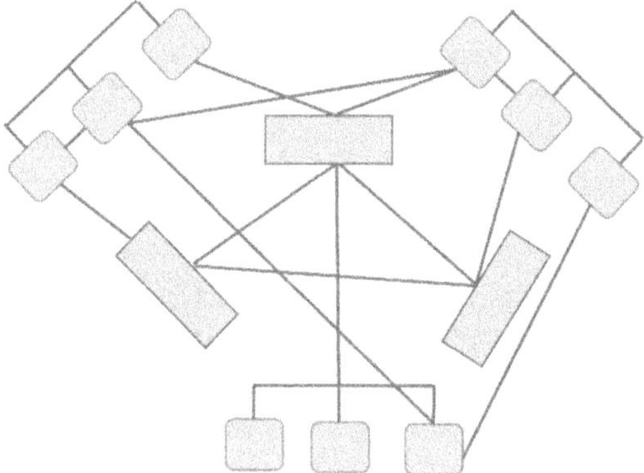

Advantages

This structure is probably one of the most detailed, it is also thought that employees can be more productive in an environment where there is less hierarchy-related pressures. The structure may also make staff feel like the managers they have are more like equals or team members rather than intimidating superiors.

Disadvantages

When teams in a flat organisation disagree on something, such as a project, it can be hard to realign and get back on track without executive decisions from a leader or manager. The complicated structure's design makes it difficult to determine which manager an employee should go to if they need approval or an executive decision for something. When using a flat organisation, there should always be a clearly marked tier of management or path that employers can refer to when they run into these scenarios.

Matrix Structure

The matrix structure is the most confusing and the least used. This structure matrixes employees across different superiors, divisions, or departments. An employee working for a matrixed company, for example, may have duties in both sales and customer service.

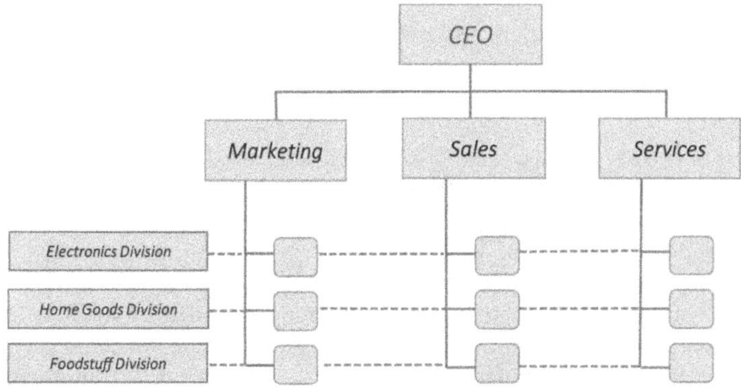

Advantages

The main appeal of the matrix structure is that it can provide both flexibility and more balanced decision-making (as there are two chains of command instead of just one). Having a single project overseen by more than one business line also creates opportunities for these business lines to share resources and communicate more openly with each other -- things they might not otherwise be able to do regularly.

Disadvantages

The primary pitfall of the matrix organisational structure is its complexity. The more layers of approval employees must go through, the more confused they can be about who they are supposed to answer to. This confusion can ultimately cause frustration over who has authority over which decisions and products -- and who is responsible for those decisions when things go wrong.

Circular Structure

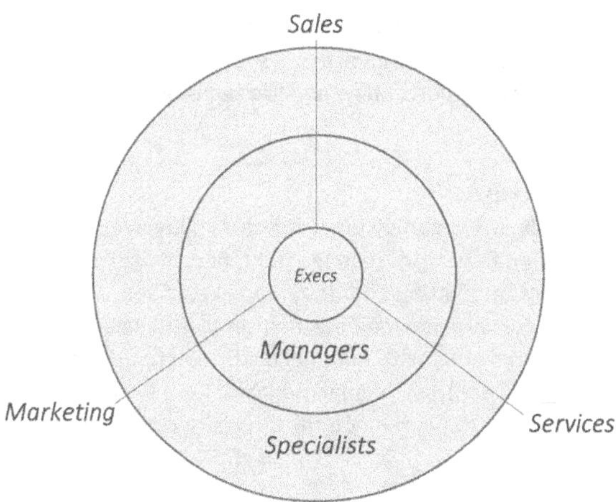

Advantages

Whilst it appears markedly different from the other organisational structures. The circular structure still relies on hierarchy, with more senior employees occupying the inner rings of the circle and lower-level employees occupying the outer rings.

The leaders or executives in a circular organisation should not be seen as sitting at the top of the organisation, sending directives down the chain of command, instead, they are at the centre of the organisation, spreading their vision outward.

The circular structure is meant to promote communication and the free flow of information between different parts of the organisation. A traditional structure shows different departments or divisions as occupying individual, semi-autonomous branches, the circular structure depicts all divisions as being part of the same whole.

Disadvantages

From a practical perspective, the circular structure can be confusing, especially for new employees. A circular structure can make it difficult for employees to figure out who they report to and how they are meant to fit into the organisation.

Benefits of Organisational Structures

Putting an organisational structure in place is beneficial to a company. The structure not only defines a company's hierarchy, but it also allows the firm to set out the pay structure for its employees. The structure also makes operations more efficient and much more effective. By separating employees and functions into different departments, the company can perform different operations at once seamlessly.

Job Descriptions to Allow for Growth

When an organisational structure is implemented, job descriptions can be developed to not only meet the organisation's goals but allow for organisational and employee growth. Internal equity and employee retention are a key to successful operations. Recruitment is also one of the highest investments for organisations, so ensuring employees have promotional opportunities and job security can assist in reducing recruitment costs.

Allow for Organisational Expansion

If an organisation expands, the organisational structure allows room for growth. This can include adding additional layers of management, new divisions, expanding one or several functional areas or appointing additional top executives. When the structure is reorganised for expansion, it provides the mechanism to edit salaries and job descriptions quickly and efficiently with minimal disruption to an organisation's operations. Within these structures, management will have a variety of roles and functions and these will differ depending on the structure chosen for the organisation.

Organisational Roles

Management roles may include but are not limited to responsibility, accountability, authority, autonomy, reporting structures, inter-dependences between functional areas (e.g., HR, finance, marketing, customer services and production), teams, colleagues, customers, suppliers, contractors, partnerships, communication, managing budgets and resources, procurement, input into strategic planning.

What is a team?
There are numerous definitions, but a team can be simply defined as:

> ***a limited number of people who have shared objectives at work and who co-operate, on a permanent or temporary basis, to achieve those objectives in a way that allows each individual to make a distinctive contribution.***

Types of Teams

There are many types of teams. What follows is not a comprehensive list, and there are other typologies or classifications.

Production and service teams - *examples are in production, construction,* **sales** *and health care. They have a relatively long lifespan, providing an ongoing product or service to customers or the organisation.*

Project and development teams - *including research and product development teams. They are dedicated to a particular objective and have limited lifespans and a clear set of short-term objectives. They are often cross-functional, with members selected for the contribution their expertise can make.*

Advice and involvement teams - *with the aim of improving, for example, working conditions or quality. Members will not devote a great deal of time to them, and once they have achieved their objectives they should be disbanded.*

Crews - *such as airline crews, who may be formed from people who have rarely worked together but through prior training clearly understand their respective roles.*

Action and negotiation teams - *such as surgical and legal teams, consist of people who tend to work together regularly. They have well-developed processes and clear objectives.*

Virtual teams - *who work in separate buildings and who may even be in different countries. Such teams may also fit into one of the above categories, such as project and*

development. They may need to communicate by telephone, e-mail and tele-conferencing rather than face-to-face.
Managing virtual teams is particularly difficult, not least because remote working can exacerbate misunderstandings.

Self-managed teams *- where much decision-making is devolved from line managers to team members. (Also known as semi-autonomous or fully autonomous teams according to the degree of self-management.) Again, such teams may also fit into one of the above categories. The 1998 Workplace Employee Relations Survey suggested that the positive benefits of team working may be largely associated with such teams, rather than teams in general. Fully or semi-autonomous teams tend to have higher than average levels of labour productivity; a lower rate of voluntary resignations; lower levels of employee dismissals, and a better than average employee relations climate.*

Normally, teams will consist of people from the same employer, but sometimes there may be teams from different employers: examples are design project teams in construction, which bring together architects and engineers from different firms, or teams which include customers or suppliers.

Benefits of Team Working

Organisations have introduced team working for the following reasons, among others:

- *to improve productivity*
- *to improve quality of products or services*
- *to improve customer focus*
- *to speed the spread of ideas*
- *to respond to opportunities and threats and to fast-changing environments*
- *to increase employee motivation*
- *to introduce multi-skilling and employee flexibility.*

There can be benefits for employees too. The most quoted outcomes are greater job satisfaction and motivation, and improved learning. But the introduction of team working needs skilful management and resources devoted to it, or initiatives may fail.

Characteristics of Effective Teams

An effective team has the following characteristics:

- *a common sense of purpose*
- *a clear understanding of the team's objectives*
- *resources to achieve those objectives*
- *mutual respect among team members, both as individuals and for the contribution each makes to the team's performance*
- *valuing members' strengths and respecting their weaknesses*
- *mutual trust*
- *willingness to share knowledge and expertise*
- *willingness to speak openly*
- *a range of skills among team members to deal effectively with all its tasks*
- *a range of personal styles for the various roles needed to carry out the team's tasks.*

Roles in a Team

In the past thirty years or so, team working has grown in importance. Until relatively recently, roles at work were well-defined. In the traditional factory, for example, there was strict division of responsibilities and most job titles conveyed exactly what people did. With advances in technology and education, employers began to place a growing emphasis on versatility, leading to an increasing interest in team working at all levels. The gradual replacement of traditional hierarchical forms with flatter organisational structures, in which employees are expected to fill a variety of roles, has also played a part in the rise of the team.

A team made up of people with the same ability, skills, beliefs and attitudes might be considered ideal, as their needs would be the same and therefore easily satisfied. The absolute opposite, however, is true.

Team members need to very different to each other as it is these differences in skills, capability, ideals, cultures, etc. which helps to make the team a strong independent unit with team members looking after and supporting each other. The goal when creating a team is to find people with complimentary skills. What one team member does not know, another one will.

It has been argued that the optimal team with have this level of diversity and Dr Meredith Belbin conducted some pioneering work on team roles in the 1970s. He identified nine team roles in addition to the necessary technical and specialist skills which need to be satisfied to achieve successful teamwork. He identified:

Belbin's work has been criticised on the grounds that individuals rarely fit neatly into these categories – most fit into more than one, and arguably the best team workers will adapt their behaviour to fill different roles as circumstances require. However, knowing that one tends to fit a certain profile arguably has value in understanding one's own and others' strengths and weaknesses.

Role	*Characteristic*
Plant	*creative, imaginative, unorthodox. Solves difficult problems.*
Resource investigator	*extrovert, enthusiastic, exploratory. Explores opportunities. Develops contacts.*
Co-ordinator	*mature, confident, a good chairperson. Clarifies goals, promotes decision making.*
Shaper	*dynamic, challenging. Has drive and courage to overcome obstacles.*
Monitor evaluator	*sober, strategic, discerning. Sees all options.*
Team worker	*co-operative, mild, perceptive, diplomatic. Listens, builds, averts friction.*
Implementer	*disciplined, reliable, conservative. Turns ideas into practical action.*
Completer	*painstaking, conscientious, anxious. Searches out errors and omissions, delivers on time.*
Specialist	*single-minded, self-starting, dedicated. Provides knowledge and skill in rare supply.*

Team selection is not an exact science and instinct should come into play as well. A mix of types is necessary, as is a mix of skills – for example, selecting a team of IT specialists to look at an IT project would be wrong (although it happens!); users of the IT system will need to be included in the team.

Teams can include senior and junior people (for the latter, team membership may also be a development opportunity) and someone relatively junior may be a team leader. To reiterate, what is most important is the team's mix of skills and types.

Team Size

Most commentators suggest that between five and eight people is the ideal size for teams. Teams need to be large enough to incorporate the appropriate range of expertise and representation of interests, but not so large that people's participation, and hence their interest, is limited.

Team Leadership

Leadership is vital for successful teams.

There is no one recipe for successful team leadership. Like other team members, team leaders have their own personal styles, which they need to understand and work within.

Some people, by instinct, will be directive – they will want to tell people what to do. Those with directive tendencies will need to temper their approach to avoid causing resentment; otherwise, other team members may ask 'If he knows all the answers, why are we involved?'.

Others will be democratic and ask questions to gain commitment and get people on board, even if they themselves have clear ideas about how things should be done. Leaders with democratic tendencies will need to be aware that there is a danger of drift and lack of direction if there is too much debate.

Some leaders will be more involved, while others will let team members get on by themselves.

Whatever their personal styles, leaders should:

- *listen to team members*
- *question them to understand their points of view*
- *be responsive to feedback.*

In this way they act as facilitators or coaches to get the most out of team members, and to encourage learning and creativity. The roles that leaders play, and hence the ways in which they behave, may differ at different stages of team development. Helping to overcome conflict in the early stages may develop to setting tasks at a later stage. It can also be argued that successful team leaders need a high degree of emotional intelligence.

In some situations, leadership may rotate. Different individuals may take the lead at different stages of a project for which a team is responsible. Some semi-autonomous or fully autonomous teams may also appoint their own leaders as they see fit.

Team Training and Learning

Team building training is often necessary to assist the move from working in a traditional hierarchy to being part of a team, and in circumstances where team members have not worked together previously and may not even know each other. Such training may consist of exercises carried out jointly under a facilitator, sometime outdoors to enable people to get to know each other and to work together, understanding each other's strengths and weaknesses.

Communications, knowledge-sharing and problem-solving may often be on the agenda, but the areas covered will depend on the nature and role of the team, so it is impossible to generalise.

Social events may also be used to get team members to know each other. Separate training may take place for team leaders. As projects develop, there may be additional training that emerges from the team's needs. An important role of the team leader is to act as a coach or facilitator to encourage learning.

Team Reward

It is a criticism of traditional appraisal systems that they do not give sufficient weight to individual contributions to teams, but this is starting to change. A few organisations have introduced team pay systems, aimed at encouraging group endeavour rather than individual performance. Research has found that such schemes are less important for success than management style, culture and the working environment. If team pay is to be introduced, it should be done with great care, and the complementary impact of non-financial reward should always be acknowledged.

The importance of team working

The principle of working together in a team should underpin how an individual operates. Managing or leading people does not just mean acting as overseer, to see that they get their work done satisfactorily. It means involving people throughout the team in a creative role, to ensure that together you are all able to succeed.

Involving people on broad issues is motivational. Never underestimate people. Their views can enhance everything from methods, standards, processes to overall effectiveness.

Managers are not paid to have all the ideas that are necessary to keep their section working well in a changing world, but they are paid to make sure that there are enough ideas to make things work and go on working.

The Organisational Purpose

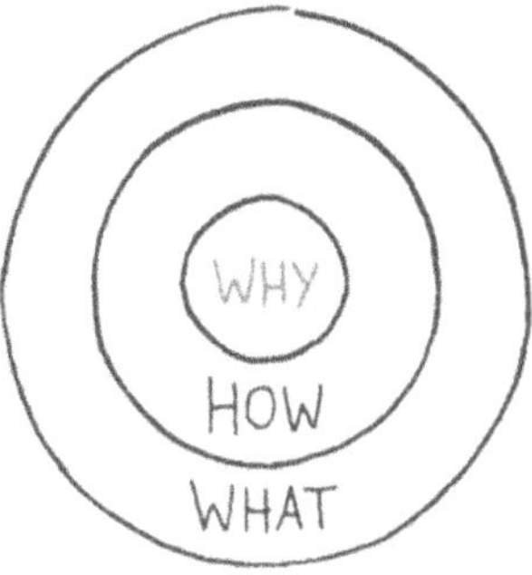

The Organisational Purpose does not explain what it does, but rather defines why it exists – what purpose does it serve.

Rather than asking the question - What do you do? it asks the question Why is the work you do important? The organisational purpose of a fast-food outlet might be to serve the public quickly and safely. It does not consider how it will achieve profits, set goals or targets, but simply states why it exists, what is it there to do.

Organisational Purpose is fundamental to an organisation because it is the basis for all aspects of the business.

Employees must genuinely believe that the purpose is meaningful. If the purpose is not supported by employees, then a key factor in gaining employee engagement is missing.

In the bigger picture of any organisation, the purpose is at the very heart of its existence, everything else sits around this core purpose.

The management and employees must agree on the organisation's Purpose.

The table below contains some examples of purpose statements.

Organisation	*Purpose*
Facebook	*We bring the world closer together*
IKEA	*We make everyday life better*
Private Healthcare	*We help people on their path to better health*
Virgin Group	*Changing Business for Good*
Kellogg's	*Nourishing families so they can flourish and thrive*

The statement should be meaningful for employees, and easily understood. It must be more than just a cliched set of words. It must capture the emotion of the business. It must encourage employees to feel part of something positive and inspire them with the energy to achieve more. It should also be directed but improving society as a whole.

Purpose becomes even more important when you think about the world today and the challenges we all face.

Organisations today are part of communities, societies and the planet. Purpose focusses on how the organisation makes a difference and this is a goal that can be extended to achieving a better world.

The understanding and use of organisational purpose has changed over the years.

Organisations used only to view their purpose as way to make money. Managers believed that making money was the only reason they were in business. They believed employees would be motivated and engaged with this narrow view.

Organisations must make money to stay in business, and employees need to make money to support themselves and their families. However, once a worker has sufficient money to live, making money as a purpose is no longer valid and therefore the purpose ceases to be of importance.

Organisations also view their purpose from their customers perspective. If what the organisation does made things better in some way for those they serve, then that too is a meaningful purpose. It does not take long to realise that purpose is not just a contribution to external issues. It must also be a contribution for the people who work there.

If an organisation chooses improving health and well-being as its purpose, it would be wrong if the company only sought to improve the health and wellbeing of their customers. Employees cannot be expected to work each day to improve the health of "others" when the company neglects the health and well-being of its employees. The focus of purpose has grown from just being customer focused to also being employee focused.

Today, the visionary organisations have expanded their view on Purpose still further. An organisation is more than a vehicle for serving employees and customers. Organisations today recognise they must also make a meaningful impact on the communities it serves, to the society at large and even to the planet.

If you are creating a purpose statement, you must - inspire your staff to do good work for you, find a way to express the organisation's impact on the lives of all stakeholders and make sure it has an emotional impact so they can "feel" it.

Mission, Vision and Value Statements

In the latter part of the 20th century organisations began to introduce Statements or Charters which were aimed at telling people why the organisation existed, what it did and how it did it. Today, successful businesses have moved on from issuing lengthy, wordy, statements that no employee can understand, never mind remember.

Today it is common to have three concise company statements:

The Vision Statement

A vision statement is a statement of an organisation's overarching aspirations of what it hopes to achieve or to become. Here are some examples of vision statements:

> ***Disney:*** *To make people happy*
> ***IKEA:*** *To create a better everyday life for the many people*
> ***British Broadcasting Company (BBC):*** *To be the most creative organisation in the world*
> ***Avon:*** *To be the company that best understands and satisfies the product, service and self-fulfilment needs of women—globally*
> ***Sony Corporation:*** *To be a company that inspires and fulfils your curiosity*

The vision statement does not provide specific targets. Notice that each of the above examples could apply to many different organisations. Instead, the vision is a broad description of the value an organisation provides. It is a visual image of what the organisation is trying to produce or become. It should inspire people and motivate them to want to be part of and contribute to the organisation.

Vision statements should be clear and concise, usually not longer than a short paragraph.

The Mission Statement

The vision statement and mission statement are often confused, and many companies use the terms interchangeably. However, they each have a different purpose. The vision statement describes where the organisation wants to be in the future – the dream! the mission statement describes what the organisation needs to do now to achieve the vision – the how!

The vision and mission statements must support each other, but the mission statement is more specific. It defines how the organisation will be different from other organisations in its industry. Here are examples of mission statements from successful businesses:

> ***Adidas:*** *We strive to be the global leader in the sporting goods industry with brands built on a passion for sports and a sporting lifestyle.*
> ***Amazon:*** *We seek to be Earth's most customer-centric company for four primary customer sets: consumers, sellers, enterprises, and content creators.*
> ***Google:*** *To organise the world's information and make it universally accessible and useful*

Each of these examples indicates where the organisation will compete (what industry it is in) and how it will compete (what it will do to be different from other organisations). The mission statement conveys to stakeholders why the organisation exists. It explains how it creates value for the market or the larger community.

Because it is more specific, the mission statement is more actionable than the vision statement. By describing why, the organisation exists, and where and how it will compete, the mission statement allows leaders to define a coherent set of goals that fit together to support the mission.

The mission statement leads to the creation of strategic goals.

Strategic goals are the broad goals the organisation will try to achieve.

Today, most businesses have a Mission Statement – whether it is a formal statement emblazoned on publicity materials, websites, etc or an informal statement which is used in house as a reference.

It is important for every organisation to have its mission and vision statements as it serves as a guide when it comes to decision making and alignment.

The Values Statement

The values statement, also called the code of ethics, differs from both the vision and mission statements. The vision and mission statements define where the organisation is going (vision) and what it will do to get there (mission). They direct the efforts of people in the organisation toward common goals.

The values statement defines what the organisation believes in and how people in the organisation are expected to behave—with each other, with customers and suppliers, and with other stakeholders. It provides a moral direction for the organisation that guides decision making and establishes a standard for assessing actions. It also provides a standard for employees to judge exceptions.

Managers cannot just create a values statement and expect it to be followed.

For a values statement to be effective, it must be reinforced at all levels of the organisation and must be used to guide attitudes and actions. Organisations with strong values follow their values even when it may be easier not to. Levi Strauss & Co is an excellent example of a company that is driven by its values.

When Levi Strauss began to outsource its manufacturing overseas, the company developed a set of principles for overseas operations and suppliers. One of the principles covered the use of child labour:

> *Use of child labour is not permissible. Workers can be no less than 15 years of age and not younger than the compulsory age to be in school. We will not utilise partners who use child labour in any of their facilities. We support the development of legitimate workplace apprenticeship programs for the educational benefit of younger people.*

Levi Strauss found that one of its contractors was employing children under 15 in a factory in Bangladesh. The easy solution would be to replace the contractor, but in Bangladesh, the children's wages may have supported an entire family. If they lost their jobs, they may have had to resort to begging on the streets.

Levi Strauss came up with a different solution, one that supported its values of empathy, originality, integrity, and courage: it paid the children to go to school. Levi Strauss continued to pay salaries and benefits to the children and paid for tuition, books, and supplies. Even though it would have been easier to just fire the child laborers and consider the problem settled, Levi Strauss was driven by its values to find a better solution.

Together, the vision, mission, and values statements provide direction for everything that happens in an organisation. They keep everyone focused on where the organisation is going and what it is trying to achieve. They define the core values of the organisation and how people are expected to behave. They are not intended to be a straitjacket that restricts or inhibits initiative and innovation, but they are intended to guide decisions and behaviours to achieve common ends.

Customer Service Statement

In the 21st century, competition has never been greater, customer choice has never been wider and the needs and demands of customers is constantly changing. As a result, these three statements are no longer enough – today a business must also address Customer Service with a clear statement about Customer Service within the organisation.

In some instances, this may be included in the Mission Statement, but increasingly organisations are producing separate statements which detail exactly what type of customer service you want your company to provide to its customers.

Think of a mission statement for a football team – it may be "to win the Premier League title". However, that is not what the defenders or midfielders will say to each other at the start of the match!

Winning the Premier League is a result, not the action.

The Customer Service Statement would be how the game would be played. This one statement is the one every employee in the organisation must be able to understand and know it backwards and forwards.

The Customer Service Statement is what each and every employee, regardless of department, level, or wage, must deliver to every Customer, every time. It provides a meaningful purpose for the employees.

The Customer Service Statement is never shared with the outside public, i.e., Customers. It is only used by the employees.

The Disney vision: – To make people happy – is just that - a vision. It is the Customer Service Statement which will define how the employees can achieve that.

Organisational Strategies

Organisational strategy is a combination of a clear vision, coupled with a meaningful mission and purpose, underlined with some clear steps to make sure the right resources and plans are in place to achieve outcome-based goals.

An organisational strategy is the sum of the actions a company intends to take to achieve long term goals, and these will help to form a strategic plan.

The strategic plans will need involvement from all levels within the organisation. Whilst managers at the top will create the organisational strategy, middle and lower management will help by looking at the step-by-step actions that are needed to fulfil the goals to achieve the overall strategy. This collaboration is like a journey, where each step must be satisfied to enable the journey to continue which leads to the ultimate destination.

Building a culture where employees understand the organisational strategy and purpose, have buy-in to the business and team objectives, and want to develop ideas that creates continuous improvement, is a culture that has the 'hearts and minds' of the people.

Together, these actions make up the organisation's strategic plan.

Strategic Plans

Strategic plans take at least a year to complete, requiring involvement from all company levels. Top management creates the larger organisational strategy, while middle and lower management adopt goals and plans to fulfil the overall strategy step by step.

This unified effort can be likened to a journey. The journey starts at the point we are at today and ends at the ultimate destination. The route to get there will be formulated and the road conditions encountered on the journey are the challenges which need to be overcome to complete each stage of the journey, which will eventually lead to the ultimate destination.

Effective planning usually results in a written strategic plan. This is a formalised document that describes the business' goals, and the actions needed to achieve them.

The Purpose of Strategic Planning

Strategic planning is a systematic process that helps to set an ambition for the business' future and determine how best to achieve it. Its primary purpose is to connect three key areas:

the mission *- defining your business' purpose*
the vision *- describing what you want to achieve*
the plan *- outlining how you want to achieve your ultimate goals*

The Importance of Strategic Planning

Strategic planning is necessary to determine the direction for an organisation. It focuses effort and ensures that everyone in the business is working towards a common goal. It also helps to:

- *agree actions that will contribute to business growth*
- *align resources for optimal results*
- *prioritise financial needs*
- *build competitive advantage*
- *engage with your staff and communicate what needs to be done*

Another significant purpose of strategic planning is to help to manage and reduce business risks.

Growing a business is inherently risky. Detailed planning may help to:

- *remove uncertainty*
- *analyse potential risks*
- *implement risk control measures*
- *consider how to minimise the impact of risks, should they occur*

There are a variety of models and approaches which can be beneficial in strategic planning. Many businesses include a SWOT analysis or a PESTLE analysis as key elements of their strategic plan.

SWOT Analysis

Managers can produce these quickly and simply to help to clarify their thinking and focus their attention on all aspects of the problem. A SWOT analysis is particularly useful for gathering, interpreting and analysing information. For each realistic possible solution, managers can analyse the following:

S – *Strengths*
W – *Weaknesses*
O – *Opportunities*
T – *Threats to success*

If your car has been breaking down and causing you problems, a SWOT analysis could show, for example:

	Option A – *have it fixed every time to keep it going for as long as possible – maybe another year*	**Option B** – *replace the car with a brand-new, up-to-date version that should last ten years*	**Option C** – *replace it with a second hand, model that should last five years*
Strengths	*Not too expensive to run The problems are well-known and familiar*	*Good reliability Up-to-date technology Good warranty support*	*Reasonable cost Its service history should indicate reliability Know how to operate it*
Weaknesses	*Cost of repairs Frequent disruption of your life that cannot be planned Drop in your efficiency and performance*	*Very expensive May have to make sacrifices Will be difficult to look after properly*	*Does not benefit from the most up-to-date technology and design Only a short warranty Could develop problems at any time*
Opportunities	*Easy to arrange with garage for repairs*	*Three possible suppliers Available in about two months*	*Plenty available if researched online Could be bought quickly as changes to storage arrangements not needed*
Threats	*Garage staff may refuse to repair it when it breaks again. Repair costs are high. Wages could be lost due to delays*	*Cost and budget constraints Might be outdated after a few years Personal benefits may not justify cost*	*Cost might not be justifiable if planning to keep it for less than five years*

Although a SWOT analysis does not give a magic answer to the problem, it does help managers to identify the pros and cons of each option. Once they know their budget constraints and the long-term targets, the decision makers would be able to identify the best solution to the problem.

PESTLE Analysis

Another system that could be used when wishing to make well-informed decisions is a PESTLE analysis.

This can be particularly useful when there are areas of concern, outside of the control of the organisation, and for gathering, interpreting and analysing information.

For example, if the problem is that the company has outgrown its present site and is considering solutions to the problem, it will have to consider many things that are outside its control. When doing a PESTLE analysis, managers would look at these areas:

P	*Political*	*e.g., government funding for expanding in the same area or setting up in a different location*
E	*Economic*	*e.g., the overall economic climate and whether stakeholders would support investment and expansion if the economy is slow or in recession*
S	*Social*	*e.g., the effect on the local population if the company moves away/stays put and expands*
T	*Technological*	*e.g., the scope for using new technology as part of the expansion plans*
L	*Legal*	*e.g., legal requirements about redundancies or relocation of staff*
E	*Environmental*	*e.g., the regulations on emissions and waste management in the current area and the potential new area*

You may also want to include an implementation schedule, key performance indicators (KPIs) and other accountability measures.

Factors Affecting an Organisation

You may often hear the term *trend* in relation to the way an organisation of the economy is performing. These trends are often caused by a variety of influences which might include:

- *Governments*
- *International trading activity*
- *Speculation and expectation*
- *Supply and demand*

These are known as Market Forces and are the factors that influence the price and availability of goods and services in a market economy, i.e., an economy with the minimum of government involvement.

Market forces push prices up when supply declines and demand rises and drive them down when supply grows or demand contracts. When demand equals supply for a product or service, the market is said to have reached equilibrium

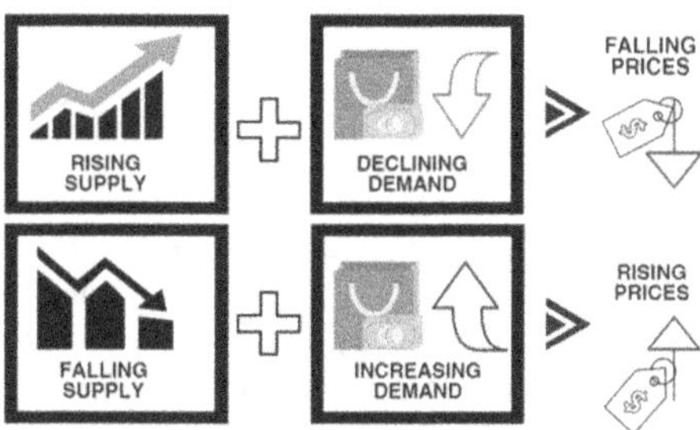

Government

Governments across the World have a great deal of influence how business trades both within their own borders and more widely at an international level. The fiscal and monetary policies that governments and the central banks put in place will have a profound effect on the economy.

The Government will increase or decrease taxes as it sees necessary. If it needs to raise money, it will raise taxes. If it wants to stimulate the economy, create jobs and encourage investment, it will reduce taxes, freeing up money to be spent thus boosting the economy. This is known as monetary policy.

The Bank of England has the power to set and adjust interest rates and these are used as a brake or accelerator on the UK economy. Lower interest rates mean it is cheaper to borrow money and therefore there is an inclination to spend. This will lead to an upturn in trade as people buy goods and services meaning the volume of trade increases and business becomes mor profitable.

Conversely, when interest rates are increased, it causes the economy to shrink. Money becomes more expensive to borrow and because repayments against debts is increasing, there is a reduced amount of money available for spending elsewhere and so the economy contracts. This is known as monetary policy.

International Trade

The way in which money flows between countries affects the strength of a country's economy and its currency. The more money that is leaving a country, the weaker the country's economy and its currency becomes. Countries that are predominantly exporters of goods and services are continually bringing money into their countries. This money can then be reinvested and can stimulate the financial markets within those countries.

Prior to Brexit, the United Kingdom traded goods and services around the World under trade agreements which were agreed by the European Union. This meant that the international trade helped to support the Euro as well as the Pound. Now the UK has left the European Union, it is now seeking trade agreements around the World to enable independent trade which will boost the UK economy and strengthen the value of the pound against other international currencies.

Speculation and Expectation

Speculation and expectation are integral parts of the financial system. Huge amounts of money are made on the international money markets by trading in foreign currencies and shares. News of a major takeover of an organisation will prompt dealers to buy shares because such activity is a sign the business is doing well, and the share value will rise. Likewise, the money markets will respond in a similar way to the news that Governments are to reduce taxes or lower interest rates, indicating that the economy is buoyant. Future action is dependent on current activity and this type of speculation shapes both current and future trends.

Supply and Demand

Supply and demand has long been a key theme for economists' organisations which manufacture or sell goods or services. The greater the demand, the higher the price that can be charged for an item. If there is no demand for a product the price will be reduced to tempt people to buy something which is far less popular than other items on the marketplace. This is true for everything from consumer goods to aeroplanes! Who wants to buy a Turkey in January? Think about new cars = how many people are still buying petrol- or diesel-powered cars when we know that they will be banned in the near future and fuel may become difficult and expensive to buy.

If something is in demand and supply begins to shrink, prices will rise. If supply increases beyond current demand, prices will fall. If supply is relatively stable, prices can fluctuate higher and lower as demand increases or decreases.

Policy and Regulatory Change

Policy and regulatory change means that the government are changing the rules. These changes will impact heavily on organisations across all sectors and because the change is a government action, they must be complied with businesses must change to meet their new requirements.

This may be changes to taxation such as increases to VAT, corporate taxation, personal taxation or a range of other levies and duties which the government is able to apply. All of this will have an impact on the businesses which it affects.

One of the most common examples of policy and regulatory change is the annual change to the national minimum wage. Each year the government decides what the national minimum wage should be based on a number of criteria including the retail price index,

inflation, etc. and then sets the minimum amount of money an employer must pay an employee per hour for the next 12 months.
There may also be changes to tariffs and training policies. This is currently affecting the United Kingdom as, following Brexit, the United Kingdom must renegotiate trade deals with other countries across the world otherwise there is a requirement to trade under World Trade Organisation rules which apply fixed tariffs to the import and export of goods.

Free trade agreements allow all such trade to take place without there being any tariffs applied. The United Kingdom now has a limited trade policy with the European Union whereby the majority of goods may be traded free of tariff, providing that certain quotas are not exceeded, or the other policy changes do not make those particular goods more favourable than those available in the EU states.

Another example of policy and regulatory change is the use of subsidies. Governments may choose to subsidise certain sectors or industries using government money to allow the goods or services to be sold internationally or locally at discounted prices. It is common for Governments to subsidise the cost of public transport to encourage people to use it rather than using their own personal transport to reduce congestion or emission. This is a practise which is also being used in China where the government subsidises the cost of production of some goods and in some cases, the cost of postage to other countries around the world for goods which are sold online from China.

GDPR is another example of regulatory activity which is impacted on businesses. GDPR was introduced to protect data which is being collected and stored in every increasing quantities, from abuse or misuse by other organisations or countries. The impact on business has been significant.

Many organisations have had to introduce new policies, procedures and methods of working to ensure compliance with GDPR and others have also had to make major changes to the information they collect from websites, social media and other platforms in common use today. This has not only affected businesses in the UK, the GDPR regulations were part of European law, which has further impacted across the World as the regulations apply to data which is collected from citizens of the nations who fall under the GDPR regulations. This means other continents have also had to accommodate these changes, but more importantly, it serves as a warning that they too may soon be subject to similar policy changes to ensure data protection within their borders as well.

Chapter 3: The Need for Learning and Development

Learning and Development

In its broadest terms, Learning and Development covers all professional development within an organisation and is considered a core function of Human Resource (HR) operations. This learning and development includes formal, tutor-led educational programs and informal, employee-driven learning.

At the highest level, Learning and Development is about understanding the organisational strategy and from that, anticipating the future capability needs of the business. This will help identify the current and future learning priorities for the organisation.

At an individual level, it is about creating an environment where employees can continuously develop and support them to be their best.

The difference between Human Resources and Learning and Development

The principal difference between Learning and Development and Human Resources is that Human Resources covers all aspects related to employees, whilst Learning and Development focuses on the specific task of employee development.

The Human Resources department will deal with payroll, employee relations, recruitment, and employee benefits, whilst the Learning and Development role focusses on the growth of employees and their acquisition of new skills.

There is a significant overlap between the two in terms of induction, change management, succession planning, and employee performance assessment.

Given the umbrella role of the Human Resources department, Learning and Development is typically overseen by the HR department.

Irrespective of how an organisation structures its Learning and Development and Human Resources operations, both must work in parallel to create a workforce capable of achieving the wider business goals

Human Resources	*Learning and Development*
Manages all aspects relating to employees	*Focusses exclusively on employee development*
Deals with Payroll, employee relations, recruitment and employee benefits	*Focusses on the growth of employees and the development of new skills*
Is reactive to employee management – when problems arise Human Resources solve them	*Proactive in influencing employee satisfaction and retention*

The Need for Learning and Development

The need for Learning and Development in every organisation should never be underestimated. However, Learning and Development is a costly practice which needs close control and management.

Learning and Development which is unnecessary, not relevant, above or below the capabilities of the learner or does not directly benefit the organisation is a waste of time, effort and money and should be avoided at all costs.

Investing in employee learning and development is a reliable way for organisations to derive a greater return from their employment costs leading to improved overall profitability. Additionally, learning and development initiatives can increase employee engagement and retention rates and foster an addictive work culture or learning ecosystem.

Learning and Development is also vital to an organisation's talent acquisition and management strategy, by offering new opportunities to help attract and maximise employee performance.

With the digitisation and automation of many business practices, organisations now, increasingly require a technically skilled and capable workforce. Learning and Development is a critical tool to bridge the skills gap and future-proof employees by ensuring they have the necessary skills to operate effectively in the modern economy.

Employee learning and development interventions can take many forms, from classroom-style teaching to online learning to coaching and personalised educational programs designed to maximise each individual's skills.

Learning and development is essential in a number of situations:

- *Induction / Onboarding*
- *Improving performance*
- *Employee development*
- *Compliance*
- *Business Change*

Induction Training

This is the process of introducing new starters to both their role within the organisation and the organisation itself. It is necessary to ensure that new employees are integrated as quickly as possible in order to ensure they become productive as quickly as possible.

It is also the opportunity for the organisation to set the tone, impart company values, outline the cultural, ethical and professional stance of the business as well ironing out any potential teething problems during the early, formative, days of their time with the organisation

The content of induction training will depend on the job role being filled, however, there will be common elements across all levels of employee and these can include:

- *The company history*
- *The company structure and their role within it*
- *Company objectives and plans*
- *Ethical and Cultural Values*
- *Health and Safety*
- *Fire Safety*
- *Sickness Reporting*
- *Grievance and Disciplinary*
- *First Aid*
- *Pension*
- *Practices, policies and procedures*

This list is really just a small snapshot of what might be included. Depending on the industry there may be specific training needs which must be completed before work can begin.

Employees dealing with personal data will need to be trained on the issues surrounding GDPR. Those involved in financial services may need to be made aware of practices and procedures required by the authorities responsible for services they provide.

There may be a career development plan withing the business and inductions can be an ideal time to explain about the learning and development plans which are in place within the organisation. There may also be social activities within the organisation which may need explanation.

It is vital to ensure that the induction covers as many areas as necessary, but more importantly, that it does it in slick professional manner to create ethe very best view of the organisation given the importance of first impressions. By defining what is and what is not acceptable at the outset can prevent many problems later on.

Improving performance

Staff will need training for a variety of reasons which may include:

- *increase their productivity and quality of work*
- *increase overall profits*

- *improve employee motivation*
- *improve customer satisfaction*
- *give you a competitive advantage*
- *reduce staff turnover and absenteeism*

Performance Management will use Learning and Development as a tool to align performance with standards or expectations. An employee who is not meeting expected targets or failing to achieve KPIs will often be given support to help develop their knowledge and skills as part of any performance management process.

The training may take the form of coaching or more formalised methods of learning; however, the training will have a specific purpose with clearly defined objectives. This is a specialised form of training which will be tailored to the needs of the individual and their specific needs and circumstances. It is important to ensure only the areas in need of development are identified.

Employee development

Having considered the scope, scale and cost of induction training, it is clear that any attempts to reduce the frequency that this L&D activity needs to be carried out are beneficial for the organisation on many levels.

By developing existing employees the organisation is able to plan for the future, identify those who have the necessary qualities to progress through the organisation, but may not at this stage have the necessary skills for progression.

By supporting this organic development, the need for induction training is reduced, the employees are already aware of the company ethics, culture, values and policies and procedures. They need only to develop their skills in identified areas in order to perform at a higher level. This type of development is often outsourced by the organisation, using specialist providers or facilitators to oversee the delivery of the learning, typically in the form of apprenticeships and distance learning degree courses.

Compliance

Development will be necessary in situations where there are legislative or procedural changes which are mandated and it is essential that the organisation complies with the new rules.

GDPR was a classic example of this. The strict regulations imposed on business by the Data Protection Act meant many procedures which had been carried out for years by organisations, suddenly became illegal under the GDPR regulations and processes and practices had to be changed which resulted in there being a widespread need for Learning and Development to ensure everyone who was affected by the regulations was fully trained and skilled in the procedural changes.

At a simpler level, this could include refresher training for food safety or first aid. In some industries, staff must be regularly reassessed and their knowledge checked – all of this will require Learning and Development in order to maintain the standards necessary.

Business Development

All businesses undergo periods of change and this is becoming more common as they strive to keep pace with changes in technology, customer preferences, legislation, a changing labour market, etc.

This change is often delivered by creating project teams who will work of specific aspects of delivering business growth. These project teams work with clearly defined objectives which are formed as part of the organisations strategic plan.

Whilst these are usually very well considered and planned the one area which is most frequently forgotten is the impact it will have on the employees of the organisation. Without the support and buy in of the employees, the project will never work if they are not supportive of the planned changes.

Alongside a Project Team, there should always be a Change Management team whose responsibility it is to prepare the employees for the change by ensuring that they are aware of the change through first-hand information and not coffee machine gossip. That they are provided with training to ensure they are appropriately prepared for the change and that this continues to be reinforced with backup training and support after the changes have taken place.

The Importance of Learning and Development

The importance of Learning and Development should never be underestimated. The benefits it can deliver to an organisation are diverse and numerous. Some of the most important ones are detailed below.

Employees

Today, employees care about whether organisations invest in Learning and Development. To them it shows the leadership is committed to their personal growth and is willing to develop existing staff members rather than looking to progress through recruitment.

Organisations where Learning and Development is embedded in the culture of the organisation can reasonably expect employees to remain longer with the organisation, reducing staff turnover and reducing recruitment costs.

- *Employees will remain 2.5 years longer with an organisation which invests in Learning and Development*
- *87% of millennials value development opportunities as being important when looking for jobs.*
- *59% rate development opportunities as critical in a job search.*
- *92% of Learning and Development personnel believe L&D Strategies increase the sense of belonging*
- *Employees are 5.2 times more likely to be engaged in their work as a result of Learning and Development activity.*

Recruitment

Companies that demonstrate their commitment to Learning and Development, making it part of their employer branding, do better when looking to recruit new employees. Employees are motivated to work for organisations that invest in them, potentially helping their careers long-term.

People want to work for companies which invest in them and support them to develop their careers. In turn, this leads to:

- *Higher quality applicants*
- *Reduces expenditure on recruitment*
- *Reduces time to fill new roles*
- *Increases the number of potential applicants*

Retraining

The cost of recruiting and training new employees is significantly more than retraining employees who are already employed. Think about all the additional training needed to get a new employee to the same level of competence as an existing employee. By retraining the existing employee, all of these costs are saved.

- *Replacing an employee can cost the organisation up to twice their annual salary*
- *79% of Learning and Development professionals believe it is more expensive to recruit than retrain*

Customers

When dealing with a company, customers want to deal with enthusiastic, engaged employees who are experts in their field and clearly understand the product or service being discussed. The application of development solutions can reduce the time it takes to answer queries and improve the quality of responses, so customers are more likely to get a quick and accurate solution the first time. This boosts customer satisfaction and helps produce repeat customers willing to return after a successful experience.

The customers who use organisations which have highly skilled and competent employees will benefit significantly over others which will lead to increased loyalty, advocacy and therefore improved margins.

Profitability

There is an increasing amount of unquestionable evidence linking Learning and Development with increased profitability in organisations with planned L&D programmes. Organisations today simply cannot afford to ignore the benefits to be derived from Learning and Development.

- *Skilled workforces in L&D driven organisations are 10% more productive that their counterparts in other organisations*
- *Learning and Development can lead to a 14-29% increase in profitability*
- *An investment of around £1500 per employee per annum n L&D activity will generate 24% more profit than those spending less*

Learning and development is essential for staff, leadership, and customers. It helps employees develop their skills and expertise to allow the business to open new opportunities and advance their careers.

Businesses can build the workforce they need, improve performance, and increase profitability.

Finally, customers have a better experience interacting with well-trained, competent and knowledgeable staff who know how to help them and can make qualified and constructive suggestions

Benefits of Learning and Development

The benefits of planned, structured Learning and Development programmes far exceed the cost of development and implementation and furthermore, the benefits continue to be reaped over an extended period of time.

Some of these benefits are:

- *Higher employee retention*
- *Reduced stress in the workplace with competent and confident staff capable of delivering*
- *The discovery of hidden potential within the workforce*
- *More outstanding work-life balance among staff members*
- *Increased job security*
- *Increasing productivity and the number of work employees can complete*
- *Higher customer satisfaction*
- *Attracting new customers and spotting emerging opportunities in the market*
- *Greater efficiency and better use of company resources to reduce outlays*

Challenges facing Learning and Development Practitioners

The challenges which face todays Learning and Development teams are different to those they faced even a few years ago. Today the workforce is becoming increasingly diverse and its needs continue to evolve and expand. Tutors re delivering to multigenerational teams which include tech savvy younger employees, but who lack operation knowledge and skills to those older employees who have the operational skills but lack the technology skills they need in today's workplace. The training courses which are delivered, must take this into account.

Teaching the hard skills needed for the workplace is a fairly straightforward practice, however, helping staff to develop the soft skills needed in today's business environment requires far more consideration and planning.

Hybrid working has introduced new challenges for the Learning and Development departments. Programmes now need to accommodate this and an increase in online and e-learning activity is being increasingly relied upon at the expense of collaborative learning.

Engagement is become increasingly difficult to achieve. Employees today become absorbed in computer games and they expect a similar level of absorption in the learning they undertake, where this does not happen, they become disengaged and the learning opportunity is lost.

It is also important to consider the effectiveness of the Learning and Development activity. The cost of activities today and it is important to be able to assess the effectiveness and the benefit to be derived from every intervention. Training activity which is not effective or does not achieve the planned outcome is an unnecessary expense which must be avoided. Measuring the effectivity of training is therefore a critical part of the Learning and Development function.

The level of investment in Learning and Development continues to grow and it is increasingly important that this investment is justified by measuring the return being achieved on the investment. Training programmes must at least be self-financing and should achieve more besides. A failure to achieve this could result in the demise of the Learning and Development function!

Roles in Learning and Development

There is no right or wrong way to structure a Learning and Development team and therefore, there is no right or wrong way of assigning job titles and/or roles within that team.

Who does what is simply a matter for each individual organisation and the needs of the Learning and Development function within the organisation.

Some typical roles might include:

Trainers – the people that facilitate learning within the organisation, running classroom-style sessions, one-on-one interactions, or demonstrating on-the-job skills. Trainers need to have a firm grasp of the educational material and the ability to deliver it engagingly, maximising the knowledge employees learn and retain.

Coaches – practitioners who partner with specific employees or teams in order to enhance their skills and maximise their potential. Coaches will be implicit in employee training programs and will set goals based on their pre-existing skillset and what they want to achieve.

Content designers – the Learning and Development role that designs and develops learners' educational content and experiences within the organisation. This content can include anything used during learning, such as slides, guides, assessments, etc.

E-learning specialists – employees who create and deliver digital learning experiences such as online self-study, virtual classrooms, and digital collaborations.

Learning and Development managers – also known as talent development managers, oversee the work of the Learning and Development team discussed above and ensure they meet the broader leadership goals.

The Learning and Development Practitioner

Learning and Development Practitioners will put in place development programmes and learning activities which are designed to meet the current and future skills needs across the organisation. This allows the business to be responsive to operational and technological changes by ensuring that staff are developed and prepared for change with a skillset to match.

It is the role of the Learning and Development team to identify the areas for skills development and respond by designing, developing and delivering learnings solutions to resolve the skills shortages in the most effective and cost-effective way.

The Learning and Development Practitioner will need most, if not all of the following skills in order to be effective in their role.

- *Passion for learning and education*
- *Strong knowledge of Learning and Development theories and delivery methods*
- *The interpersonal skills to deal with a range of possible learners*
- *Professional capabilities to operate successfully in business*
- *Organisational capacity to track, monitor, and deliver development programs for a large number of people, often with very different Learning and Development requirements*
- *Conduct training needs assessments across the organisation*
- *Design, develop and deliver learning solutions*
- *Utilise digital solutions to create flexible and innovative learning*
- *Apply adult learning theory to maximise the return on investment*
- *Drive a culture of continuous professional development*
- *Facilitate learning interventions*
- *Instilling a coaching culture across the organisation*
- *Monitor and assess the effectivity of learning*
- *Evaluate the benefit to the organisation of the intervention*

Change Management and Project Management

Project Management and Change Management are often confused.

Although they both involve managing people and processes (and often work together to meet organisational goals), they are quite different disciplines.

Understanding what those differences are and how both practices can (and should) work together to manage projects and their resulting change, is crucial for the success of an organisation.

Project management focuses on the processes and activities needed to complete a project (such as a new software solution), change management focuses on those people affected by the project being implemented.

Project Management

Project management is about the process required to bring a team or product from point A to point B.

To do this, project managers and the team will deploy and manage processes within five main project stages:

- *Initiating*
- *Planning*
- *Executing*
- *Monitoring and Controlling*
- *Closing*

These stages help organise the huge number of tasks and demands of a project and as a result drive the project forward.

A project team is often made up of stakeholders from various departments and backgrounds. The project team will focus on the strategic goals of the project which means they are not always able to address the collateral impact the project may have on stakeholders outside of the team.

This uncertainty can lead to anxiety, confusion, and resistance from the people on the ground who may not fully understand the need for the changes or how to adopt and adapt to new processes. Without buy-in from the rest of the organisation, a project's outcomes can be limited.

Change management is the solution to this employee resistance problem

Change managers help the stakeholders impacted upon by a project to transition smoothly from the former ways of working to the new methodology. They fulfil this goal through three process stages:

- *Planning for change*
- *Managing change*
- *Reinforcing change*

In many ways, change managers are the facilitators for a project. They must design and deliver the messaging around the project and communicate the reason for the changes with employees and other stakeholders. They will also help them understand how the changes may impact on different departments and roles and how to move forward effectively and efficiently.

Projects, by design, have a significant and lasting impact on the business and its stakeholders. Project and Change management must work hand in hand to ensure a project's long-term success.

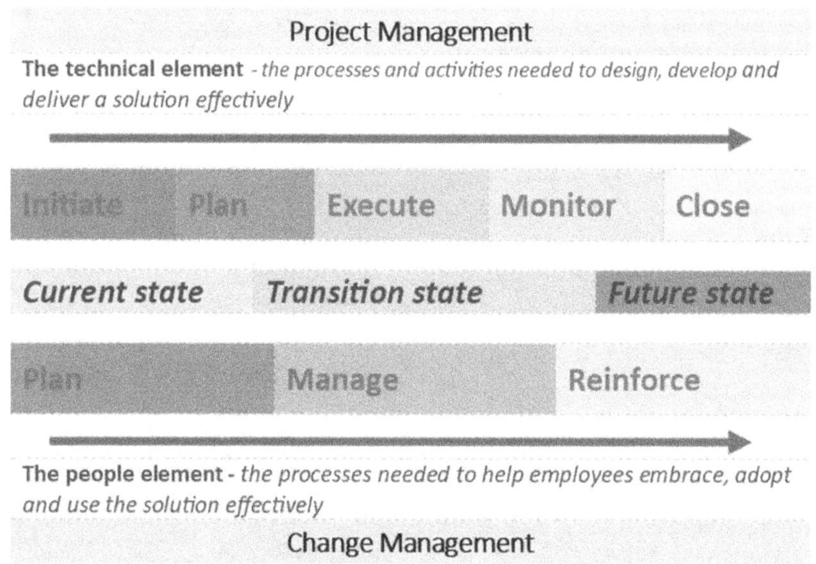

Project management and Change management focus on different aspects of a project, however they must work in tandem to ensure the project's intended outcomes and overall organisational success is achieved.

Change Management

Change management is the process used to ensure that changes to a business created by a project, are smoothly implemented, with as little resistance as possible to achieve lasting benefits.

Definition of Change Management

> ***Change management is the overarching approach used to transition from the current to a desirable future state by engaging a coordinated and structured approach in collaboration with stakeholders.***

This type of change is not the organic evolution which happens, inevitably, over time in every organisation, but the planned and considered change an organisation will undertake to significantly change the way it operates. The important term here being the word planned.

Business change should never be considered without extensive planning having taken place before hand and every effort made to identify potential problems which could arise and undermine or prevent the change from taking place or being successful.

The net effect of a failed program of business change can devastate an organisation and lead to the loss of substantial amounts of money.

The Need for Change

Change management has become one of the most important business functions an organisation undertakes.

Change management will be necessary to successfully implement changes including:

- *Implementation of a new technology*
- *Mergers & acquisitions*
- *Change in leadership*
- *Change in organisational culture*
- *Time of crisis*

Resistance to Change

People do not like change – they enjoy routine as it allows them to operate within their comfort zone. The moment change is proposed, the status quo is under threat and people automatically react negatively to the prospect of change. A major part of the change process is making sure the change is accepted and adopted by the people who are affected by it. Without proper buy-in, there is a risk that employees will reject or even sabotage the change project, resulting in wasted time and money.

Proactively managing the people-side of change can help to reduce fear and anxiety and ensure the new goals are embraced.

Research shows that only 38% of people actually like to leave their comfort zone. When these people are presented with a change, they think, "This is exciting!" The positive interpretation of change results in positive emotional reactions, which result in greater employee productivity.

The other 62%, however, look at the same statement and immediately feel fear and discomfort. They may think, "Oh great, this change will slow my career development." or "I will not enjoy my job anymore." or "Will they keep me on?".

The acceptance and adoption of change by employees at all levels is the biggest problem to overcome when managing change.

Types of Change

The change undertaken can be relatively small, such as improving the organisation's invoicing procedures, to a complete transformation, such as changing the entire product

and service offerings in response to unexpected competition. In most instances though, it will cause major disruption to daily operations.
There are three main types of change in business: developmental, transitional and transformational change.

Developmental Change

Developmental change occurs when the organisation wishes to improve a process or procedure, such as updating a computer system or refining a manufacturing process. These changes are minor and incremental in nature - the workflow is not being redesigned, but rather, being refined to make it better.

This type of change usually occurs in response to technological upgrades or efforts to improve the efficiency of a work process. Provided the employees are given the training necessary to implement the changes, there should be minimal impact associated with this type of change.

Transitional Change

Transitional change is the act of replacing major organisational processes with new ones. This might include automation of processes or upgrading IT solutions. It will also include mergers and acquisitions and other such courses of action. Transitional change is usually caused by a desire to remain competitive in the marketplace. The organisation is not moving into the unknown when executing a transitional change, but it may have to reconsider its job functions, processes, culture and relationships to manage the change effectively. If handled badly this can cause doubt and insecurity in staff.

Transformational Change

Transformational change is the most disruptive since it requires a fundamental shift in the way an organisation operates. An organisation might decide to completely change direction or restructure the whole organisation using new, proprietary operating systems. Because of the upheaval caused, these types of changes happen only rarely. Managing a transformational change is complex, requiring significant skill from the management team and outside help from change specialists. When the change process is complete, the organisation is unrecognisable from what it was before.

The Impact of Change Management

Change management is needed whenever an organisation undertakes a program or event that interrupts day-to-day operations. Such an undertaking will impact on:

The work content of individual jobs.

Many job roles require employees or teams to repeatedly perform the same task. An accounts department has daily, weekly, monthly, and annual activities. Over time, most people become comfortable with the tools provided and the rhythm of the work calendar. Even simple changes can disrupt workflow and be disconcerting for the staff.

The roles of individual employees.
Many people view their value to the organisation as being a good technician, administrator, or data entry clerk. When asked to take on a different role, they may become very uncomfortable. People with excellent practical skills often struggle when asked to become managers. Rather than performing the practical tasks, they now have to work through other people. Once they are no longer rewarded for the practical skills that made them successful, those affected may question their purpose.

The organisation itself.
Management teams debate major changes for months before making final decisions, enabling each member of the team to gain a deeper understanding of the effects the change will have on the organisation. Even if they do not agree with the final decision, they have time to determine whether to accept the new direction or to depart gracefully. Employees lower in the organisations structure rarely have time to process major changes. Managers do not want employees to worry about events that may never happen until it is clear the change will take place. If the change involves a merger, acquisition, or divestiture there will also be strict controls on sharing information to prevent the possibility of insider dealing. As a result, individuals who are not part of the management team have much less time to prepare for the planned change and may decide to leave while the change is undertaken, making change management even more difficult.

Managing Change

The responsibility for delivering the change is usually assigned to an individual who will take on the responsibility for all aspects of the process.

Some tasks a change manager is responsible for include:

- *Making sure the benefits are achievable.*
- *Preparing affected business areas for transition to new ways of working.*
- *Establishing and implementing mechanisms to measure and deliver benefits.*
- *Optimising the release timing of the project deliverables*
- *Liaising with managers to ensure operational benefits.*
- *Communicating with people and senior leaders about the business vision.*
- *Defining and monitoring the benefits and outcomes expected from the project.*
- *Managing the activities effectively that are associated with the desired benefits.*

- *Leading the transition, ensuring that changes are integrated into the business.*
- *Measuring the benefits after the work is complete.*

To achieve all of this the change manager will require a number of competences including

- *Detailed knowledge of the business environment.*
- *An understanding of the management structures, politics, culture and vision of the organisation*
- *Effective marketing and communication skills to sell the vision to all stakeholders.*
- *Knowledge of business change techniques such as business process modelling and gap analysis.*
- *Training in change management, project management or strategic management.*
- *Knowledge in applying best practices in project management.*
- *Knowledge of organisational change models such as Kotter's change model.*

For business change to be successful the process must be underpinned by:

- *A clear vision of the future that is articulated at both an individual and organisational level.*
- *Senior management buy-in and a 'balanced' leadership team.*
- *Change management processes must be embedded in the project delivery lifecycle – they are not an optional extra.*
- *Engagement, communications and 'big' stakeholder relationships.*
- *A team-based culture where the aims of the project are recognised and valued.*
- *Mechanisms to define, measure and monitor success.*

Common challenges in Change Management

Successful business change is all about getting employees' buy-in and embedding new behaviours in the workplace. As noted above, this is not always easy. In addition to the challenges presented by employees, there are additional issues which must be overcome as part of the process.

Defining goals in a timely manner

Change is typically implemented with the goal of improving current processes, products, services or organisational cultures. It is critical to identify clear goals and milestones for every stage of the process.

Change management goals and objectives include:

- *Building a culture of innovation*
- *Changing or updating organisational best practice*
- *Implementing new technology*
- *Establishing milestones and incentive programs*
- *Implementing knowledge sharing initiatives*
- *Shift in targeted customer base*

Poor leadership and lack of alignment
Leaders have a big impact on employee engagement. If leaders are not convinced about the benefits of change, it will be hard to implement it.

Poor leadership and a lack of unity among the leaders are some of the key reasons why organisational change fails. Great leaders know how to inspire their team and embrace the change.

Identifying the resources needed to make change a success
Correctly identifying the necessary resources and individuals that will facilitate the change process and lead it is crucial for success. It can be hard to identify those resources and budgets before the change process begins.

A Lack of agility and slow approval process
Agile organisations struggle less when implementing changes. Delays in the approval processes can cause subsequent delays in change implementation. It is important to have everyone on the same page in to implement change smoothly and on time.

Planning the next steps
Every change management process should have a well-defined plan. It should consist of a timeline and change milestones which are concurrent with those in the project plan. Without such a plan, it will be hard to define the overall success of the change process.

Fear and conflicts
Changes within organisations can develop emotions of uncertainty and fear. This may cause employees take their frustrations out on each other. It is the leaders' responsibility to overcome the difficulties and resolve conflicts. An active leader should always be ready to dive deeper into the problem while working in accordance with their organisational change management.

Resistance to change and lack of commitment
Some employees are resistant to change, do not want to collaborate or commit to new practices. Leaders should be able to address resistance on a psychological level and proactively remove behavioural barriers that restrict change.

Poor communication in the workplace
Effective communication is critical for success in change management. The cost of poor communication can be significant. Every organisation which has a successful change management team, expresses the need for constant communication throughout the change process.

Aligning all the teams with the new strategy
Having everyone on board and informed before and during the implementation process may be a challenge. This is especially true for large organisations with various offices and departments across the world. Global as well as interdepartmental communication become critical to ensure change success.

Updating everyone on the new materials, policies and procedures in a timely manner
The planned change should be documented and the resulting documents should be readily and easily accessible and shared with all stakeholders affected by the change. A well-documented change management strategy keeps all changes well-documented and transparent.

Best Practice in Change Management

Change management processes can be highly complex. Additionally, change in the workplace can cause high levels of stress among employees.

However, there are some rules and best practices every organisation should follow.

Define clear goals
SMART goals are not easy to define for change management, however, organisations should strive to define goals with as much clarity as possible. This provides stakeholders with a point of reference when evaluating change management.

Be honest and transparent
Over 30% of employees suggest that their employer is not always honest and truthful. Employers must be honest and transparent especially during a period of change. As most stakeholders do not feel comfortable with change, transparency at every step of the change management process helps build trust and engage employees.

Train and reassure your teams

Support employees with constant reassurance. Offer ongoing training sessions and provide the time they need to adapt to new practices. Empathy and reassurance help build engagement and commitment and ease future organisational changes. All too often, managers do not understand why the change is happening!

Encourage conversations and communicate regularly

Stakeholder relations have a big impact on encouraging conversations before, during and after the changes are implemented. Start a conversation among employees in order to find out how they feel about the new initiatives. Understand that true communication is a two-way conversation.

Listen to your employees

When driving engagement and communication, actively listening a key practice. Listen to what the employees have to say. Allow them to lead the conversation. Let stakeholders ask questions, comment and suggest their ideas for improvement.

Bring your leaders on board

Effective change management increases the benefits to be derived from change initiatives. Companies should work on proving the real return on investment derived from change management and communicate that to the business leaders to bring them on board and support the change.

Choose the right communication tool

Millennials in the workplace expect an easier way of communication than through emails. In fact, many emails are never read which causes important information to get lost.

Apply the most effective communication and engagement solution that employees will actually want to use. Make sure the solution is mobile friendly. Younger generations are used to being able to do everything on their mobile phones. Organisational communication should, for that reason, be mobile-friendly.

Empower your employees

Change managers and employees should be empowered to engage in the change process by giving them freedom to make their own decisions and implement new ideas.

If employees do not feel empowered, engagement levels will drop leading to resistance to change.

Encourage knowledge sharing
Some employees will learn and adapt to change faster than the others. However, knowledge sharing among employees can speed up this learning process significantly. Collaborative tools enable the sharing of organisational knowledge in a way that is easy and fun for employees.

Document and make information easily accessible
Documenting everything does not help if this information is not easily accessible to employees. An accessible, central repository where all important documents and information are kept, makes change management much more efficient.

Recognise and reward
77% of employees say that they would work harder if they were recognised for their work. Therefore, this approach can be a great motivation to comply with and implement the changes faster. Recognise and reward employees for accomplishments and for adopting new behaviours during the transformation process. Celebrate the wins and milestones.

Make it social
When implementing new technology, share it publicly! Modern communication tools allow information to be easily shared inside and outside the organisation. Having employee champions can also be a significant benefit to recruitment and talent acquisition.

Change Management Theory and Models

There are many change management models but the most common ones are as follows:

Kotter's Change Management theory

Kotter's theory is one of the most popular and most widely adopted. It is divided into eight stages where each focuses on a key principle that is associated with the response of people to change.

- ***Increase urgency*** – *Creating a sense of urgency among stakeholders helps to motivate them to move forward towards the change objectives.*
- ***Build the team*** – *Assign the right people to the team by selecting a broad mix of skills, knowledge and commitment.*
- ***Get the vision correct*** – *Consider not just the strategy but also creativity, emotional connect and objectives.*
- ***Communicate*** –*Communicate openly, freely and frequently to inform stakeholders about the change.*

- ***Get things moving*** – *Get support, remove the roadblocks and implement feedback in a constructive way.*
- ***Focus on short term goals*** – *Break down the change process into smaller, staged, goals to achieve success without applying too much pressure.*
- ***Do not give up*** – *Persist with the change process irrespective of how tough things may seem.*
- ***Incorporate change*** – *Reinforce the need for change and embed it as part of the workplace culture.*

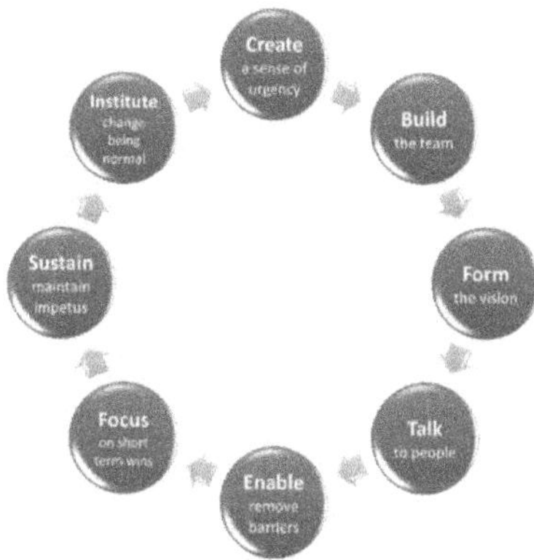

Kotter's change management model focuses on preparing employees for change rather than change implementation itself. The focus on stakeholder experience and proper workplace communication is a key reason why this is one of the most commonly used change management models.

McKinsey 7-S Change Management Model

McKinsey 7-S framework or model is one of the most enduring change management models.

This model consists of 7 crucial categories that companies should be aware of when implementing change:

- ***Strategy*** – *Strategy is the step-by-step process of how change management will be implemented*
- ***Structure*** – *This factor is related to the structure in which the organisation is divided or the structure it follows.*
- ***Systems*** – *This stage focuses on the systems that will be used to complete day-to-day tasks and activities.*
- ***Shared values*** – *These are the core values of an organisation upon which it runs or works.*
- ***Style*** – *The manner in which change is adopted or implemented is known as 'style'.*

- ***Staff*** – *The staff refers to the workforce or employees and their working capabilities.*
- ***Skills*** – *The competencies as well as other skills possessed by the employees working in the organisation.*

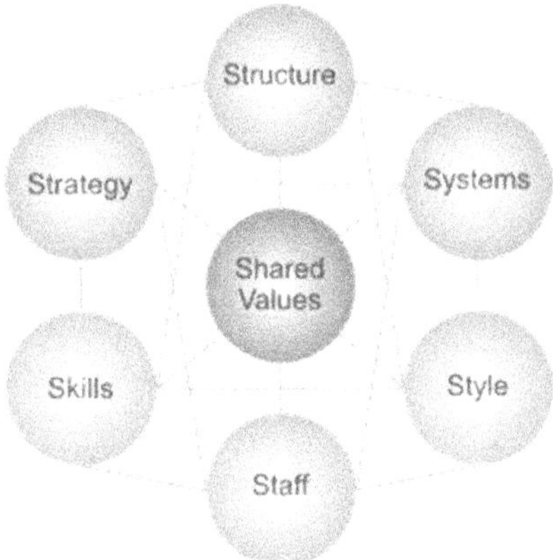

This model focuses on the areas that change may impact upon.
While most other models represent some kind of a process or workflow, McKinsey's model simply reminds that all the business aspects should be defined before the change strategy is implemented.

ADKAR Model

This model is based on the premise that change can only happen when individuals are willing to change. The ADKAR model or theory of change is goal oriented. The model allows change management teams to focus on activities that are directly related to the goals the organisation is trying to achieve. It guides individuals through change and addresses any roadblocks or barriers along the way.

The model identifies the challenges which should be anticipated in the process of change management, so timely and effective training can be provided.

ADKAR Model acronym defines:

- ***Awareness*** – *of the need and requirement for change*
- ***Desire*** – *the motivation to effect change and participate in it*
- ***Knowledge*** – *of how to bring about this change*
- ***Ability*** – *to incorporate the change on a regular basis*
- ***Reinforcement*** – *to keep it implemented and reinforced later on as well.*

Pre-contemplation	*Contemplation*	*Preparation*	*Action*	*Maintenance*
A	D	K	A	R
Awareness	**Desire**	**Knowledge**	**Ability**	**Reinforcement**
Why is change necessary?	*How do you motivate people to want to change?*	*What will be their involvement in the change?*	*Address issues which may prevent someone from changing*	*Maintain the change – do not let them slip back top old ways*
Make employees aware of the change.	*Instil a desire to change*	*Teach employees how to make the change*	*Transform knowledge into the ability to make the change.*	*Make the change permanent by reinforcing new methods*

This change management model is a good solution for organisations that are trying to look at both the business and people dimensions of change.
ADKAR focuses on the reasons why change is working or not and why the desired goals are not being obtained.

Kübler-Ross Five Stage Change Management Model

This model is different from the others in the sense that is 100% employee oriented. The model can also be applied to other life situations such as loss of job, changes in work and other less serious health conditions.

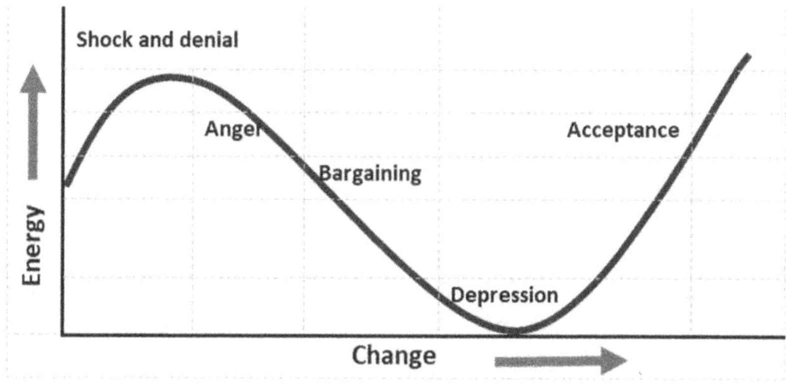

This model helps employers understand employees reaction to change better and thereby empathise with them. The model consists of five stages through which most employees will transit during organisational change.

- ***Denial*** – *In this stage, employees are not willing to or unable to accept change. Most people show resistance to change and may not want to believe what is happening.*
- ***Anger*** – *The model assumes that when the news of pending change is first presented, anger follows. Denial becomes anger when employees realise that the change is inevitable.*
- ***Bargaining*** – *During this stage, employees try to derive the best possible solution out of the situation. Bargaining is a way for people to avoid ending up in the worst-case scenario.*
- ***Depression*** – *When employees realise that bargaining is not working, they may end up getting depressed and may lose faith. Symptoms may include low energy, non-commitment, low motivation and a lack of happiness.*
- ***Acceptance*** – *When employees realise that there is no point in fighting change any more, they may finally accept what is happening and may begin to resign to it.*

This is an effective change management model due to its focus on employees, their feelings, concerns and needs.

Organisations which understand their employees are far more likely to eliminate the barriers towards successful change management.

It is because of the feelings identified by this model that it is extremely important to keep employees informed and to have an effective communication strategy.

Lewin's Change Management Model

Lewin's Change Management Model makes it possible for organisations to understand structured change.

This model comprises three stage: ***Unfreeze, Change and Refreeze***.

- ***Unfreeze:*** *Preparation for change. Employers are prepared for the change by explaining why the change is necessary. Given most people are reluctant to change, this step helps to break the ice!*
- ***Change:*** *The change takes place. Good leadership and effective employee communications are crucial for this step.*
- ***Refreeze:*** *The change has been implemented and accepted. This is the time when the employees revert to business as usual. Leaders must ensure that changes are adopted and continue to be used, even after the change management objectives have been achieved.*

Unfreeze	Change	Refreeze
Recognise the need for change *Determine what needs to change* *Encourage the replacement of old behaviours and attitudes* *Ensure there is strong support from management* *Manage and understand the doubts and concerns*	*Plan the changes* *Implement the changes* *Help employees to learn the new concept or points of view*	*Changes are reinforced in stabilising* *Integrate changes into the normal way of doing things* *Develop ways to sustain the change* *Celebrate success*

Lewin's change management model describes in a very simple way the main 3 stages that every change management process has to go through: pre-change, during change and post-change. Because of its simplicity, many organisations choose to follow this model when implementing change.

Communication Strategy

Communicating change is not a one-off effort. Communication will be needed again and again throughout the change process. Reiterate the vision, retell the story, chart and re-chart the path when challenges arise and enable employees to be the heroes. The organisation will be more motivated and equipped to make that change effort with continued communication.

Change is possible. Individuals make real changes every day.

Organisations shift gears and become increasingly successful as a result. The communication strategy can play an important role in enabling transformation and lasting impact.

Businesses have to find effective ways to communicate the abrupt changes they are implementing so that employees can understand the new strategies and adjust their work accordingly.

Broadly speaking, when driving change, you need to:

- *Explain to employees the changes being implemented as well as the different steps the organisational change plan includes.*
- *Tell them the reasons why change is being implemented, the specific changes and the impacts they may have on their work*
- *There is no organisational change plan without objectives and goals. Clearly explain to employees the objectives set and help them identify the impacts their work will have on the team's ability to reach these goals.*
- *Encourage employees to ask any questions they may have in mind and most importantly, make sure they are all answered in full.*

This is also one of the best ways to connect and build trust with remote teams. Appoint a spokesperson for the employees who will keep the dialogue with employees open.

Some common examples of best practices for communicating change are as follows:

- *Share the new company policies and procedures with teams in a timely manner*
- *Share safety tips with employees on a daily basis. Sharing with them informative and educational materials such as short videos is a great way to help them.*
- *Monitor updates from management and other stakeholders and instantly share them with employees*
- *Inform employees about urgent matters as soon as possible*
- *Know the employees and then care about the things they are interested in*
- *Make it easy for teams to keep up with the latest news related to the change*
- *Track the effectiveness of the change plan*
- *Use a mobile app so you can reach all employees, no matter where they are, and they can update themselves*
- *Align communication efforts so messages are consistent, no matter who they are shared with. It is all about building trust!*

Employee communication is the keystone of every change management model and the key to successful change.

Within organisations, change initiatives mostly come from the top down. However, it is ultimately the employees of the organisation who have to change how they do their jobs. If these individuals are unsuccessful in their personal transitions, if they do not embrace change and learn a new way of working, the initiative will fail.

Aligning employees with business goals is not an easy task. Communication is the central part of every change management model meaning; if employees are not on board, implementing change will be extremely challenging and failure must be considered a realistic possibility.

A recent survey has revealed that 70% of change management projects fail!

Only 14% of business change managers said that change failures can be attributed to a company's inability to cope with technology.

The other 86% of failures are related to:

- *Improperly defined objectives (17%),*
- *Unfamiliar scope (17%),*
- *Lack of effective communication (20%)*
- *Poor project management skills (32%)*

Communicating Organisational Change

Internal communication plays a critical role in change management today. Effective communication plays a vital role in making organisational change possible. There are two questions which need to be asked when communicating change:

- *Do the employees have the motivation to change?*
- *Are the employees equipped with the ability to change?*

Both of these responses are incredibly important. One without the other can jeopardise attempts at organisational change.

When communicating change, focus should be on increasing motivation and the company's ability to adapt.

Four steps to communicate organisational change

1. Share a Vision

When communicating change, share the vision of how the organisation can benefit from the transition. Stakeholders need to know the change is beneficial for them and the organisation alike. The vision can be created by answering these questions:

- *How will the organisation operate once the change is made?*
- *What will employees experience as a result of making the necessary transitions?*
- *Will there be tangible results? What will those results look like?*
- *Will there be a sense of accomplishment? What will that feel like?*

- ***What will the rewards be, both for the individuals and your organisation as a whole?***

By answering these questions, employees will have a better understanding of why organisational change is imminent, which is critical to success. Clarifying the motivations behind organisational change helps team members reach a mutual understanding, allowing everyone to work toward one shared vision.

Businesses around the world are coping with challenges caused by the COVID-19 pandemic and a stalled economy. Organisations have been forced to undergo rapid organisational change initiatives, such as embracing remote work. Those which have successfully adapted have been transparent in their efforts and communicated a clear vision for employees to rally around.

2. Tell a Story

Telling a story enables everyone to understand where the company needs to be, but also where it currently is and how to transition.

Take the example of Scandinavian Airlines.

> *Scandinavian Airlines needed to make an organisational shift in the early 1980s. The airline industry was struggling. The company was losing money at the tune of £17 million a year. The market was stagnant.*
>
> *Through its change efforts, the company not only met its goal of increasing earnings by £20 million in the first year; Scandinavian Airlines increased them by £70 million! Within a couple of years, it was named the best airline for business travellers. Employees were on board with the change, which was making a difference. How did Scandinavian Airlines do it?*
>
> *All 20,000 employees received a short handbook communicating the change, focussing on the business flyer as a way to turn the company around. This was not a typical corporate communication. Titled "Let's Get in There and Fight," the booklet included characterisations of airplanes, complete with cartoons and large typeface fonts that highlighted where the company was and the vision for where it wanted to be. It told how "storm clouds" and "bad weather" had struck the business and how it faced challenges in being profitable. It described its competition and how employees could help it stay competitive.*

Your strategy may not involve cartoons and large text like Scandinavian Airlines but communicating the story of the change initiative can have a powerful effect on illuminating the vision.

Communicating change in this manner can allay some of the fear and uncertainty employees may be feeling, while simultaneously rallying them around common goals.

We are going to be much more punctual. Everyone can help. "Operation Punctuality" is starting soon. It's going to give everyone a chance to help us one of Europe most punctual airlines.

3. Make those in the Organisation the Heroes

The change communication strategy should focus on telling the members of the organisation what to do and what they need to change. Does it inspire and enable them to be change agents as well?

In the book "***Winning 'Em Over"***, author Jay Conger shares Scandinavian Airlines' message to employees, which was:

> ***"We have to fight in a stagnating market. We have to fight competitors who are more efficient than we are and who are at least as good as we are, in figuring out the best deals. We can do it, but only if we are prepared to fight. side by side. We are all in this together."***

Every employee received Scandinavian Airlines' handbook. Everyone was able to understand where the company wanted to go and what role they played. Telling a story where the employees were not only part of that change, but could be heroes in the story, provided a rallying cry that allowed them to stand side-by-side as active players in the change initiative.

How can the individuals in the organisation be made active participants in the change effort? How can they be made to feel that changing with the organisation will make them the hero and not the victim?
By making the employees the heroes of the change story and defining the specific role each person plays, they will be empowered to exercise agency in helping the organisation meet its goals.

4. Chart the Path

Equip those in the organisation to become leaders in the change communication. Once the vision is shared - one that your employees believe is good for the company – they must be shown the path that will get them there.

> *Japan's largest online retailer, Rakuten, wanted to change the working language of the organisation. Instead of the majority of the company speaking their native Japanese, the CEO wanted his 7,100 Tokyo employees to transition to conducting business in English.*
>
> *This change was to drive the company's effort to become number one in internet services across the globe. In two years, the CEO expected his employees to be proficient in English. With just a few months left to go in his change initiative, however, surveys found that a large percentage of employees, especially native Japanese speakers, felt afraid, frustrated, nervous, and even oppressed by the initiative.*
>
> *The employees of Rakuten were not experiencing the change as something positive for them, personally. They may have believed it was good for the company, and possibly good for them, but they were finding themselves challenged and discouraged.*

A leader should not need the change to be good for employees every step of the way. Some change will be gruellingly difficult. It will involve scaling steep inclines and, for some, working harder than they have before. The solution is to identify what can be done to increase their ability to keep going on this path.

While the initial change initiative shared by the CEO was clear, there needed to be additional communication that would help employees chart the path. Rakuten provided funding for language learning programs, communicating to employees that the company was there for them. They would not have to make the change alone. Action, as well as words, were powerful tools.

Chapter 4: Governance and Compliance

Governance and Compliance

Compliance is the term used for the way the organisation complies with the legal aspects of its operation, whilst governance refers to the systems by which it is directed and controlled.

Aims of Governance and Compliance

Organisations need to operate in compliance with a wide variety of financial rules, regulations and legislation that vary according to the type of organisation and the activities it undertakes.

There will be internal governance to ensure compliance with the requirements set out in the organisation's policies and procedures, for example:

- *how sales need to be recorded*
- *how often reports need to be generated*
- *how to use systems that track banking activities*
- *information needed for monthly reports sent to head office*
- *how to prepare quarterly reviews for shareholders*
- *systems to check and monitor compliance*

Issues that governance and compliance aim to avoid and mitigate

Broadly speaking, governance and compliance aim to avoid and mitigate issues such as:

- ***fraud*** – *e.g., procedures to shred documents to prevent identity theft*
- ***theft*** – *e.g., using CCTV to monitor staff using a cash till*
- ***tax evasion*** – *e.g., procedures to make sure that cash payments are declared*
- ***criminal activity*** – *e.g., taking bribes or trafficking workers*
- ***misuse of funds and resources*** – *e.g., monitoring budgets closely to reduce waste and unnecessary spending*
- ***inefficiency*** – *e.g., from not monitoring waste or opportunities to steal cash or goods*
- ***money laundering*** – *e.g., disposal of large sums of money which have been derived from illegal activity*

Sometimes actions are deliberate and have a criminal intent – e.g., knowingly employing people who are illegal immigrants or those who have been trafficked, stealing products or cash.

Some actions are due to negligence and ignorance – e.g., from someone not realising that they need to provide workplace pensions for their employees; under-declaring VAT due to lack of knowledge about the rules.

There many legal requirements imposed by external stakeholders which must be complied with. It is a requirement of all organisations to satisfy these legal requirements by, for example:

- ***paying the right amounts of tax*** *– e.g., PAYE tax and national insurance, VAT or corporation tax*
- ***paying the correct level of minimum wage***
- ***making contributions to workplace pensions*** *– e.g., to comply with the Pension Regulator's requirements*
- ***keeping adequate records*** *– e.g., audited accounts for large companies*
- ***using, storing and disposing of financial information correctly*** *– e.g., in accordance with the General Data Protection Regulations 2018 (GDPR)*
- ***submitting accurate returns on time*** *– e.g., to HMRC or Companies House*
- ***avoiding making bribes*** *– e.g., to conform with the Bribery Act 2010*
- ***satisfying industry-specific requirements*** *– e.g., FCA requirements for financial services organisations*

There can also be costs associated with compliance – e.g., accountancy fees for preparing and submitting accounts; consultancy fees for compliance advice and strategy making and audit fees for verification.

In order to achieve compliance with legislation, organisations need good governance – the systems by which organisations are directed and controlled, imposed by management such as a board of directors or trustees.

Financial governance is necessary to enable organisations to:

- ***keep up to date with new legislation and stakeholder expectations***
- ***increase efficiency and revenue***
- ***lower the costs of compliance***
- ***avoid fines and penalties***
- ***avoid damage to their reputation***

Compliance

All organisations must comply with the laws and regulations which relate to its industry, environment, legal entity and circumstances. Financial compliance must be demonstrated through the accounts of the business and the financial returns it makes to the necessary enforcement bodies.

The following are just a small sample of the laws which apply to every business in the UK.

- *Health and Safety Act*
- *Financial Laws including tax laws*
- *Employment law*
- *General data Protection Regulations (GDPR)*
- *Freedom of Information Act*
- *Privacy and Electronic Communications Regulations*
- *Copyrights, Design and Patents Act*
- *Human Rights Act*
- *Equality Act*

In addition, there is also the legislation which defines how a business should conduct itself.

These can include:

Legislation	*Purpose*
Companies Act	*Defines the duties of the Directors of all companies registered in the UK*
Financial Services and Markets Act	*Regulates shares and securities*
Financial Services Act	*Applies criminal offences for making false claims or misrepresentation and creating false impressions*
Insolvency Act	*Governs the winding up of companies including liquidation and bankruptcy*
Consumer Credit Act	*Protects credit cards, loans and hire purchase agreements*
Consumer Rights Act	*Protects and assigns rights to the consumer including the right to compensation*
Misrepresentation Act	*Protects consumers from false or fraudulent claims*
Payment Services Regulations	*Protects consumers who are victims of fraud*
Unfair Terms in Consumer Regulations	*Defines the terms which are considered unfair in consumer agreements*
Consumer contracts Regulations	*Protects customers when buying items online*

The type and nature of the legislation which must be complied with, will vary from organisation to organisation. Not all legislation will apply to all business, however, a few do and include employment law, equality law, data protection and health and Safety.

The Health and Safety Act 1974

The thought of being hurt at work is not very appealing but on average, 300 people a year lose their lives at work in Britain. In addition, around 158,000 non-fatal injuries are reported each year and an estimated 2.2 million people suffer from ill health caused or made worse by work. Some £16 billion is lost each year through accidents and injuries.

Accidents don't happen. They are caused!

The Health and Safety Executive (HSE) was set up under the Health and Safety Act and it is the HSE who enforces workplace health and safety and apply. The Act contains powers for the HSE to enforce these employer duties and apply penalties for non-compliance.

The Health & Safety at Work Act 1974 applies to all employees, the self-employed, government offices and in some circumstances the general public.

When it was introduced, the Act did three things.

- *Introduced the concept of criminal liability.*
- *Introduced the concept of you are guilty until proven innocent.*
- *Gave wide, sweeping, powers to Health & Safety Inspectors to enter businesses at any time that work is in progress, carry out inspections and if necessary, serve notice that practices are dangerous.*

Its main concept is that employers have a duty to protect their employers and members of the public affected by their work and must inform them about matters relating to their health, safety and welfare.

The employer's duty under the Health and Safety at Work Act is to provide staff with a safe and healthy workplace, and this includes:

- *a safe system of work*
- *a safe place of work*
- *safe equipment, plant and machinery*
- *safe and competent people working alongside you, because employers are also liable for the actions of their staff and managers*

- ***carrying out risk assessments as set out in regulations, and taking steps to eliminate or control these risks***
- ***informing workers fully about all potential hazards associated with any work process, chemical substance or activity, including providing instruction, training and supervision***
- ***appointing a 'competent person' responsible for health and safety*** *(competent persons, such as a head of health and safety, oversee day-to-day safety management, oversee safety inspections, and liaise with staff safety reps)*
- ***consulting with workplace safety representatives*** *(if a union is recognised, your employer must set up and attend a workplace safety committee if two or more safety reps request one)*
- ***providing adequate facilities for staff welfare at work***

The Health and Safety at Work Act 1974 states:

> ***"All employers are required to have a health and safety policy, carry out risk assessments and provide health and safety training for their employees."***

The Health and Safety at Work Act allows the government to issue regulations, guidance and Approved Codes of Practice (ACOPs) for employers. These set out detailed responsibilities for an employer in every aspect of workplace health and safety, from working safely with computers, to stress and hazardous chemicals.

Approved Codes of Practice (ACOPs) are guidance with specific legal standing. They deal with a wide range of hazardous materials and working practices.

Employers who are prosecuted for a breach of health and safety law, who have not followed an ACOP, are likely to be found at fault by the courts.

A failure to follow an Approved Codes of Practice is not an offence in itself, but an employer will need to be able to show that equally effective methods have been adopted to demonstrate compliance with the law.

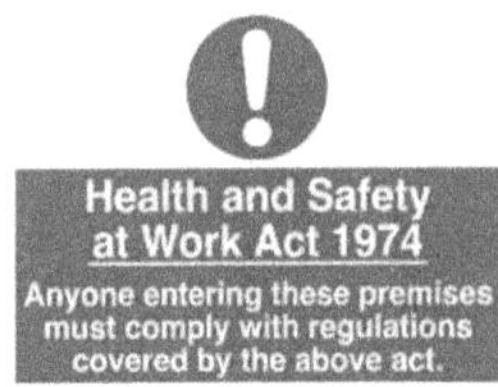

Safety Regulations

The Health and Safety at Work Act is a huge piece of legislation as it covers all industries and sectors. To address this diversity, the Act is underpinned by Regulations which are designed to meet the needs of different industry sectors.

Safety regulations are the strongest form of official advice that employers have to follow, and they are legally enforceable. Regulations are made by government ministers, often following proposals from the Health and Safety Executive (HSE) and approved by Parliament.

They broadly cover the general management of health and safety at work, work processes (e.g., manual handling, use of display screen equipment) and specific standards (e.g., exposure to chemicals).

The main set of regulations is the Management of Health and Safety at Work Regulations 1999, also known as the 'Management Regs'. They place a legal duty on employers to carry out a risk assessment as a first step in ensuring a safe workplace and lie at the heart of the modern approach to health and safety at work.

The Management of Health and Safety at Work Regulations 1999

The Management of Health and Safety at Work Regulations 1999 were introduced to reinforce the Health and Safety Act 1974.

Also known as the 'Management Regs', these came into effect in 1993. Main employer duties under the Regulations include:

- *making 'assessments of risk' to the health and safety of its workforce, and to act upon risks they identify, so as to reduce them (Regulation 3).*
- *appointing competent persons to oversee workplace health and safety.*
- *providing workers with information and training on occupational health and safety*
- *operating a written health and safety policy.*

They explicitly outline what employers are required to do to manage health and safety and apply to every work activity. The regulations place a set of duties on both employers and employees to maintain a safe and healthy workplace.

Risk Assessments

The main duty placed on employers by the Management of Health and Safety at Work Regulations is to undertake risk assessments to identify potential hazards to employee health and safety and anyone who may be affected by their work activity. Employers with five or more employees must record in writing any significant findings.

Separate risk assessments should be conducted for young people (under the age of 18) – taking their inexperience and immaturity into consideration – and new and expectant mothers.

As a result of conducting a risk assessment, employers must then plan for implementing health and safety measures to control the hazards identified by the risk assessment.

Where the risk assessment has identified that health surveillance of an employee is needed, it is necessary for a system of regular checks to be carried out. These are used to detect ill-health due to working conditions such as noise, vibration, solvents or dust early to prevent severe damage or deterioration caused by the workplace.

Finally, the risk assessment should determine the procedures required to manage serious and imminent danger. For example, an evacuation procedure in the event of a fire or other emergency situations. It also needs to advise how and when an employee should contact the emergency services.

Competent Persons

Employers are required to appoint at least one competent person (preferably from within the organisation) to oversee, supervise and assist in all matters of health and safety and complying with legislation.

Information and Training

Employees must be provided with all necessary safety information in an understandable format. Similar appropriate health and safety information also needs to be provided to temporary and non-employees (e.g., contractors).

Adequate health and safety training must be received by every employee. In addition, workers should not be given tasks beyond their competence or physical capabilities.

Shared premises

Where employers are sharing premises with another employer, it is necessary for the employers to co-operate and co-ordinate health and safety activities. Information from risk assessments — and the resulting preventative measures — must be exchanged between employers.

The Six Pack

The 'six-pack' is the name given to the most widely quoted sets of health and safety regulations. These can cover heating, lighting and ventilation at work, the safe use of computer screens and keyboards, handling heavy or awkward loads, rest breaks, and personal protective equipment.

The six pack of regulations include:

- *The Workplace (Health, Safety and Welfare) Regulations 1992*
- *The Health and Safety (Display Screen Equipment) Regulations 1992*
- *The Personal Protective Equipment at Work Regulations 1992*
- *The Manual Handling Operations Regulations 1992*
- *The Provision and Use of Work Equipment Regulations 1998*
- *The Reporting of Injuries, Diseases and Dangerous Occurrences Regulations 1995*

The Workplace (Health, Safety and Welfare) Regulations 1992

The main provisions of these Regulations require employers to provide:

- *adequate lighting, heating, ventilation and workspace (and keep them in a clean condition).*
- *staff facilities, including toilets, washing facilities and refreshment*
- *safe passageways, i.e., to prevent slipping and tripping hazards.*

Toilets and handwashing facilities along with a rest area where staff can eat their meals is a minimum requirement, but the requirement may be more far reaching. Some tasks are known to cause problems for some people and steps must be taken to minimise this or make provision to limit the exposure to the problem.

The Health and Safety (Display Screen Equipment) Regulations 1992

The main provisions here apply to display screen equipment (DSE) 'users', defined as workers who 'habitually' use a computer as a significant part of their normal work. This includes people who are regular users of DSE equipment or rely on it as part of their job. This covers you if you use DSE for an hour or more continuously, and/or you are making daily use of DSE.

Employers are required to:

- *make a risk assessment of workstation use by DSE users, and reduce the risks identified.*
- *ensure DSE users take 'adequate breaks'.*

- *provide regular eyesight tests.*
- *provide health and safety information.*
- *provide adjustable furniture (e.g., desk, chair, etc.)*
- *demonstrate that they have adequate procedures designed to reduce risks associated with DSE work, such as repetitive strain injury (RSI).*

The Personal Protective Equipment at Work Regulations 1992

The main provisions require employers to:

- *ensure that suitable personal protective equipment (PPE) is provided free of charge "wherever there are risks to health and safety that cannot be adequately controlled in other ways." The PPE must be 'suitable' for the risk in question, and include protective face masks and goggles, safety helmets, gloves, air filters, ear defenders, overalls and protective footwear*
- *provide information, training and instruction on the use of this equipment.*

The Manual Handling Operations Regulations 1992

The main provisions of these Regulations require employers to:

- *avoid (so far as is reasonably practicable) the need for employees to undertake any manual handling activities involving risk of injury*
- *make assessments of manual handling risks and try to reduce the risk of injury. The assessment should consider the task, the load and the individual's personal characteristics (physical strength, etc.)*
- *provide workers with information on the weight of each load.*

The Provision and Use of Work Equipment Regulations 1998

This requires that equipment provided for use by employees in the workplace is safe.

The main provisions require employers to:

- *ensure the safety and suitability of work equipment for the purpose for which it is provided.*
- *properly maintain the equipment, irrespective of how old it is.*
- *provide information, instruction and training on the use of equipment*
- *protect employees from dangerous parts of machinery.*

The Reporting of Injuries, Diseases and Dangerous Occurrences Regulations 1995 (RIDDOR)

Under these Regulations, employers are required to report a wide range of work-related incidents, injuries and diseases to the Health and Safety Executive (HSE), or to the nearest local authority environmental health department.

The Regulations require an employer to record in an accident book the date and time of the incident, details of the person(s) affected, the nature of their injury or condition, their occupation, the place where the event occurred and a brief note on what happened.

The following injuries or ill health must be reported:

- *the death of any person.*
- *specified injuries including fractures, amputations, eye injuries, injuries from electric shock, and acute illness requiring removal to hospital or immediate medical attention.*
- *'over-seven-day' injuries, which involve relieving someone of their normal work for more than seven days as a result of injury caused by an accident at work.*
- *reportable occupational diseases, including:*
    - *cramp of the hand or forearm due to repetitive movement.*
    - *carpal tunnel syndrome, involving hand-held vibrating tools.*
    - *occupational asthma.*
    - *tendonitis or tenosynovitis (types of tendon injury).*
    - *hand-arm vibration syndrome (HAVS), including where the person's work involves regular use of percussive or vibrating tools*
    - *occupational dermatitis.*
- ***near misses*** *(described in the Regulations as 'dangerous occurrences')*

Health and Safety Policy Statements

All employers are required by law to have a Health and Safety Policy. If there are five or more employees, including any owners who work in the business, this policy must be in written form.

Health and Safety Policies are very important documents. They set out the aims and objectives of the company in terms of how it intends to provide and maintain safe and healthy working conditions, safe systems of work, equipment and plant for all its employees and how it will provide information, instruction, training and supervision for all its employees. It will also set out how it will ensure that all its legal requirements are met, how the policy shall be made known to its employees and how it will be monitored and regularly reviewed to make sure that its aims and objectives are achieved.

Health and Safety Policies also contain valuable information about the nature of the business. It also describes who in the company is responsible for what aspects of Health and Safety as well as stating any company specific Health and Safety Rules that apply to all employees.

Although it is the employer's legal responsibility to make employees aware of its Health and Safety Policy, it is equally the employees responsibility to make sure they fully understand it!

Employees are strongly urged to adopt a positive approach to working safely, to be aware of hazards, correct anything that might cause an accident (unless this would involve risk) and report it to your manager or Supervisor.

Any employee who contravenes or fails to observe relevant health and safety rules could normally expect to be subjected to disciplinary action by their employer.

What you should know poster

A Health and Safety Law Poster is a brief guide to health and safety law and provides a list of the key point's employees and employers have to know.

Every business in the UK must display a copy of this poster, regardless of the number of staff they employ.

Employment Legislation

Employment law, while designed to protect the rights of the employee, covers most of the aspects regarding the relationship between the employer and the employee. The business must comply with all aspects of employment law to avoid the negative impact of not doing so, including costly fines, employment tribunal's, adverse publicity and loss of their brand reputation, for example.

There are several pieces of legislation that can be connected with the delivery of work including:

- *Employment Rights Act 1996*
- *Human Rights Act 1998*
- *Equality Act 2010*
- *Working Time Regulations*

It is not uncommon to hear some people dismissing employment legislation as "red tape" or "health and safety gone mad". However, employment law is aimed at protecting and supporting everyone in the workplace – without it, there would be no guarantee of sickness or holiday pay, for example, and workers might not be able to challenge discrimination, bullying or wrongful dismissal.

Employment law is constantly under review and revision, with additions and changes happening every year, so it is important for managers and their organisations to keep up to date with the latest legislation and regulations.

Employment Rights Act 1996

The main employment legislation in the UK is the Employment Rights Act 1996. This law is very detailed and deals with a huge number of aspects about employment. Some of the main points covered by the Act are:

- *the employee's right to have a statement or contract of employment*
- *the employee's right to have an itemised pay statement*
- *protection of wages*
- *protection from suffering detriment in employment from taking time off work* – *e.g., taking time off for jury service, family reasons or antenatal care*
- *sickness*
- *maternity, paternity and adoption payments and leave*
- *suspension from work*
- *procedures for discipline, grievance, dismissal and redundancy*
- *Sunday working and time off*

Statutory rights ensure all workers are treated fairly by their employers under law. These rights apply to most, though not all, workers. The self-employed or those working for an agency may not have the same rights.

The only universal rights for every worker are the right to minimum wage and to not be discriminated against.

UK workers have 8 key legal rights

The right to maximum working hours

Employees cannot be forced to work more than 48 hours in one week so must agree to put in additional hours in writing. Workers also have a legal right to paid holiday every year. Full-time employees can get up to 5.6 weeks (depending on the company) and part-time workers get pro rata holiday.

Workers can also legally take unpaid time off for reasons such as additional training, taking part in trade union activities, and for emergencies, like looking after dependants.

What people often do not realise is if you have been working somewhere for six months you have the right to submit a request for flexible working. The business does not have to accept your request but must give a compelling reason why not if so.

The right to equal pay & minimum wage

UK workers must be paid at least National Minimum Wage. All employees should receive a payslip breaking down their pay and deductions soon after starting, and employers cannot make any illegal wage deductions.

Under the Equal Pay Act 1970, unequal treatment between men and women overpay and employment conditions became completely prohibited. It was repealed but then many of its provisions were replicated in the Equality Act 2010. It is important to distinguish between unequal pay – which is illegal – and the issues surrounding the gender pay gap, where one sex is earning more than the other within a company because one dominates the higher up positions, which is not illegal but is an issue many businesses are tackling.

The right to health and safety at work

Health and safety laws state every worker has a legal right to daily and weekly time off. This means anyone working more than six hours must have a break of at least 20 minutes and everyone must get at least one day off in every seven days.

All workers also have a right to work in an environment where any risks to their health and safety are properly dealt with and controlled. This is the duty of the employer, who must also ensure they communicate with employees on all health and safety matters. This responsibility includes ensuring staff have a clean environment to work in, any necessary protective clothing, water for drinking, and first aid equipment.

The right to parental leave

Every woman who has a baby is entitled to up to a year of maternity leave, no matter how long they have worked for the company. Statutory leave for fathers is currently only two weeks and the fathers must have worked for the company for at least 26 consecutive weeks by the end of the 15th week of the pregnancy.

Leave is very different to pay, which can be more complex and varies depending on how long you have worked for a company.

Fathers qualifying for paternity pay must earn at least £113 a week before tax and the rate is either £140.98 a week or 90% of your weekly earnings, whichever is lower.

Mothers are only entitled to pay for 39 weeks of their leave, and this changes over time. They get 90% of their pre-tax weekly earnings for the first six weeks, £145.18 a week or 90% of their earnings if it is less for the next 33 weeks and nothing after that.

Shared Parental Leave is a recent ruling which allows both parents to share up to 50 weeks of leave and 37 weeks of pay between you. *(Please check the accuracy of these details before using them as they change frequently)*

The right to trade union membership

Trade unions are organisations of workers who join together to achieve a common goal, like improving wages and working conditions and protecting their trade's integrity.

Employees have the right to belong to a trade union, join or not join a trade union, and leave or remain a member of one at any time during their employment.

Employers are not allowed to treat you unfairly or dismiss you because you do any of these things.

Workers decide to join trade unions because they give you the power to negotiate a better deal through collective bargaining.

The right to not be discriminated against

Under no circumstances can anyone be discriminated against at work for gender, sexuality, age, background, race, religious beliefs, marriage and partnership, pregnancy, or disability. Examples of how this could happen include not choosing someone for a job or promotion, not paying them the same, and it could even occur indirectly through rules which put certain employees at a disadvantage.

Employers can actively prevent discrimination from occurring by ensuring they recruit inclusively, have an equal opportunities policy, and ensuring all staff follow these practices, by providing training on this topic, encouraging universal respect, and dealing with any complaints quickly. There is no situation when it is legally acceptable to harass or victimise anyone at work if they complain or expose a wrongdoing.

The right to fair dismissal

Employees must usually give employees at least the notice stated in their employment contract or the legal minimum notice period, whichever is longer.

An employer can only dismiss a worker without notice if it considers someone to have done something which constitutes gross misconduct, for example committing fraud or being violent.

Dismissals related to the following are considered automatically unfair:

- *health and safety concerns*
- *assertion of statutory rights*
- *request for flexible working*

Employers must always pursue a fair procedure when considering dismissal.

If you are threatened with, or receive what you consider to be, unfair dismissal, you can get help from a third party to resolve the issue by mediation, conciliation, and arbitration. Trade union members can speak to their unions.

You must have worked for the company for a minimum period of time before you have the right to claim unfair dismissal This varies depending on when you started working for the company and how long you have worked there, due to changes in the law.

The right to reasonable adjustments

Under the Equality Act 2010 employers must also ensure there are reasonable adjustments so that workers with disabilities are not disadvantaged, neither in the job application process or in the job itself. A person is classed as disabled under this law if they have a mental or physical impairment which has a substantially adverse and long-term impact on whether they can do day-to-day activities.

Reasonable adjustments remove or minimise disadvantages disabled people face and, while some businesses will spend a lot on expensive equipment, this does not have to happen. Examples of reasonable adjustments include a keyboard for someone with arthritis, a wheelchair ramp, changing performance targets, and a phased return to work after a period off sick.

The Human Rights Act 1998

This Act is designed to provide legal protection to all human beings. It embraces all other Equality & Diversity Acts and ensures human rights are protected in areas not covered by them.

The Human Rights Act was set out and agreed in 1948. It was reaffirmed by all nations on its 50th anniversary in 1998 and led to the introduction of the European Convention on Human Rights.

It came into force as law in the UK on 2nd October 2000.

The Human Rights Act declares that:

> *'All human beings are born free and equal in dignity and rights. They are endowed with reason and conscience and should act towards one another in a spirit of brotherhood.'*

It also states that 'Everyone is entitled to all the rights and freedoms set forth in the declaration, without distinction of any kind such as race, colour, sex, language, religion, political or other opinion, national or social origin, property, birth or other status'.

In an equal and fair society all people have rights and these are protected by legislation

For example:

- *The right to be treated as equal as human beings regardless of sex or race*
- *The right to be treated properly at work*
- *The right to be free from discrimination*
- *The right not to be bullied or harassed*
- *The right to be healthy and safe at work*

Harassment

No one should be deliberately harassed at work. Neither should they be bullied or made to feel bad. Employees do not have to put up with it!

Harassment can take many forms such as:

- *Threatening or abusive language*
- *Insulting language or behaviour*
- *Disorderly behaviour*

- *Displaying any writing, sign or other visible representation that alarms or distresses and was intended to do so*

Sexual Harassment
It is perfectly acceptable to court and pay attention to someone if it is wanted or invited, but it is illegal to pester people.

If you are told once 'No, I don't like it', but you do it again, you are in danger of breaking the law, both Civil and Criminal. No one has to put up with sexual harassment at work. Be careful and think. Even a thoughtless comment may cause offence.

- *It might be OK for a man to say to a woman, 'You look smart today'*
- *But it might not be so good to say, 'I like that top you are wearing'*

Bullying
Bullying at work can also take many forms such as:

- *Aggressive or violent behaviour*
- *Threatening postures*
- *Putting you in a position where if you do not do something a threat of some kind hangs over you*
- *Excluding you from a group by intimidation*

Anyone who feels they are being harassed or bullied at work, should inform their line manager.

Remember, there are laws that exist to protect employees such as:

- *Sex Discrimination Act 1975*
- *Race Relations Act 1976*
- *Protection from Harassment Act 1997*
- *Gender Reassignment Regulations 1999*
- *The Human Rights Acts of 1948 and 1998*

Equality Act 2010

The Equality Act 2010 is the current legislation that deals with equality and discrimination in the UK.

The term equality and diversity has become a watch word in both the workplace and society. It is vital that everyone is aware of the implications on the workplace.

Equality

Equality in the workplace means equal job opportunities and fairness for employees and job applicants.

In the wider world, you must not treat people unfairly because of reasons protected by discrimination law ('protected characteristics'). For example, because of a person's sex, age or race.

Diversity

Diversity is the range of people in the workforce. For example, this might mean people with different ages, religions, ethnicities, people with disabilities, and both men and women. It also means valuing those differences. Managing equality and diversity involves creating and maintaining a positive environment where the differences of all employees are recognised, understood and valued so that they can reach their full potential and maximise their contributions.

It has also been described as:

> *"promoting equality of opportunity for all, through diversity, giving each individual the chance to achieve their potential, free from prejudice and discrimination."*

Inclusion

An inclusive workplace means everyone feels valued at work. It lets all employees feel safe to:

- *come up with different ideas*
- *raise issues and make suggestions to managers, knowing this is encouraged*
- *try doing things differently to how they have been done before, with management approval*

An inclusive workplace can help lower the risk of bullying, harassment and discrimination.

The Act gives individuals rights as it is unlawful to discriminate against anyone because of a protected characteristic. The protected characteristics include:

- ***age*** *– all people over 18 are protected at work or in work training*
- ***disability or impairment*** *– organisations must make 'reasonable adjustments' to accommodate staff, customers and visitors with disabilities*
- ***gender*** *– equal pay, training and opportunity for males and females*
- ***gender reassignment*** *– people changing from male to female, or female to male*
- ***marriage or civil partnership*** *– preventing discrimination on the grounds of being married or in a civil partnership, at work or in work training*
- ***pregnancy or maternity (including breastfeeding)*** *– only reasons of safety are not covered – e.g., equality may not be possible for pregnant women in some circumstances if the activity could harm them or the baby*
- ***race*** *– wherever they were born, their parents' and their own race, colour, ethnicity are protected*
- ***religion or beliefs*** *– any religion, lack of religion or personal belief is protected*
- ***sexual orientation*** *– heterosexual, gay, lesbian and bisexual people are covered*

Genuine Occupational Requirements

There are limited exemptions from liability in all the discrimination legislation. Thus, where the sex, race, age, sexual orientation or religion or belief of an employee is required for the specific job he or she is required to do, that characteristic may amount to a genuine occupational requirement (GOR).

There must be a clear connection between the duties of the post in question and the characteristics required. An example might be the need to recruit a person from a particular racial group to act in a role written for a character from that racial group.

It is permissible to specify gender when:

- *A man or woman is needed to act in a particular role in a play*
- *The job is one of two when is to be held by a married couple*
- *The work is in a single sex prison or hospital ward*
- *Carers for the mentally ill must be of the same sex*

Discrimination can occur in several different ways, as follows:

Direct discrimination

This is where one individual is treated less favourably than another, and the less favourable treatment is because of a protected characteristic they have, or are thought to have (see perception discrimination), or because they associate with someone who has a protected characteristic.

Indirect discrimination
This is where a provision, criterion or practice applies equally to everyone but has, or would have, a disproportionate impact on those people who share a protected characteristic (e.g. it is more difficult for someone to comply with a requirement because of their religion or belief).

Discrimination by association
This is direct discrimination against an individual because they associate with another person who possesses a protected characteristic.

Perception discrimination
This is direct discrimination against an individual where the person is treated less favourably than another, and the less favourable treatment is because others think they possess a protected characteristic. It will apply even if the person does not actually possess that characteristic.

Harassment
This is defined as:

unwanted conduct related to a relevant protected characteristic which has the purpose or effect of either:

a) violating another person's dignity
b) creating an intimidating, hostile, degrading, humiliating or offensive environment for that other person.

Victimisation
This occurs where an individual is subjected to less favourable treatment by reason of the fact that they have done a 'protected act' under the discrimination legislation – e.g., someone has made a complaint about discrimination on grounds of their age or sex, or helped somebody else to do so, and they are now being treated less favourably by their manager.

Employees also have a responsibility to make sure that they do not breach their employer's equality and diversity policies, codes of conduct or guidelines. The law requires each individual to take responsibility and avoid discrimination, and the employer needs to give clear guidelines in contracts of employment, equality and diversity policies, training sessions and so on.

If an individual fails to follow the guidelines, the employer can implement disciplinary action or claim a breach of contract (the employment contract).

Employee Responsibilities

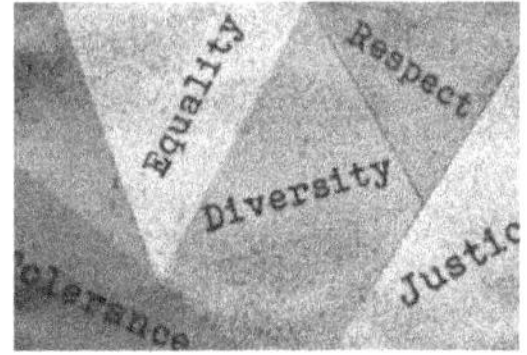

The principles of legislation have to be applied at work and in all dealings with other people. This means that everyone must be treated fairly and equally by you. It is important that you are clear about your personal responsibilities and liabilities under equality legislation and any relevant codes of practice.

Failure to comply with equality legislation could lead to legal action against you or the organisation. If you are unsure of any of your responsibilities it is important that you clarify them with your manager or equality and diversity representative.

Working successfully as a team with your colleagues depends upon all parties involved behaving in a fair and equal manner towards one another.

This does not mean you have to like everyone, but you must respect others and not treat people differently because of their individual characteristics and preferences. No matter what your personal views are, your behaviour at work should not be based upon them. A good employee always behaves professionally.

Professional behaviour requires that you are:

- *Respectful towards others in your dealings with them*
- *Consistent in your treatment of others at all times*
- *Honest in your communications with others*

Some organisations may choose to have a written equality and diversity policy. It is important that this policy is communicated quickly and clearly to the relevant people in your area of responsibility e.g., all employees, visitors and contractors.

treat others as you would expect them to treat you!

Working Time Regulations 1998

The Working Time Regulations generally provide rights for employees to have:

- *a limit of an average 48-hour working week, individuals may choose to work longer by 'opting out'*
- *5.6 weeks of paid leave a year*
- *11 consecutive hours' rest in any 24-hour period*
- *a 20-minute rest break if the working day is longer than 6 hours*
- *1 day off each week*
- *a limit on the normal working hours of night workers to an average 8 hours in any 24-hour period, and an entitlement for night workers to receive regular health assessments*

Extra protection is available to young workers (workers aged 15 to 18). In particular, young workers:

- *are entitled to a daily uninterrupted rest break of 30 minutes after working more than 4.5 hours.*
- *are entitled to an uninterrupted 12-hour break in each 24-hour period of work.*
- *are entitled to weekly rest of at least 48 hours in each seven-day period (and unlike adult workers, they cannot be made to take this rest over two days averaged over two weeks); and*
- *cannot normally work more than eight hours a day or 40 hours a week. These hours cannot be averaged out. There is no 'opt-out' for young workers.*

All full-time workers are entitled to 5.6 weeks' paid holiday each year, reduced pro-rata for part-time workers.

These basic limits on the working week make a vital contribution to health and safety at work.

Employers have the right to ask their staff to enter into a written agreement to opt out of the 48-hour limit, for a specific period or indefinitely. However, if such an agreement is opted into, a worker is entitled to bring the agreement to an end without the employer's consent.

Other Employment legislation and regulations

There are numerous other regulations and pieces of legislation that apply to certain industries or circumstances. Employees and management need to check the organisation's policies and procedures to find out which ones affect them, and what their responsibilities might be. These might include, for instance:

- ***Trade Union and Labour Relations (Consolidation) Act 1992*** *– the ACAS code is issued under this Act*
- ***National Minimum Wage Act 1998*** *– dealing with the minimum wage for different age groups*
- ***Pensions Act 2014*** *– dealing with contributions to occupational pension schemes and state pensions*
- ***Modern Slavery Act 2015*** *– dealing with people trafficking and slavery*
- ***Part-Time Workers (Prevention of Less Favourable Treatment) Regulations 2000***
- ***Fixed-term employees (Prevention of Less Favourable Treatment) Regulations 2002***
- ***Statutory Paternity Pay and Statutory Adoption Pay (General) Regulations 2002*** *– and later amendments*
- ***Work and Families Act 2006***
- ***Enterprise and Regulatory Reform Act 2013***

Operational Legislation

The Data Protection Act 2018

The Data Protection Act 2018 controls how your personal information is used by organisations, businesses or the government.

The Data Protection Act 2018 is the United Kingdom's implementation of the General Data Protection Regulation (GDPR).

Everyone responsible for using personal data must follow strict rules called data protection principles. They must make sure the information is:

- *used fairly, lawfully and transparently*
- *used for specified, explicit purposes*
- *used in a way that is adequate, relevant and limited to what is necessary*
- *accurate and, where necessary, kept up to date*
- *kept for no longer than is necessary*
- *handled in a way that ensures appropriate security, including protection against unlawful or unauthorised processing, access, loss, destruction or damage*

There is more strict legal protection for more sensitive information, such as:

race	*ethnic background*
political opinions	*religious beliefs*
trade union membership	*genetics*
biometrics *(where used for identification)*	*health*
sex life or orientation	

There are separate safeguards for personal data relating to criminal convictions and offences.

Rights

Under the Data Protection Act 2018, people have the right to find out what information the government and other organisations store about them. These include the right to:

- *be informed about how your data is being used*
- *access personal data*
- *have incorrect data updated*
- *have data erased*
- *stop or restrict the processing of your data*

- ***data portability*** *(allowing you to obtain and reuse your data for different services)*
- ***object to how your data is processed under certain circumstances***

People also have rights when an organisation is using personal data for:

- ***automated decision-making processes*** *(without human involvement)*
- ***profiling, for example to predict your behaviour or interests***

The General Data Protection Regulation 2016

GDPR stands for General Data Protection Regulation. This was a Europe wide initiative.

The GDPR is a regulation from the Data Protection Act and covers any information related to a person or data subject that can be used to identify them directly or indirectly.

It can be anything from a name, a photo and an email address to bank details, social media posts, biometric data and medical information. It also introduces digital rights for individuals.

When the GDPR came into effect in May 2018, set new standards for data protection, and kickstarted a wave of global privacy laws that forever changed how we use the internet.

The purpose of GDPR

Personal data is highly valuable — in fact, it supports a trillion-dollar industry. Companies like Facebook and Google make their profits by selling personal information to advertisers. With this much money at stake, do you trust them to have your best interests at heart?

The GDPR defines what companies of all sizes can and cannot do with customer information.

What Is Classified as Personal Data Under GDPR?

Personal data is information that can be used to identify an individual. Put simply, it is any private details that they would not want to fall into the wrong hands.

These are some examples of personal data:

Name	*social media posts*
phone number	*geotagging*
address	*health records*
date of birth	*race*
bank account	*religious and political opinions*
passport number	

Think of personal data like a jigsaw. One piece alone might not say much but connected together they reveal a vivid picture of your life.

What Is a 'Breach' under GDPR?

Any incident that leads to personal data being lost, stolen, destroyed, or changed is considered a data breach. Today, breaches happen all the time.

Here are some examples of note from before the GDPR started cracking down:

- ***Almost half the population of the US had their name, date of birth, and social security number stolen from credit reporting agency Equifax as the result of a data breach.***
- ***Political consulting firm Cambridge Analytica secretly took information from 50 million Facebook profiles and gave it to the 2016 Trump campaign.***

These incidents illustrate how data breaches have serious real-world consequences. This is exactly what GDPR and similar laws hope to regulate.

What are the penalties for violating the GDPR?

GDPR threatens would-be violators with some severe penalties. To ensure companies handle personal data in a legal, ethical way, the fines for noncompliance are:

Up to £18 million or 4% of annual global turnover.

Some big organisations have already been hit with these noncompliance fines:

- ***British Airways — £165 million.*** *The UK airline set the record for fines when the booking details of 500,000 customers were stolen in a cyberattack.*

- ***Marriott — £90 million.*** *After buying the Starwood Hotels group, Marriott failed to update an old system belonging to the group. Their system was hacked, revealing information about 339 million guests.*
- ***Google — £40 million.*** *Important information was hidden when users set up new Android phones, meaning they did not know what data collection practices they were consenting to. The Google GDPR fine shows even tech giants are not immune to GDPR enforcement.*

Although smaller businesses would not be hit for such high amounts, they are held to the same standards.

A business owner now has to make sure their operations comply with the GDPR.

The only thing most people will need to do is read the cookie consent banners that now appear on websites and click agree (or not). The GDPR works mostly behind the scenes but it affects everything people do online.

Freedom of Information Act 2000

The Freedom of Information Act 2000 provides general public access to information recorded and held by public authorities.

Recorded information includes documents, computer files, letters, emails, photographs, and sound or video recordings.

It does this in two ways:

- *Public authorities are legally required to publish certain information about their activities*
  and
- *Any member of the public is entitled to request information from public authorities.*

The Act covers any recorded information that is held by a public authority in England, Wales and Northern Ireland, and by UK-wide public authorities based in Scotland. Information held by Scottish public authorities is covered by Scotland's own legislation.

These organisations include:

- *schools*
- *councils*
- *government departments*
- *health trusts and hospitals*
- *libraries*
- *museums*

Anyone is able to request information, regardless of age, location or nationality.

The Act does not automatically cover every organisation that receives public money. For example, it does not cover some charities that receive grants and some private sector organisations that perform public functions.

Requests must be made in writing, either by letter or by email. The organisation then has 20 working days to provide the information.

Public bodies do not always have to give requested information if:

- ***The information required is regarded as sensitive*** *- the Data Protection Act 2018 overrules in this instance. Aa request to find out how much an employee earned would be rejected as that information is sensitive to the specific employee.*
- ***Information will be too costly or time consuming to produce. For a public organisation, such as a school, or a council, the cost limit is £450.*** *Organisations determine costs based on £25 per hour per person. Therefore, if the information requested would take longer than 18 hours (18 x £25 = £450) to produce, the request would be rejected. For the government and armed forces, this limit is raised to £600 (24 hours).*

The Act does not give access to an individual's own personal data (information about themselves) such as their health records or credit reference file. If a member of the public wants to see information that a public authority holds about them, they should make a data protection subject access request.

Digital Economy Act (2017)

The Digital Economy Act 2017 (the Act) makes provision about electronic communications infrastructure and services, including the creation of a broadband Universal Service Order (USO), to give all premises in the UK a legal right to request a minimum standard of broadband connectivity, expected to be 10 megabits per second (Mbps). The Act also reforms the Electronic Communications Code and provides greater clarification on data sharing between public bodies.

The Digital Economy Bill was introduced in the House of Commons on 5 July 2016, completed its parliamentary stages and received Royal Assent, becoming law, on 27 April 2017.

The Bill followed an announcement made in the Queen's Speech to introduce legislation seeking to make the United Kingdom a world leader in the digital economy.

The Act is made up of six parts as follows:

1. *Access to digital services*
2. *Digital infrastructure*
3. *Online pornography*
4. *Intellectual property*
5. *Digital government*
6. *Miscellaneous.*

Copyright, Designs and Patents Act (1988)

The Copyright, Designs and Patents Act 1988 exists to protect peoples' creations.

When a person creates something, they own it. What they create might include:

- *a picture, drawing or photograph*
- *a video, television programme or film*
- *text, such as a book, article or report*
- *a game*

Copyright is a legal means of protecting the work produced by authors, artists, designers, etc. It applies to certain types of creative work, including artwork, books and computer programs.

Copyright does not apply to ideas.

Copyright is applied automatically as long as certain criteria are met. There is no requirement to formally register the work or use the © symbol.

Work is automatically protected by copyright unless the copyright holder chooses to surrender that right.

Copyright gives the copyright holder exclusive rights to publish, copy, distribute and sell their work as they see fit. No one else can use the work without permission.

Copyright on a piece of work lasts for a long time. In the UK, copyright on artistic work, literature, music and films lasts for 70 years after the death of the creator.

When you buy someone's work, such as a book, film or music CD, the copyright holder grants permission to use it as part of the sale. This is called a licence. The licence is generally only for the purchaser to use.

It is illegal to:

- *make copies of copywritten material*
- *publish it and sell it without permission*
- *share it with other people*
- *sell copies to other people*

This applies to any copywritten material, such as music, films, games and television programmes.

The internet has made it easy to access copyrighted material illegally. If a music track, film, game or programme which is downloaded without the copyright holder's permission, it is breaking the law.

For example, shops earn their money by selling goods. If someone takes them without paying, the shop does not make any money. In the same way, musicians, photographers, filmmakers and artists earn their money by selling the material they produce. If someone takes their work without paying, the person who created the work does not make any money.

There are some situations where it is legal to copy, publish, distribute or sell copyrighted material. These are:

- *when you own the copyright*
- *when the copyright holder has given permission*
- *when the copyright holder has surrendered their copyright*

The Computer Misuse Act (1990)

The extensive use of computers in business has led to new types of crime. The Act strives to discourage people from using computers for illegal purposes. There are three separate parts to the Act:

- *It is illegal to access data stored on a computer unless you have permission to do so. Unauthorised access is often referred to as hacking.*
- *It is illegal to access data on a computer when that material will be used to commit further illegal activity, such as fraud or blackmail.*
- *It is illegal to make changes to any data stored on a computer when the user does not have permission to do so. If the contents of another person's files are changed without their permission, you are breaking the law. This includes installing a virus or other malware which damages or changes the way the computer works.*

The maximum punishment for breaking this law is a £5,000 fine or several years' imprisonment.

BUT: One key part of the law is that **intent** must be proved. If a computer is not well protected, someone could accidentally access its data without meaning to. They might also accidentally change a document without realising it. For anyone to be found guilty, it has to be shown that they **intentionally** accessed and changed data.

Other employment related legislation and regulations

There are numerous other regulations and pieces of legislation that apply to certain industries or circumstances. Organisations need to review their policies and procedures against all legislation to establish which ones affect them, what their responsibilities might be and whether they are compliant.

These might include, for instance:

- *Trade Union and Labour Relations (Consolidation) Act 1992 – the ACAS code is issued under this Act*
- *National Minimum Wage Act 1998 – dealing with the minimum wage for different age groups*
- *Pensions Act 2014 – dealing with contributions to occupational pension schemes and state pensions*
- *Modern Slavery Act 2015 – dealing with people trafficking and slavery*
- *Part-Time Workers (Prevention of Less Favourable Treatment) Regulations 2000*
- *Fixed-term employees (Prevention of Less Favourable Treatment) Regulations 2002*
- *Statutory Paternity Pay and Statutory Adoption Pay (General) Regulations 2002 – and later amendments*
- *Work and Families Act 2006*
- *Enterprise and Regulatory Reform Act 2013*

Consumer-Related Legislation

Whenever goods or services are provided to customers there are expectations from both the supplier and the customer of the goods and/or services being provided.

There is a minimum expectation that the goods or services will be fit for purpose.

A window cleaner that does not leave clean windows will not have many happy customers nor will they be in business for long. The customer, however, will have paid to have their windows cleaned and if they are not clean, they have a right to demand a refund of the monies paid.

Similarly, promises made by suppliers must be met in full – A new sofa in your home before Christmas is a common message on TV advertising, they are making a promise that they will achieve the delivery deadline – if they do not, they will be in breach of contract and the purchaser can make a claim against them for failing to fulfil the contract.

All these rights are defined and covered by The Consumer Rights Act which came into force on 1 October 2015 and replaced a number of old laws which had become outdated.

The law has now been clarified, meaning that consumers can buy with confidence and businesses can sell to them with similar confidence.

When problems arise, disputes can now be sorted out more quickly and cheaply.

Alternative Dispute Resolution, for example through an Ombudsman, offers a quicker and cheaper way of resolving disputes than going through the courts. The changes apply to all consumers and every business which sells directly to them.

UK consumers spend £90 billion a month across all sectors. This new, clear, statement of consumer rights helps them to make better choices when they buy and save both time and money.

The Consumer Rights Act

The Consumer Rights Act came into force in October 2015.

From that date new consumer rights became law covering:

- *what should happen when goods are faulty*
- *what should happen when digital content is faulty*
- *how services should match what has been agreed and what should happen when they do not, or when they are not provided with reasonable care and skill*
- *unfair terms in a contract*

- *what happens when a business is acting in a way which is not competitive?*
- *written notice of routine inspections by public enforcers, such as Trading Standards*
- *greater flexibility for public enforcers, such as Trading Standards, to respond to breaches of such consumer law, by seeking redress for consumers who have suffered harm.*

Most of these changes were important updates to existing laws. But two new areas of law were also introduced.

- *For the first time, rights on digital content has been set out in legislation. The Act gives consumers the clear right to the repair or replacement of faulty digital content, such as online film and games, music downloads and e-books. The law previously had been unclear and this change has brought it up to date with how digital products have evolved.*
- *There are now also new, clear rules for what should happen if a service is not provided with reasonable care and skill, or as agreed. For example, the business that provided the service must bring it into line with what was agreed with the customer or, if this is not practical, must give some money back.*

In terms of what is covered by the new Act, the old standards remain, and these are as follows:

- *Claims about goods - It is an offence for the business or any member of staff to issue false statements about services, accommodation and facilities, or to give misleading information about prices, discounts or special offers.*
- *Description of goods – Examples are labels such as 'home-made', 'made in France', 'fresh vegetables', etc. There is still a sale by description even where the customer selects the goods, for example, in a self-service restaurant, if he or she relied in some way on the description.*
- *Satisfactory Quality – Goods must be fit for the purpose for which they are usually bought*
- *Fitness for a particular purpose – Reasonable fitness for a purpose known to the seller*
- *Samples – Ensuring that goods when sold correspond with samples*

Other legislation affecting the Learning and Development Practitioner

As mentioned above, the sector in which the Learning and Development Practitioner typically operates is not regulated and there is seldom any involvement from OfSTED. As a result, the Learning and Development Practitioner enjoys a greater degree of freedom from rules and regulations, however, they do remain subject to all normal workplace regulation and may also be affected by sector specific legislation.

A typical list of applicable legislation is listed below:

- *Human Rights Act (1998)*
- *Equality Act (2010)*
- *Children Act (2004) - Every Child Matters*
- *Freedom of information Action (2000)*
- *Safeguarding Vulnerable Groups Act (2006)*
- *Protection of Children Act (1999)*
- *The Further Education Teachers' Qualifications (England) Regulations (2007)*
- *Code of Professional Practice ETF*
- *Copyright Designs and Patents Act (1988)*
- *Health and Safety (Display Screen Equipment) Regulations 1992*
- *Food Hygiene Regulations (2006)*
- *Personal Protective Equipment at Work Regulations 1992*
- *Provision and Use of Work Equipment Regulations 1998*
- *Manual Handling Operations Regulations 1992*
- *Control of Vibration at Work Regulations 2005*
- *Electricity at Work Regulations 1989*
- *Control of Substances Hazardous to Health Regulations 2002 (COSHH)*
- *Workplace (Health, Safety and Welfare) Regulations 1992*
- *Health and Safety (First Aid) Regulations 1981*
- *The Health and Safety Information for Employees Regulations 1989*
- *Employers' Liability (Compulsory Insurance) Act 1969*
- *Reporting of Injuries, Diseases and Dangerous Occurrences Regulations 2013 (RIDDOR)*

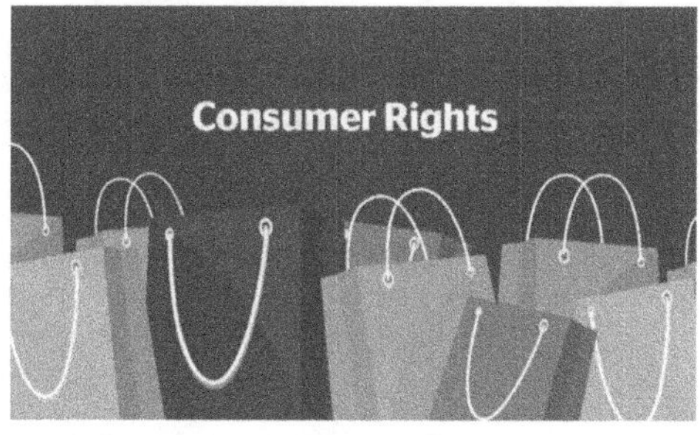

Governance

The term Governance refers to the actions taken by those who run the organisation to ensure legal compliance and uphold the company's integrity.

Governance should promote good relations with stakeholders, including shareholders and employees.

Governance is the exclusive responsibility of the person, or group of people accountable for the performance and conformance of the organisation. In a commercial organisation, this is the Board of Directors or the management team which operate on their behalf.

There is a formal code of governance which is enshrined in company law for organisations listed on the London Stock Exchange. This sets a code of practice for the governance of financial matters; however, governance is required in all organisations and is also across the spectrum of activities.

The most tangible form of governance in an organisation is it policies, practices and procedures. These are put in place not only to ensure legal compliance, but also to ensure the business is operated in a way which maximises the benefit for the owners and employees.

Governance along with compliance aims to avoid and mitigate against:

- ***fraud*** – *e.g., procedures to shred documents to prevent identity theft*
- ***theft*** – *e.g., using CCTV to monitor staff using a cash till*
- ***tax evasion*** – *e.g., procedures to make sure that cash payments are declared*
- ***criminal activity*** – *e.g., taking bribes or trafficking workers*
- ***misuse of funds and resources*** – *e.g., monitoring budgets closely to reduce waste and unnecessary spending*
- ***inefficiency*** – *e.g., from not monitoring waste or opportunities to steal cash or goods*
- ***money laundering*** – *e.g., Disposal of large sums of money which have been derived from illegal activity*

Accountability

An organisation is not just accountable to HMRC and Companies House, it is also accountable to its Shareholders, Stakeholders, Investors, Suppliers, Customers and the staff within the organisation.

Internal stakeholders will need to be satisfied that the organisation looks after its financial affairs properly and could include:

- ***business owners*** *– e.g., sole proprietors or partners who need to know the levels of profit and cash flow*
- ***shareholders*** *– e.g., employees or others who own shares in a company who need to keep an eye on their investment*
- ***employees*** *– e.g., who rely on the organisation to operate payroll and bonus systems*

External stakeholders could include, for example:

- ***banks and other lenders*** *– e.g., who provide business loans to the organisation*
- ***national and local government agencies*** *– e.g., who collect taxes and provide grants*
- ***external customers*** *– e.g., individuals and companies who buy and use the organisation's products and services*
- ***charity commission*** *– e.g., who examine accounts and regulate registered charities*

The actions taken by some people are deliberate and have a criminal intent – these may include knowingly employing people who are illegal immigrants or stealing products or cash. Some actions are due to negligence and ignorance such as someone not realising that they need to provide workplace pensions for their employees or under-declaring VAT due to lack of knowledge about the rules.

By ensuring an organisation is compliant with legislation and is governed fastidiously and fairly, everyone involved with the business will have confidence in the way the business is being operated and satisfied that the business is being managed equitably and legally.

Systems of Governance

A system of governance needs to be created for every organisation and this can be achieved through the design, implementation and ensuring compliance with the five functions of governance.

These are:

Determining the objectives of the organisation
These are expressed through the vision and mission statements and implemented through its strategic plan. The objectives define the purpose of the organisation and describe how its purpose will be fulfilled.

Determining the ethics of the organisation
It is important to define what aspects of behaviour are really important. The question needs to be asked; how much importance is to be given to factors such a sustainability, corporate social responsibility and stakeholder engagement over profits?

Ethics are based on morals and values and define the rules or standards governing the conduct of people within the organisation. The ethical standards of any organisation are set by the behaviours of people at the top and cascade down the hierarchy.

Creating the culture of the organisation
This is a more subtle process and deals with the way people interact with each other. The governing body decides on the culture and influences the operating culture of the organisation through the people it appoints to executive positions.

'Governmentality', the willingness of people to 'be governed' and to support the governance system is at the centre of an effective culture. Other aspects include how supportive the organisation is, how innovative, how risk seeking or risk averse, how open and transparent, how mature and professional, and how tolerant it is.

It is impossible to have a culture of innovation and sensible risk taking if the organisation is intolerant of failure.

Ensuring compliance by the organisation
Governance is implemented to ensure the organisation meets its regulatory, statutory and legal obligations, as well as ensuring its management and staff work towards achieving the organisation's objectives, while working within the ethical and cultural framework which has been defined by the governing body.

Designing and implementing the governance framework for the organisation.
The governing body is accountable for the performance of the organisation and retains overall responsibility for the organisation it governs; however, in most organisations the governing body cannot undertake all of the work of governance itself.

To ensure the efficient governance of the organisation, various responsibilities need to be delegated to people within the organisation's management. The appropriate levels of authority and responsibility will be delegated to managers and other entities to ensure accountability.

The governing body appoints, provides direction to and oversees the functioning of the organisation's management and makes the 'rules' the organisation's management and staff are expected to conform to.

The Management's role is to achieve the objectives of the organisation; working within its ethical and cultural framework, while complying with the 'rules' and providing assurance back to the governing body that this is being accomplished.

The governance system and the management system are derived from each other. The management system is dependent on the governance framework and the governance system is driven by the management.

A well-governed organisation allows systems to work together to the benefit of the organisation's overall stakeholder community.

A good system of corporate governance will strive to:

- *Ensure that the management of an organisation considers the best interests of everyone*
- *Help organisations deliver long-term corporate success and economic growth*
- *Maintain the confidence of investors and as consequence organisations raise capital efficiently and effectively*
- *Has a positive impact on the price of shares as it improves the trust in the market*
- *Improves control over management and information systems (such as security or risk management)*
- *Provides guidance to the owners and managers the strategy of the company*
- *Minimises wastages, corruption, fraud, risks, and mismanagement*
- *Helps to create a strong brand reputation*
- *Most importantly – it makes organisations more resilient.*

Creating a framework for the governance of an organisation can be immensely challenging. You need to spend only a few moments thinking about the number of policies and procedures which are followed each day within one department to realise scale of the task of producing a framework for the governance of a whole organisation. In order to begin to make sense of the process it can be broken down into four elements often known as the four Ps'

These are:

- *People*
- *Purpose*
- *Process*
- *Performance*

People

People come first because people exist on every side of the business equation. They are the founders, the board, the stakeholder and consumer and impartial observer.

It is people who determine a purpose to work towards, develop a consistent process to achieve it, evaluate their performance outcomes, and use those outcomes to grow themselves and others as people.

This is a cyclical process, but it must start with people.

Purpose

Purpose is the next step. Every piece of governance exists ***for*** a purpose and to ***achieve*** a purpose.

The '***for***' is the guiding principles of the organisation. Their mission statement. Every one of their policies and projects should exist to further this agenda.

The '***achieve***' is a small step on the road to achieving that larger goal. It might seem pointless to type up minutes for a meeting that felt irrelevant, but those minutes and all the other governance from that meeting contribute to making the business effective at achieving its stated purpose.

Process

Governance is the process by which people achieve their organisation's purpose, and that process is developed by analysing performance. Processes are refined over time in order to consistently achieve their purpose, and it is good practice to constantly review the governance processes.

The questions should be asked of all processes - Can they be streamlined? Are they efficiently achieving their purpose? It takes work and endeavour to make processes function effectively, but once they do, they will quickly allow an organisation to grow.

Performance

Performance analysis is a key skill in any industry. The ability to look at the results of a process and determine whether it was successful (or successful enough), and then apply those findings to the rest of the organisation, is one of the primary functions of the governance process.

The analysis of these performance results should then be used to identify developmental needs in order to refine the process. The question to be asked regularly is: Governance: is it performing?

Examples might include:

- *how sales need to be recorded*
- *how often reports need to be generated*
- *how to use systems that track banking activities*
- *information needed for monthly reports sent to head office*
- *how to prepare quarterly reviews for shareholders*
- *systems to check and monitor compliance*

Developing Governance

The leaders of organisations will not sit around a boardroom table and begin to discuss which policy or procedure of governance they will start with, it is very much more likely to be an organic process.

At day one of the organisation there will probably be only a few people involved and one or two people will be able to manage all four of the elements listed above so the need for detailed, documented governance will be negligible.

As the organisation grows, volumes will increase, more staff will be required and suddenly the business needs far more controls. New policies and procedures will be required and existing ones will need to be reviewed. Organisations will continue on this cycle of designing, developing, documenting and implementing new policies and procedures as the needs of the business require.

The key word here is documenting. If an organisation relies on word of mouth to implement new standards, governance is immediately under threat as it is open to interpretation or omission and people will not follow the prescribed processes.

It may seem that the number of policies an organisation has is excessive, however, it should be remembered that many policies and processes will not apply to all departments.

The key policies will be those that are directly linked to ensuring compliance with legislation. There will then be a number of policies and procedures which relate specifically to a department or team. These will be developed to ensure consistency in behaviour and performance and it is essential that those people affected by the policy adhere to it.

An example might be an escalation policy.

> *A problem which cannot be dealt with by a junior team member will need to be escalated to someone in a more senior role, but who is the appropriate person?*
>
> *This will be defined in the process. If it is a supply issue, it may be directed to an identified member of a sales team. If it involves a quality issue it may need referring to a defined member of the production team. If the issue relates to a refund, it may need a certain level of authority to authorise the refund.*
>
> *If the staff member knows this policy or has immediate access to it, they can explain to the stakeholder how they will deal with the problem and pass the query on quickly, to the right person, to ensure a speedy resolution.*

It is important that all staff are conversant with the policies which relate to their job role to ensure problems are resolved in a standardised manner to protect all stakeholders involved.

Typical framework

A framework for governance will necessitate the creation of policies and procedures or processes. These reflect – how a process should be performed in practice – and can be a separate document or a section of the same. Clarity is important as a policy change may or may not alter the procedure, whilst a necessary change in procedure should not be allowed to change the policy by default either. It should be clear in every procedure to which policy or policies it relates.

Basic requirements

- *Health and Safety Policy and Procedure. Could include:*
  - *Workstation assessment procedure.*
  - *Fire safety.*

- *Equal Opportunities Statement of Intent. Could include:*
  - *Harassment.*
  - *Reference to recruitment procedure.*
  - *Confidentiality Policy (including Data Protection).*

Office Management

- *Green office policy/Environmental impact.*
- *E-mail/internet use policy.*
- *Personal, or associated group, use of office facilities.*
- *Security.*

External

- *Partnership working.*
- *Media handling* – *who is authorised to say what*
- *Supplier selection*

Staff

Basic terms of employment
Expenses policy (regarding HMRC rules)
Staff disciplinary procedure
Staff grievance procedure
Staff appraisal procedure
Supervision
Staff loans (travel, cycle, car)
Union recognition policy
Sick leave policy and procedure
Leave policy and procedure
Time off in lieu policy and procedure
Public duties
Recruitment procedure
Redundancy policy
Induction procedure and checklist.
Exit interviews
Job evaluation
Retirement policy

Ethics, Empowerment, Improvement

- *Complaints procedure (for members, service users, public).*
- *Service user/member involvement.*
- *Training policy.*
- *Quality/monitoring policy*
- *Staff involvement policy.*
- *Ethical investment policy.*
- *Whistleblowing.*
- *Child/vulnerable adult protection – 'safeguarding'.*

Finance

- *Insurances*
- *Other accounting policies often part of audit process (e.g., valuation of assets).*
- *Financial policies and procedures.*

Governance

- *AGM procedures.*
- *Committee procedures (standing orders).*
- *Management committee/board (and sub-committee) terms of reference.*
- *Job descriptions for directors / board members – chair, secretary and any others.*
- *Conflicts of interest*

Implications of unresolved Governance and Compliance issues

There can be serious implications if governance and compliance issues are unresolved. Failure to address governance and compliance can cause internal issues that, for example:

- ***result in theft and loss of income*** *– e.g., if sales and transactions are not monitored correctly*
- ***cause longer-term financial problems for the organisation*** *– e.g., from paying compensation and having to repay money that has been taken; from a drop in share value as investors lose confidence*
- ***lead to a breach of contract*** *– e.g., being sued for releasing information*
- ***cause a security problem*** *– e.g., a personal attack or terrorist threat if security arrangements are leaked; passwords and access codes being used by unauthorised people*
- ***cause embarrassment*** *– e.g., if personal details or financial records are made public*
- ***give competitors an advantage*** *– e.g., from gaining access to confidential operational data*
- ***increased compliance costs*** *– e.g., restructuring costs as a consequence of prosecution or loss of reputation*
- ***increased staff turnover and related costs*** *– e.g., from staff not wanting to work for an employer with a poor reputation*

There can also be serious implications if an organisation's external stakeholders act in response to governance and compliance failures – e.g., government agencies or customers who take enforcement or legal action. Actions could result in:

- ***fines and penalties*** *– e.g., from paying insufficient tax*
- ***compensation payments*** *– e.g., to customers when financial data has been mishandled*
- ***the organisation losing customers*** *– e.g., from having a bad and unprofessional reputation*
- ***financial problems for customers*** *– e.g., if their bank accounts are hacked as a result*
- ***prosecution of the employer and/or employees*** *– e.g., under the Data Protection Act, Bribery Act or Money Laundering regulations*

The consequences of failure can seriously affect an organisation's ability to survive and thrive due to additional costs and loss of reputation.

Policies

All businesses must have Policies, Processes and procedures which apply Governance and Compliance to its operations.

The policies used within an organisation fall into two categories. There are those which are formed out of compliance and are the key business policies for an organisation and those which are formed to maintain governance which can be considered internal policies as they do not affect any external stakeholders directly.

Policies are used to establish high levels of standards and behaviour

Internal policies will include:

Dress Code policy
Dress codes are used to maintain a positive and professional image of the organisation to both internal and external stakeholders. A dress code will include the use of PPE at all appropriate times. Any dress code which is used should be inclusive toward members of staff, not discriminatory in anyway and not put financial strains on any employee or hinder their productivity.

Use of Equipment
The use of equipment policy will define how and when employees can use corporate assets such as computer equipment, mobile telephones, a company car, office supplies and stationery, printers and any other equipment that they may require to carry out their job role. The misuse of equipment is widely regarded to be a major cost against many businesses

Social Media policy
A social media policy will define what is acceptable and unacceptable behaviour when using the internet and social media at work. A social media policy will define what is acceptable as far as profile updates and photograph updates. It is normal for such a policy to prevent the uploading of any organisational data or images from being uploaded to personal or the organisations social media accounts. It will also state when and how to reply to customers comments. Such responses to customers will normally be restricted to those who have received specific training on what information it is appropriate to post on social media due to the very public nature of the information posted. The abuse of social media platforms is becoming an increasing concern for organisations.

Annual Leave policy
An annual leave policy is used to outline employee leave entitlements. The policy will explain the process for requesting leave and to provide a fair policy for all. The policy will normally highlight the notice period an employee may need to give their employer when they are requesting time off for holidays or other purposes. They may also be

limits set on the total number of consecutive days which may be taken and also restrictions at particularly busy times of the year.

Data Protection

There are many reasons why an organisation needs a data protection policy. The most important being legal compliance with GDPR. The policy should highlight the company's commitment and approach to the collection and handling of data. It should also advise employees how their own personal data will be handled.

Hours of Work

Most organisations have set operating hours; however, these hours may be flexible at times and therefore some organisations will allow flexible start and end times for employees. It is important that an organisation provides their employees with clear guidance on the number of hours per day or week that they are expected to work. An hours of work policy should state:

- *the number of hours full time and/or part time you are expected to work per week*
- *the length of lunch breaks*
- *the length of other breaks if provided*

Equal Opportunities policy

An equal opportunities policy is simply a written policy that allows the organisation to set out how it intends to ensure it will not discriminate against minority or disadvantaged groups.

The policy is usually separated into sections, section one will include a statement of intent and section 2 a code of practice. The statement of intent tells employees why the organisation is adopting the policy and what it intends to do, Section 2 will provide more detail about how intends to implement the statement of intent.

The code of practice must be realistic and practical.

Many organisations also add a third section, called the code of conduct. This is very clear statement that can be displayed and circulated within the organisation, making it clear that everybody will be treated equally and with respect. It will also highlight the steps that will be taken to ensure this happens.

Health and safety

All organisations must have a health and safety policy however, if a business has fewer than five employees, it does not need to be written down

Health and safety policies are often set out in three sections:

- *General policy*
- *Responsibilities*
- *Arrangements*

The statement of general policy on health and Safety at Work sets out the organisations commitment to manage health and safety, stating what the organisation wants to achieve

The responsibilities section explains the responsibility of managers, team leaders, employees and visitors. It will also define responsibility for specific areas including fire safety, first aid, first workplace safety and safety training, highlighting those who are responsible for these areas.

The arrangement section contains details on what the organisation is going to do in practise to achieve the aims that have been set out in the statement of general policy on health and Safety at Work.

All sectors are different and will have different policies in place and these have been covered in more detail in the earlier part of this document. Some policies will be found in all businesses and include:

- *Health and safety*
- *Equal opportunities*
- *Data protection*

Some will be bespoke to individual organisations and sectors such as:

- *Annual leave*
- *Social media*
- *Dress code*

You have a responsibility to the organisation that you work for to follow the organisation's policies and procedures and promote these to other team members.

This can be done by:

- *discussing the policies at team meetings*
- *making employees aware of any changes to the policies*

If policies are not being followed it could cause a health and safety issue and put other people at risk.

The Role of the Learning and Development Practitioner

The role of the Learning and Development Practitioner is one of responsibility and duty. There is a responsibility to serve the needs of the learner to the best of one's ability and to carry out those responsibilities in a manner which complies with the professional standards expected by the organisation and the professional standards expected by the profession and as set out in regulatory framework.

Although Training and Coaching is less formal and a more spontaneous practice than teaching, the need for professionalism and equitable conduct is implicit in both.

Training and Coaching is often unregulated and therefore there are no standards which are enforced in legislation, other than those which are covered in normal statute law. This does not for one moment suggest that such standards are not a prerequisite for anyone working in a coaching role.

The standards expected from Learning and Development Practitioners may be drawn from two primary sources. The first is from the Department for Education which defines the standards expected from those involved in education and the second are the standards which are set by the Education and Training Foundation (ETF).

The Teaching Standards

The Teaching Standards set a clear benchmark of expectations for the professional practice and conduct of teachers and define the minimum level of practice expected. They were developed by an independent review group made up of leading teachers, headteachers and other experts. They can be used to review own practice and inform plans for continuing professional development.

The standards are also used to assess trainee teachers when considering their competence for qualified teacher status and often used when assessing the competence of practising teachers during the interview process.

Part Two of the Teaching Standards is often used during a disciplinary process to establish whether an act of serious misconduct has been committed and this may be in any educational setting.

The Department for Education (DoE) defines the following standards:

> ***Teachers make the education of their pupils their first concern and are accountable for achieving the highest possible standards in work and conduct. Teachers act with honesty and integrity; have strong subject knowledge, keep their knowledge and skills as teachers up-to-date and are self-critical; forge***

positive professional relationships; and work with parents in the best interests of their pupils.

Part One: Teaching

A teacher must:

1. Set high expectations which inspire, motivate and challenge pupils
   - *establish a safe and stimulating environment for pupils, rooted in mutual respect*
   - *set goals that stretch and challenge pupils of all backgrounds, abilities and dispositions*
   - *demonstrate consistently the positive attitudes, values and behaviour which are expected of pupils.*

2. Promote good progress and outcomes by pupils
   - *be accountable for pupils' attainment, progress and outcomes*
   - *be aware of pupils' capabilities and their prior knowledge, and plan teaching to build on these*
   - *guide pupils to reflect on the progress they have made and their emerging needs*
   - *demonstrate knowledge and understanding of how pupils learn and how this impacts on their teaching*
   - *encourage pupils to take a responsible and conscientious attitude to their own work and study.*

3. Demonstrate good subject and curriculum knowledge
   - *have a secure knowledge of the relevant subject(s) and curriculum areas, foster and maintain pupils' interest in the subject, and address misunderstandings*
   - *demonstrate a critical understanding of developments in the subject and curriculum areas and promote the value of scholarship*
   - *demonstrate an understanding of and take responsibility for promoting high standards of literacy, articulacy and the correct use of standard English, whatever the teacher's specialist subject*
   - *when teaching early reading, demonstrate a clear understanding of systematic synthetic phonics*
   - *when teaching early mathematics, demonstrate a clear understanding of appropriate teaching strategies.*

4. Plan and teach well-structured lessons
   - *impart knowledge and develop understanding through effective use of lesson time*
   - *promote a love of learning and children's intellectual curiosity*
   - *set homework and plan other out-of-class activities to consolidate and extend knowledge and understanding pupils have acquired*
   - *reflect systematically on the effectiveness of lessons and approaches to teaching*

- *contribute to the design and provision of an engaging curriculum within the relevant subject area(s).*

5. Adapt teaching to respond to the strengths and needs of all pupils
    - *know when and how to differentiate appropriately, using approaches which enable pupils to be taught effectively*
    - *have a secure understanding of how a range of factors can inhibit pupils' ability to learn, and how best to overcome these*
    - *demonstrate an awareness of the physical, social and intellectual development of children and know how to adapt teaching to support pupils' education at different stages of development*
    - *have a clear understanding of the needs of all pupils, including those with special educational needs; those of high ability; those with English as an additional language; those with disabilities; and be able to use and evaluate distinctive teaching approaches to engage and support them.*

6. Make accurate and productive use of assessment
    - *know and understand how to assess the relevant subject and curriculum areas, including statutory assessment requirements*
    - *make use of formative and summative assessment to secure pupil progress*
    - *use relevant data to monitor progress, set targets and plan subsequent lessons*
    - *give pupils regular feedback, both orally and through accurate marking, and encourage pupils to respond to the feedback.*

7. Manage behaviour effectively, to ensure a good and safe learning environment
    - *have clear rules and routines for behaviour in classrooms and take responsibility for promoting good and courteous behaviour both in classrooms and around the school, in accordance with the school's behaviour policy*
    - *have high expectations of behaviour, and establish a framework for discipline with a range of strategies, using praise, sanctions and rewards consistently and fairly*
    - *manage classes effectively, using approaches which are appropriate to pupils' needs in order to involve and motivate them*
    - *maintain good relationships with pupils, exercise appropriate authority, and act decisively when necessary.*

8. Fulfil wider professional responsibilities
    - *make a positive contribution to the wider life and ethos of the school*
    - *develop effective professional relationships with colleagues, knowing how and when to request advice and specialist support*
    - *deploy support staff effectively*
    - *takes responsibility for improving teaching through appropriate professional development, responding to advice and feedback from colleagues*
    - *communicate effectively with parents*

Part Two: Personal and Professional Conduct

A teacher is expected to demonstrate consistently high standards of personal and professional conduct. The following statements define the behaviour and attitudes which set the required standard for conduct throughout a teaching career.

- ***Teachers uphold public trust in the profession and maintain high standards of ethics and behaviour, inside and outside school, by:***
    - *treating pupils with dignity, building relationships rooted in mutual respect and at all times observing proper boundaries appropriate to a teacher's professional position*
    - *having regard for the need to safeguard pupils' well-being, in accordance with statutory provisions*
    - *showing tolerance of and respect for, the rights of others*
    - *promoting fundamental British values, including democracy, the rule of law, individual liberty and mutual respect, and tolerance of those with different faiths and beliefs*
    - *ensuring that personal beliefs are not expressed in ways which exploit the vulnerability of pupils' or might lead them to break the law.*

- ***Teachers must have proper and professional regard for the ethos, policies and practices of the organisation in which they teach and maintain high standards in their own attendance and punctuality.***

- ***Teachers must have an understanding of, and always act within, the statutory frameworks which set out their professional duties and responsibilities.***

Michael Gove as Secretary of State for Education said of the Teachers' Standards at their launch in 2011.....

> *"The Teachers' Standard set clear expectations about the skills that every teacher in our schools should demonstrate. They will make a significant improvement to teaching by ensuring teachers can focus on the skills that matter most."*

The Education and Training Foundation

The Education and Training Foundation first published the Professional Standards for Teachers and Trainers in 2014 they were welcomed because the dealt with the unique challenges faced by practitioners at the time. The ETF has responsibility for maintaining the Standards and for ensuring their currency, including publishing guidance on their use and interpretation.

The World today is very different to that in 2014 when the standards were first written and therefore the Standards have been reviewed and updated to reflect the post COVID World in which we now operate.

The extraordinary social change witnessed following the Covid-19 pandemic also raised the importance of learner wellbeing, digital literacy and cybersecurity, and a need to work more effectively with learners with diverse backgrounds and support needs. The updated Standards recognise the increasingly vital role that practitioners play in advising and developing learners, preparing them for employment, and providing them with opportunities for personal enrichment and autonomy.

The purpose of the Professional Standards is to support educators to maintain and improve standards of teaching and learning, resulting in better outcomes for learners. For individuals and institutions, they are a national reference point for professional development.

The Standards provide clear guidance on what constitutes excellence in teaching and learning. They provide a common vocabulary for discussing teaching and learning; they help practitioners reflect on existing practices to improve their impact with learners; and they can be a valuable focus for professional development planning.

A Standards-based approach to teaching and learning is expected to be beneficial to learner outcomes, organisational development, and staff professionalism.

These professional standards are as follows:

Professional Values and Attributes

Develop your own judgment of what works and does not work in own teaching and training.

1. Critically reflect on and evaluate own practices, values, and beliefs to improve learner outcomes.
   Which means:
   - *developing and refining your judgement about what works in different learning contexts*
   - *questioning your own values, beliefs and assumptions about effective teaching, learning and assessment*

- *understanding your learners' needs, the context in which they are studying, and the factors affecting their learning and achievement*
- *evaluating and improving your impact on learner outcomes*
- *engaging learners in conversations about what works and what doesn't work*
- *discussing ineffective practices with colleagues*
- *managing your own wellbeing and minimising the impact of unhealthy working practices on your performance*

2. Promote and embed Education for Sustainable Development (ESD) across learning and working practices.
   Which means:
   - *understanding how core sustainability concepts relate to your subject specialism and/or vocational area*
   - *embedding ESD into curriculum design, delivery and assessment*
   - *creating an environment where learners consider and/or implement sustainable decisions and practices*
   - *modelling sustainable practices at work and in the classroom*
   - *compiling, creating and/or sharing resources that promote learners' understanding of ESD*
   - *using ESD examples to build learners' skills in other areas (for example, mathematics, English, enrichment, projects, and so on)*
   - *collaborating with others to develop learners' ESD knowledge, skills and behaviours*
   - *participating in and promoting whole-organisational approaches to ESD*
   - *explaining the value of ESD to others.*

3. Inspire, motivate and raise aspirations of learners by communicating high expectations and a passion for learning.
   Which means:
   - *being passionate about learning and your subject discipline*
   - *conveying this passion to learners, colleagues and other stakeholders*
   - *setting high expectations so that all learners feel they can excel*
   - *using clear, motivational language*
   - *adapting your communication to suit different learners and learning contexts*
   - *valuing learners as partners*
   - *engaging learners in purposeful discussions about their progress and future*
   - *ensuring learners are at the centre of decision-making.*

4. Support and develop learners confidence, autonomy and thinking skills, taking account of their needs and starting points.
   Which means:
   - *valuing learners as individuals*
   - *exploring the profile of your students to establish their current confidence levels and the factors that support or challenge this*
   - *being clear about the role that self-efficacy and self-belief play in a learner's success*

- *developing a learning environment that values and promotes self-direction and independent learning*
- *encouraging learners to explore the options and consequences of taking different decisions*
- *encouraging learners to participate, ask questions and see mistakes as an essential part of the learning process*
- *encouraging learners to evaluate their learning and think critically*
- *using diagnostic data and other forms of initial assessment to determine learners' current attainment and skills levels and using these to develop learning goals and plans that facilitate progress*

5. Value and champion diversity, equality of opportunity, inclusion and social equity. Which means:
   - *encouraging learners to gain an understanding of how diversity brings extensive added value to the teaching and learning process*
   - *highlighting different ways of interpreting, discussing and approaching controversial issues, and the role people's beliefs play in this*
   - *treat all learners and colleagues equally and fairly without directly or indirectly excluding anyone*
   - *giving learners a voice and being responsive to this*
   - *challenging stereotypes, biases and other forms of prejudice*
   - *actively seeking ways to include all learners in learning activities and removing barriers that inhibit learning and participation*
   - *using data to examine, monitor and reduce attainment gaps between different learner groups*

6. Develop collaborative and respectful working relationships with learners, colleagues and external stakeholders.
   Which means:
   - *championing the benefits of teamwork and creating opportunities for collaboration*
   - *recognising the value of other people's ideas and contributions*
   - *providing advice and/or support to others*
   - *developing and maintaining positive relationships with learners, colleagues and external stakeholders with shared/different characteristics*
   - *removing barriers that keep people from working together effectively*
   - *being honest and respectful in your interactions/correspondence with others*
   - *managing and resolving conflict successfully.*

7. Engage with and promote a culture of continuous learning and quality improvement. Which means:
   - *taking ownership of your professional development and proactively seeking opportunities to update/improve your knowledge and skills*
   - *adopting rigorous processes of self-assessment and quality assurance to maintain high standards of teaching and learning*
   - *implementing plans to improve the learner experience*

- *working with learners, colleagues and external partners to improve and develop the organisation in which you work – its systems, structures and policies*
- *presenting, leading or organising professional development activities for other colleagues*

Professional Knowledge and Understanding

Develop deep and critically informed knowledge and understanding of theory and practice.

8. Develop and update knowledge of own subject specialism, taking account of new practices, research and/ or industry requirements.
   Which means:
   - *constantly updating your subject/vocational knowledge and skills so that learners benefit from your currency and relevance*
   - *collaborating with employers and external partners to ensure subject and/or technical knowledge is consistent with industry requirements*
   - *consulting the latest research on how to teach your subject*
   - *liaising with subject matter experts*
   - *holding a professional membership with a relevant subject/occupational body and engaging in professional development*
   - *discussing subject pedagogy with learners and/or colleagues and using their feedback to refine your approach*
   - *working with other colleagues to support their subject development*
   - *using labour market data to make informed decisions about learning/curriculum for the local community*

9. Critically review and apply own knowledge of educational research, pedagogy, and assessment to develop evidence-informed practice.
   Which means:
   - *reading professional literature, regularly reviewing professional websites, blogs, and so on*
   - *reflecting on the latest educational theories and research with colleagues and discussing how these may be relevant to your teaching context*
   - *undertaking classroom experiments and action research to test and improve teaching and learning approaches*
   - *collaborating with and/or supporting others to develop evidence-informed practice*
   - *liaising with awarding organisations to ensure you are adopting the most recent advice on assessment, standardisation and/or examination requirements, and interpreting these consistently in line with expectations.*

10. Share and update knowledge of effective practice with colleagues, networks and research communities to support improvement.
    Which means:
    - *working with colleagues to update, develop and improve some aspect of practice*
    - *attending subject and/or teaching networks*

- *participating in a collaborative project with external colleagues which develops practice in a positive direction*
- *presenting at a conference or professional network*
- *carrying out action research or project where the focus is on exploring and reflecting on practice to increase its impact*
- *contributing to organisational committees or policy groups with responsibility for improving teaching and learning*

11. Develop and apply your knowledge of special educational needs and disabilities to create inclusive learning experiences.
    Which means:
    - *holding regular conversations with learners (and their families/carers where appropriate) to inform, adapt and improve your teaching*
    - *keeping up to date with academic and scientific developments on how learners learn and how learning differences are best supported*
    - *liaising with internal and external support teams for specialist advice/input, using this to improve the learner experience*
    - *understanding and applying appropriate equality legislation (including specific SEND legislation), policies and/or codes of practice*
    - *creating personalised learning plans that improve the learner's chances of making progress and being successful.*

12. Understand your teaching role and responsibilities and how these are influenced by legal, regulatory, institutional and ethical contexts.
    Which means:
    - *being fully aware of the requirements of your role and responsibilities*
    - *understanding fully your obligations towards safeguarding and what to do in the case of an emergency*
    - *being fully aware of, planning for, and implementing required health and safety procedures*
    - *ensuring your learners and colleagues have access to equal opportunities and are not subject to discrimination*
    - *keeping up to date with organisational policies and rules*
    - *keeping up to date with changes in legislation and regulatory frameworks that govern your practice*
    - *keeping up to date with relevant curriculum, assessment and examination arrangements*
    - *responding effectively to changes in policy and practice*
    - *accessing expert advice from colleagues or third parties*
    - *being aware of how your actions can influence people's perception of you, your role and your professionalism*
    - *defining and maintaining appropriate boundaries with learners*

Professional Skills

Develop your expertise and skills to ensure the best outcomes for learners.

13. Promote and support positive learner behaviour, attitudes and wellbeing.
    Which means:
    - *critically reflecting on the drivers that contribute to poor behaviour and wellbeing*
    - *designing and evaluating the curriculum so that it recognises the potential challenges to learners' physical and mental health*
    - *regularly discussing wellbeing with learners*
    - *experimenting with different teaching approaches to improve learner behaviour, attitudes and wellbeing*
    - *taking advice from colleagues and putting this into action*
    - *adopt suitable behaviours to act as an exemplary role model to learners*
    - *cultivating a growth mindset in learners*
    - *developing learners' resilience*

14. Apply motivational, coaching and skills development strategies to help learners progress and achieve.
    Which means:
    - *identifying the strengths and weaknesses of individual learners and working to deepen the former while ameliorating the latter*
    - *using effective non-verbal communication to enthuse learners*
    - *developing your repertoire of motivational techniques and making judgements about when to deploy them*
    - *using one-to-one coaching and skill-building approaches to set challenging goals, extend learners' skills and deepen their motivation*
    - *supporting learners to set, monitor and evaluate their own goals*
    - *using forms of peer-to-peer learning.*

15. Plan and deliver learning programmes that are safe, inclusive, stretching and relevant to learner needs.
    Which means:
    - *recognising that your learners have different experiences, abilities and needs*
    - *encouraging all learners to meet and exceed their expectations*
    - *designing and sequencing the curriculum so that it develops the knowledge, skills and attitudes demanded of learners*
    - *adopting approaches that maximise learner participation*
    - *promoting equality and diversity in your teaching and learning in order to create a positive and inclusive learning environment*
    - *ensuring at all times that the learning environment is safe, and that potential hazards are identified quickly and addressed*
    - *managing learner workloads, assessments and home study so that they are relevant, realistic and achievable*

16. Select and apply digital technologies safely and effectively to promote learning.
    Which means:

- *keeping abreast of changes in digital technologies and how they can support teaching, learning and assessment*
- *promoting to learners the value of using digital technologies to support their learning*
- *evaluating the benefits/challenges of deploying specific digital technologies to achieve learner goals*
- *using digital technologies to inform, collaborate in and/or assess learning*
- *evidencing the use of digital technologies in curriculum planning*
- *creating digital learning resources*
- *ensuring learning tools and digital resources meet accessibility needs and guidance*
- *adopting a rigorous approach to cybersecurity, online safety and confidentiality in the management of digital technologies and data*

17. Develop learners' mathematics, English, digital and wider employability skills.
    Which means:
    - *identifying the needs of individual learners in mathematics and English and finding opportunities to develop these skills in motivating and relevant ways*
    - *develop own mathematics and English skills to ensure you have the confidence to support your learners to improve these skills*
    - *planning opportunities to develop and nurture learners' digital skills, as well as investing in your own digital skills to support learners appropriately*
    - *supporting learners with the development of employability skills such as self-organisation, time management and problem-solving, and showing how these are important to learners' success and the world of work*
    - *being familiar with the changing skillsets demanded by employers so that you can advise learners accordingly.*

18. Provide access to up-to-date information, advice and guidance so learners can take ownership of their learning and make informed progression choices.
    Which means:
    - *encouraging all learners to take an active role in decisions that affect their learning and progression*
    - *giving learners access to accurate and timely information, advice and guidance so they can make informed choices about their learning and progression*
    - *helping learners access relevant careers services*
    - *encouraging learners to self-appraise in realistic ways so that they have a good understanding of where they are and what they need to do to achieve a desired progression route*
    - *setting/negotiating attainable personal goals that are consistent with learners' progression needs and choices.*
19. Apply appropriate and fair methods of assessment and provide constructive and timely feedback to support learning and achievement.
    Which means:
    - *understanding the advantages and disadvantages of different assessment methods and their application to specific learner contexts*
    - *ensuring that all learners have regular, constructive feedback*

- *understanding the social, theoretical and practical issues that contribute to high-performing and under-performing learners*
- *tracking assessment and progress data for the purposes of informing, developing and improving teaching practices.*

20. Develop enrichment and progression opportunities for learners through the collaboration with employers, higher education and/or community groups.
    Which means:
    - *organising work placements for learners*
    - *liaising/collaborating with employers and/or other organisations to develop enrichment experiences and/or progression opportunities*
    - *organising trips, excursions and guest speakers to enrich the learner experience*
    - *producing resources that support enrichment/work placement experiences*
    - *being fully aware of organisational events and activities that augment the learners' studies and help them develop desirable skills and contacts*

The Value of Professional Standards

- ***Help practitioners excel in their teaching practice***
- ***Enrich practitioners professional development conversations***
- ***Recognise the value of practitioners knowledge-sharing with peers and partners***
- ***Support practitioners innovation and creative practices to improve learner outcomes***
- ***Encourage practices to engage with education for sustainable development***
- ***Promote a fair, equitable and respectful learning culture.***

The Professional Standards can be used strategically to develop policies and procedures. For example, they may inform:

- *strategies to improve the quality of teaching and learning, and initial teacher education across the organisation*
- *induction and mentoring systems*
- *professional development processes and planning*
- *the recruitment of staff, for example informing the development of job descriptions and person specifications*
- *whole organisation approaches to training needs analysis*
- *agendas for teaching circles, quality forums and networks where the aim is to facilitate professional dialogue and exchange.*

Governance and Compliance

There is no statutory or regulatory compulsion around the need to respond to these Professional Standards. The sector's deregulated context, however, means that the Professional Standards are a convergence point around what constitutes excellence in teaching and learning which can guide and inspire professionalism and professional improvement.

The updated Standards have considered Ofsted's criteria for outstanding practice in teaching and learning and can be a mechanism to enhance personal development and organisational performance.

The updated Standards draw on Ofsted's Education Inspection Framework, the Gatsby benchmarks for effective careers guidance and the Matrix Quality Standard for their relevance.
They also establish continuity with the new Occupational Standard for initial teacher education to enable trainees to transition smoothly into the next stage of their career.

To support career progression, the Standards provide a scaffolded approach for teachers to move into leadership and coaching positions.

Society of Education and Training Code of Practice

The Society for Education and Training (SET) Code of Practice sets out the professional behaviour and conduct expected of the membership.

The Code is divided into two sections:

> ***Mandatory, actionable provisions*** – *members must comply with these provisions in order to become and remain a member. If a member does not comply with these requirements, then SET may refuse or cancel membership.*
>
> ***Aspirational provisions*** – *members are expected to work towards these requirements as part of their professional practice. They encourage members to follow these standards but will not refuse or cancel membership on this basis.*

Mandatory, actionable provisions

All SET members must:

1. Uphold the reputation of the profession – they must not behave in such a way that is likely to diminish the trust and confidence which the public places in them and in the profession.
2. Act honestly and with integrity in the educational setting.
3. Use reasonable professional judgement when discharging responsibilities and obligations to learners, colleagues, institutions and the wider profession.
4. Take reasonable care to ensure the safety and welfare of learners and comply with relevant statutory provisions to support their wellbeing and development.

5. Respect the rights of learners and colleagues in accordance with relevant legislation and organisation requirements.
6. Act in such a way which recognises diversity as an asset and does not discriminate unfairly.
7. Act in accordance with the conditions of membership which may be subject to change from time to time.
8. Comply with all reasonable requests for information from SET *(including all reasonable requests that you consent to the disclosure of information held by third parties about you).*
9. Cooperate with any investigation in the capacity as a further education professional and in accordance with the law.
10. Notify SET within 21 days of any of the following occurring:
    10.1 They are made the subject of a bar, partial bar, warning or any other action by the Secretary of State or the Disclosure and Barring Service (DBS) in relation to misconduct or working with children, young people or vulnerable adults.
    10.2. They are charged with, convicted of, or cautioned for a criminal offence.
    10.3. Their contract of employment has been terminated due to disciplinary reasons, in line with the ACAS Code of Practice.
    10.4. They are informed that they are under investigation by any professional or regulatory body, or that they will be the subject of a disciplinary hearing by any employer, in this country or abroad.
11. Notify SET of any other information which may have a bearing on their suitability for membership, including anything which is likely to diminish the trust and confidence which the public places in them and in the profession.
12. Not seek to dissuade any person from raising a concern, or act unfairly towards them if they do.

Aspirational provisions

These are based on the EFT Professional Standards detailed above and require a commitment to demonstrating:

1. Reflect on what works best in own teaching and learning to meet the diverse needs of learners.
2. Evaluate and challenge their practice, values and beliefs.
3. Inspire, motivate and raise aspirations of learners through their enthusiasm and knowledge.
4. Be creative and innovative in selecting and adapting strategies to help learners to learn.
5. Value and promote social and cultural diversity, equality of opportunity and inclusion.
6. Build positive and collaborative relationships with colleagues and learners.
7. Maintain and update knowledge of their subject and/or vocational area.
8. Maintain and update own knowledge of educational research to develop evidence-based practice.

9. Apply theoretical understanding of effective practice in teaching, learning and assessment drawing on research and other evidence.
10. Evaluate their practice with others and assess its impact on learning.
11. Manage and promote positive learner behaviour.
12. Understand the teaching and professional role and their responsibilities.
13. Motivate and inspire learners to promote achievement and develop skills to enable progression.
14. Plan and deliver effective learning for diverse groups or individuals in a safe and inclusive environment.
15. Promote the benefits of technology and support learners to use it.
16. Address the mathematics and English needs of learners and work to overcome individual barriers to learning.
17. Enable learners to share responsibility for their learning and assessment, setting goals that stretch and challenge.
18. Apply appropriate and fair methods of assessment and provide constructive and timely feedback to encourage progression and achievement.
19. Maintain and update own teaching and training expertise and vocational skills through collaboration with employers.
20. Contribute to organisational development and quality improvement through collaboration with others.

Safeguarding

Recently there has been a great deal of coverage in the news of people who have been abused. This is not limited to children and other vulnerable people in society today, there have also been many instances of historic abuse which, up until now has been hidden. It is alarming that in our modern society such things as slavery and the mutilation of human beings still exists.

Because of this, systems have been introduced which make the identification and reporting of abuse far clearer and for the victim, much safer.

The victims of abuse fall into three categories, these are Children, who are those aged under 16. Young people are those aged 16 – 18 years and adults are those aged over 18.

Definition

> *Safeguarding means protecting people's health, wellbeing and human rights, and enabling them to live free from harm, abuse and neglect. It's fundamental to high-quality health and social care.*

Safeguarding young people and promoting their welfare includes:

- *Protecting them from maltreatment or things which are injurious to their health or development.*
- *Making sure they grow up in circumstances which allow safe and effective care.*

Safeguarding vulnerable adults includes:

- *Protecting their rights to live in safety, free from abuse and neglect.*

Training providers take their responsibility in this area very seriously and most require that all staff undergo an enhanced DBS check and are trained to the highest standards in identifying and responding to suspected cases or incidents of abuse.

In the event that a learner feels vulnerable, or is suffering from any form of abuse, they are likely to raise the matter with their Coach. They will discuss the problem with them and the Coach must take steps to ensure they are safe and protected.

> *Learners should be aware that anything they tell their Tutor relating to safeguarding matters cannot be kept confidential and will be shared with people who are able to provide help and support.*

Chapter 5: Education Theory and Practice

Educating Humans

The natural evolution of human beings has led the species from the development of the wheel to a point where we have developed a powerful toolkit of predispositions that go a long way towards explaining our ability to learn a language, cooperate in groups, solve problems, plan for the future and empathise with others.

This evolutionary legacy both empowers and constrains us. Humans are born ready to learn, but the brain is wired in such a way that learning is more effectively under certain conditions.

Humans learn best when they 'go with the flow of the brain' instead of going against it.

As a race we have survived, despite physical vulnerability, by working together and solving problems as a group. It is through collaboration, not competition, that humans learn best. Competitive learning which is commonly promoted in schools (I have scored more than you have!) encourages only surface-level thinking and increases peoples dislike for school and learning, whilst decreasing both creativity and subject interest.

Humans learn best through interaction with others

Learning is about making sense of the World around us. This is done by taking in new information, comparing it and contrasting it with current understanding and then rationalising it to find new meaning.

Humans 'construct' knowledge through experience – by doing

The human brain gathers information about the World whilst operating within it, rather than by reading about it, hearing lectures on it, or studying abstract models of it. This process is most effective when it is in a context which is real – where the new knowledge and skills would actually be used.

Learning is not something that takes place outside productive activity - learning is at the very heart of productive activity

People will only learn when they are motivated to do so. They must be interested and engaged in the topic – they are more likely to remember and really understand what they are learning, if they find it intriguing.

There is profound evidence that rewards (such as scores or grades!) undermine motivation. Such rewards turn play into work, and discourage risk-taking and creativity.

People's beliefs about intelligence (whether it is something that can be developed or a 'fixed' attribute) are crucial. The most motivated and resilient learners are those who believe that their abilities can be developed through their own effort and learning.

A tutor cannot learn for the learners – the can only facilitate their learning

Learners also need choices in what and how they learn. The enthusiasm people have for learning will disappear quickly when they start to be controlled and their motivation will evaporate.

If learning really is an active process of making sense of new information, within the context of current understanding and experience, then learning – by its very nature – is personal and individual.

Every learner is different and brings different things into the learning environment. Add to that, interest in creating the motivation to learn and it becomes clear that the development process cannot rely on one-size-fits-all learning opportunities – the learner's life experiences, personalities, talents and interests are far too diverse for that to be viable.

Humans learn best when we recognise the individual, address the whole person and promote self-directed learning opportunities

Pedagogy

Education is commonly presented as young children, eager and attentive, relying on their teacher to bestow their wisdom and years of knowledge upon them.

This classic image is called "pedagogy". It is derived from the Greek words for "child" (paidi) and "guide" (ago) and literally means "the practice of teaching children".

Pedagogy refers to developing habits of thinking and acting.

Within pedagogy, a tutors main role is to provide opportunities for students to learn through experiences.

The responsible positions of "monitor" or "door holder" in a school demonstrate the importance of leadership and service to children. Or, when a teacher changes the volume and intonation of their voice from the playground to the classroom, they are exemplifying the need for behavioural awareness.

Tutors use many types of pedagogy to assist in classroom management and instruction. The four main forms of pedagogy are:

Behaviourism
The belief that learner behaviour is affected and reinforced by external forces rather than internal forces. Positive reinforcement is the most well-known form of behaviourism and is used often when teaching children by reinforcing the desired behaviour by giving a reward.

Constructivism
The idea that learners create their own learning based on previous knowledge and experience. Tutors function as a guide to help learners understand and "construct" processes and applications to further their learning.

Social Constructivism
A blend of two methods, social constructivism incorporates tutor-guided and learner-cantered instruction. This concept believes that "the group is greater than the individual" and allows learners to influence and form outcomes.

Liberationism
The practice of placing learner opinions as the focus for developing the learning environment, wherein the training room is often managed democratically.

The key word here is "children" – pedagogy relates to teaching children – not adults.

Andragogy

The Learning and Development role will seldom involve delivering learning to children. The learning cohort will always be adult.

Adults are self-driven and can refer to and rely on, past experience to solve complex problems, which equates to "enlightening the enlightened - further" is the basis of deciding how to best support them in retaining new ideas, learning new ways of problem solving, and strengthening independent thinking.

"Andragogy" - the practice of teaching adults. Derived from the Greek word for "man" (andras)

The methods used to teach adults are therefore markedly different from those traditionally used to educate children. Using a behaviour chart with colourful stickers to motivate children to remain quiet during reading time is not going to be effective in adult learning.

Most adult learners will already be actively working in a career or field of interest, from medicine, to engineering, to business and they will require specialised instruction to guide and develop the necessary skills.

The field of adult education is constantly evolving with new practices and theories.

Andragogy theory suggests that adult learners differ from children in many ways, including:

- *They need to know why they should learn something.*
- *They need internal motivation.*
- *They want to know, exactly, how the learning will help them.*
- *They bring prior knowledge and experience that form the foundation for their new learning.*
- *They are self-motivated and want control of their learning journey.*
- *They derive most benefit from task-oriented learning that aligns with their own needs.*

Andragogy focusses on enabling learners to understand ***why*** they are doing something, more hands-on experiences, and ***less*** instruction so they can tackle things themselves.

Developed in 1968 by Malcolm Knowles, Andragogy posits that the adult learner:

- *Is far better suited to directing their own learning than a child learner.*
- *Uses their own knowledge base and life experience to aid in their learning.*
- *Will be engaged, present, and ready to learn when the material is of immediate relevance, such as in a new job, social, or life role.*
- *Wants to be able to apply new information immediately, to solve problems in their life.*
- *Needs to have a voice in both the planning and evaluation of their learning experience.*

When using andragogy in learning and development, the tutor should create an environment that is conducive to collaboration, with resources that are relevant to the learner's needs. The tutor should demonstrate why the learning is important, using real-world examples of how the concept will be valuable to the learner. The learning should come through doing, rather than memorisation or repetition.

An organisation will apply andragogy in its learning and development program by identifying the common problems that the learner will encounter and then assisting them to develop solutions to those problems.

The theory of andragogy is not without criticism—some suggest that andragogy doesn't take other cultures into consideration well enough. While there are inevitably pros and cons, learners find andragogy is both accurate and helpful as they work to continue their education and learning. Learners without self-motivation, or those who value a training room experience over alternative learning, will not find as much value in this type of learning.

Six Principles of Andragogy

Why and How

Learners need to know the "why" of what they are learning. Being able to answer, "Why is this principle important to my life?" is essential for the learner to understand "how" they can apply their new knowledge.

If an individual wants to increase their income and advance to a leadership position at work but can't do so without a specialised qualification, then the qualification becomes a vehicle for their professional goal.

Experience

Adults enter the new learning environment with experience that inform their identity and their abilities. It's important to consider this experience as a key part of the learning process when teaching adults.

An expert carpenter has thousands of hours of experience in woodwork. Their ability to understand and solve a problem in carpentry is significantly greater than that of a newly qualified carpenter.

Self-concept

Most adults have moved from a dependent learning environment (school) to independent learning, a state that impacts self-awareness and autonomy. Tutors must consider this independence when building course deadlines and modules.

Readiness

Since most adult learners are already employed, their education needs to be approachable, flexible, and readily applicable.

A working mother who is planning an on-line course needs accessible education outside the normal 9–5 schedule.

Problem Orientation

A focus on practical problems and identifying solutions is imperative to engaging and effective adult learning environments. Many adult learners aren't looking for hypotheticals but real skills that can help them in their current career.

Intrinsic Motivation

Andragogy is most effective, when adults have intrinsic or internal motivation, by recognising their success and promoting increased self-esteem and confidence. With a more specific and advanced hierarchy of needs than children, adult learners place more value on self-actualisation.

Differences Between Andragogy and Pedagogy

Though there are many differences between andragogy and pedagogy, but the learners involved (adults vs. children) are the most important.

Motivation	*Pedagogy*	*Andragogy*
Dependence	*Children are dependent on the teacher to facilitate and structure their learning.*	Adults are independent and want to be empowered to direct their own learning.
Learning Motivation	*Teaching children focusses learning on the essential stages that a child must accomplish before being able to move on to the next stage.*	Teaching adults focusses on developing the necessary skills or knowledge to further personal and professional development.
Learning Resources	*Children are dependent on the teacher for all learning resources. The role of the tutor is to create and incorporate engaging methods and resources for knowledge retention*	Adults use their own experiences and the experiences of others, to gain a better understanding of the curriculum.
Learning Focus	*Child learning is a subject-focused model with prescriptive curriculum.*	Adult learning is often problem-cantered, making the impact of learning more focused on current events or real life.
Motivation	*Children are motivated by external sources (parents, teachers, tangible rewards, etc.)*	Adults are motivated through self-motivational sources (self-esteem, confidence, recognition, etc.)
Teacher's Role	*The teacher acts more as an expert, bestowing knowledge, skill, and structure to learners*	The tutor acts as a facilitator, encouraging collaboration, mutual respect, and openness with learners.

Summary

Children and adults have different needs, different motivations, and different desired outcomes when it comes to learning.

Understanding these key differences is important to the success of learners of all ages. More specifically, andragogy demands that educators innovate and connect with adult learners in meaningful and applicable ways, and value the input and experience that adults bring to the learning environment.

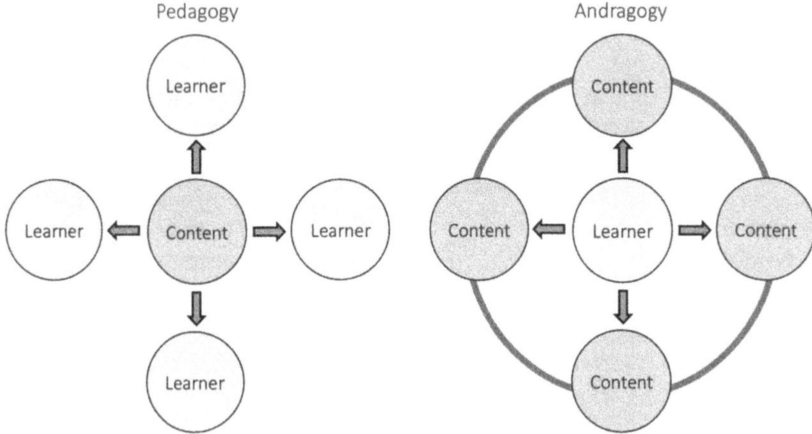

Terminology

The has been a shift in the terminology used in the L&D world over the last few years. Training had, until recently, been a term which was widely used to reference any development activity which took place, and it was not uncommon for learning to also be used interchangeably with training.

More recently, any activity which is aimed at changing the knowledge, skills or behaviours of employees is now commonly referred to as a development activity.

Definition of terms *(as defined by the CIPD)*

- ***Training*** *– and instructor led, content-based intervention designed to lead to skills or behaviour changes*
- ***Learning*** *– a self-directed, work-based process that leads to increased adaptive potential – derived through coaching, mentoring or a learning network*
- ***Development*** *– acquiring skills or knowledge by a range of different means such as coaching, formal and informal learning interventions, education or planned experience*

This redefining of terminology is as a result of the shift from a tutor led, content-based face to face training towards a broader, leaner-centred style of delivery.

The Theory of Learning

There are five widely accepted learning theories upon which teachers rely:

- ***Behaviourism learning theory***
- ***Cognitive learning theory***
- ***Constructivism learning theory***
- ***Humanism learning theory***
- ***Connectivism learning theory***

Educational theorists believe these theories can inform successful approaches for teaching and serve as a foundation for developing lesson plans and curricula.

Theories in education didn't really begin until the early 20th century, but curiosity about how humans learn dates back to the ancient Greece and the philosophers, Socrates, Plato and Aristotle. They sought to establish whether knowledge and truth could be found within oneself (rationalism) or through external observation (empiricism).

In the 1800s', psychologists began to apply scientific studies to answer this. Their goal was to understand, objectively, how people learn and then develop teaching approaches accordingly.
In the 20th century, the debate among educational theorists centred on the behaviourist theory versus cognitive psychology. Or, in other words, do people learn by responding to external stimuli or by using their brains to construct knowledge from external data?

Adult Learning Theories

A lot of organisational training is based loosely on the models of education found in schools. That is not really surprising as school is the first and longest exposure we have to a learning environment.

The reasons adults learn are different from the reasons children learn.

In school, children learn because they are placed in a controlled environment that prompts them to do so. They are placed in a classroom, matched with other children who are the same age and have the same level of expertise and are then expected to do nothing but learn for the majority of the time they are there.

Most of their motivation is external, meaning that children go through this process to please their parents and teachers.

Once they leave school things are different. When adults choose to learn something, it is because they see value or benefit in doing so. An adult might engage in a hobby because they find it interesting or relaxing. They might choose to learn a skill that will help them to advance in their career.

It is those interests and ambitions that motivate and drive their learning.

In organisational learning, this difference is usually forgotten. This results in training being based on a school model where people are grouped together and required to learn content. It is hardly surprising that model doesn't work.

After spending years in school, adults don't want to have "homework" in the form of training courses.

Adults have different levels of expertise, and so every training room will have some learners who are struggling to keep up, and some who are bored, because they already know the material. The challenge for the Learning and Development tutor is to make that training something that they WANT to do!

The simple questions - how do we make training something that adults want to do, and how do we make it effective—are what drive the field of Learning and Development.

The Importance of Adult Learning theory

For aspiring educators, the question of why adult learning theories are important is now an easy one.

Peoples understanding of theory is informed by their own personal experiences of teaching and learning.

Every day, everyone experiences something that requires them to engage in learning

There are quite a few different adult learning theories, but all of them start with the same premise:

Adults learn differently to children

The way adults and children learn differs in many ways:

- *Adults are more self-motivated, as they understand the value of education. They typically have a clear goal in mind when they begin studying. Children need higher levels of engagement, as they are less motivated in learning situations.*
- *Adults can refer to their existing knowledge base to understand new concepts, while children are often approaching a new subject from an entirely clean slate.*
- *Adults are better able to self-direct to solve problems and understand new concepts, while children have a higher need for direction.*
- *Adult learning theory highlights the fact that training programs must be developed with adults in mind to be effective. There is no one unified adult learning theory, however, there are different theories that will fit the needs of different organisations.*

Learning theories fall into two groups. These are formal and informal theories. The formal theories are those which have developed over time as a result of research and study and the informal ones are created by the individual as a starting point for developing further knowledge and understanding.

Informal Theories

Informal theories are the premise used to develop and shape our understanding of how to do things. These informal theories may then further affect how we approach teaching and learning in formal, nonformal, and informal contexts.

Informal theories are important to consider when reflecting on one's role as an educator and our assumptions as a learner, as these theories shape beliefs about teaching and learning which may then affect our actions and behaviours.

Example:

- *If you want to learn a second language and you believe the best way to learn something is just to do it, you may seek out a total immersion experience by going to France or Spain to work for a year.*
- *If you enjoy the autonomy and flexibility offered by learning through technology, you might purchase a language instruction program for your laptop.*
- *If you think the most effective strategy for learning is to go to an expert, you may sign up for a university language course.*
- *If you are convinced that the most successful learning experiences result from a shared endeavour, you could join a local conversation group at the public library.*

In addition to the limitations caused by the availability of resources in terms of time and money, the ***way*** we choose to learn something (*or how we would decide to teach it*) is often influenced by these informal theories about how teaching and learning occurs.

Formal Learning Theories

Formal theories are those which have evolved within particular academic disciplines and have gained credibility by their usage through the work of other scholars.

These are ideas that are the result of examination and assessment by academics and researchers, based on the results of practical experimentation. Formal theories provide a different kind of resource for different areas of study. Formal theories have been written down and published, shared with others through various teaching contexts, incorporated into the analysis of research studies, critiqued and debated in both written and oral formats.

There are many learning theories when it comes to adult learners, and each theory has unique applications and techniques associated with it. Different theories and techniques will work better with some leaners than others. Some of the more common learning theories in the adult learning include:

Behaviourism

Developed by B. F. Skinner in the 1940's, behaviourism theorises that people learn through being conditioned, using stimulus, reward, and punishment. Immediately this is at odds with Andragogy.

This theory proposes that the learner:

- *Gains information in response to stimuli.*
- *Benefits from instruction which repeats and reinforces information while the learner receives it. passively*
- *Requires the demonstration of either positive or negative consequences.*

There are two types of conditioning:

Operant conditioning
This involves applying either positive reward and/or reinforcement or negative reinforcement and/or punishment after a behaviour has taken place. The basis is that people will seek to gain more positive reward and so repeat the behaviours that result in this. This is unlikely to be effective in adult learning.

Operant conditioning is about changing ***voluntary*** behaviour. It is based on the premise that the learner wants to participate and wants to change their current behaviour to those behaviours that result in positive reinforcement and reward. The feedback given during skills training is a typical example of operant conditioning. It does not always work. Where managers are very sparing in providing recognition in the form of feedback, praise, reward or just acknowledgement, learners may settle for negative punishment as the only way of getting any acknowledgement of their existence.

This means that negative behaviours are reinforced; the absolute opposite of what is required.

Classical conditioning
This has its roots in the way Pavlov trained dogs to salivate when they heard a bell ring. He conditioned his dogs associate the ringing of a bell with food appearing (which made the dogs salivate). Subsequently, the dogs salivated when they heard the bell even if no food was produced.

Classical conditioning is about changing involuntary behaviour.

In the training room, the behavioural theory is key in understanding how to motivate and help learners.

Information is transferred from tutor to learners in response to the right stimulus. Learners are passive participants in behavioural learning—tutors are giving them the information as an element of stimulus-response.

Tutors use behaviourism to show students how they should react and respond to certain stimuli. This has to be done in a repetitive way, to regularly remind students what behaviour the tutor is looking for.

Behaviourist teaching strategies.

Teachers can implement behavioural strategy techniques in their classroom in many ways, including:

> ***Drills.*** *Tutors may practice skills using drill patterns to help learners see the repetition and reinforcement that behavioural learning theory uses.*
>
> ***Question and answer.*** *Teachers can use a question as a stimulus and answer as a response, gradually getting harder with questions to help students.*
>
> ***Guided practice.*** *Teachers can be directly involved in helping students go through problems to give them the reinforcement and behaviour demonstration you want them to follow.*
>
> ***Regular review.*** *Reviews are important to behavioural learning theory. Going back over previous material and providing positive reinforcement will help learners retain information much better.*
>
> ***Positive reinforcement.*** *Behaviourist training rooms utilise positive reinforcement regularly. This can be done by verbal reinforcement and praise, rewards, extra privileges, etc.*

Disadvantages of Behaviourism

While behaviourism is a good option for many schoolteachers but it is less appropriate for tutors in adult learning.

Behaviourism is best suited to second languages and maths, but is not effective for analytical and comprehensive learning.

Behaviourism is common in training programs where a standard outcome is desired, such as health and safety demonstrations or company policy training. In situations where tutors do not need participation or action from learners - this learning theory can be beneficial. However, behaviourism can quickly disengage learners and can result in them not remembering important information effectively.

Cognitivism

This theory was developed in rejection of behaviourism and cited that learners were far more active in the learning process than behaviourists claim. Cognitive learning theory explains the internal and external factors which influence an individual's mental processes to supplement learning.

It is an active style of learning that focuses on how to maximise the brain's potential. It makes it easier to connect new information with existing ideas hence deepening memory and retention capacity.

It is based on the premise that the knowledge which is already known is used to interpret new knowledge through cognitive processes (mental skills) such as recognition, recall, analysis, reflection, application, finding meaning, problem solving, evaluation, memory, and perception.

It also focusses on developing the capacity and the skills to learn better. This theory places importance on previous experiences.

When cognitive processes are not working regularly, delays and difficulties in learning can be observed. These processes include attention, observation, retrieval from long-term memory, and categorization.

Benefits of Cognitive Learning

1. *Enhances learning*
Cognitive learning theory enhances lifelong learning. Learners can build upon previous ideas and apply new concepts to their existing knowledge.

2. *Boosts confidence*
Learners become more confident in approaching tasks as they gai a deeper understanding of new topics and learn new skills.

3. *Enhances Comprehension*
Cognitive learning improves learners' understanding of acquiring new information. They can develop a deeper comprehension of new learning materials.

4. *Improves problem-solving skills*
Cognitive learning provides learners with the skills they need to learn effectively. They are thereby able to develop problem-solving skills they can apply under challenging tasks.

5. *Help learn new things faster*
Through the experience of learning, the learner will be able to recycle and use the same learning methods that worked previously. This will help them learn new things a lot faster as they already know what works for them when it comes to obtaining new knowledge.

6. *Teaches to form concept formation (think abstract)*

Cognitive learning can also teach your employees to form a range of different concepts such as easily perceiving and interpreting information that could boost creativity and lead to innovations at the workplace.

Recent developments include 'cognitive load' which is the amount of mental effort needed when using working memory and information processing. This theory states that the learner:

- ***Acquires knowledge by combining both old and new information together in a holistic fashion.***
- ***Receives information, processes it, and organises it according to existing knowledge to better be able to recall it later.***
- ***Is an active participant in their own learning process.***

Cognitivism can be particularly effective in scenarios when the learner is able to reflect on the knowledge gained and then apply it to their own work. After a week-long training seminar, a learner can be encouraged to take a morning to reflect on what they have learned and consider the ways that this new information can be applied in their role.

Traditional learning focuses on memorisation instead of trying to achieve proficiency in a particular subject.

The following are fundamental aspects of cognitive learning:

1. Comprehension
For cognitive learning to be efficient, the learner must understand the reason they are learning a specific subject in the first place.

2. Memory
Cognitive learning discourages the cramming of information, which is very ineffective in education. Having a deep understanding of a subject improves the ability to link new knowledge with previous experiences or information.

3. Application
Cognitive learning strategies help to apply new information or skills in life situations. They encourage learners as they continue to develop problem-solving skills.

Constructivism

The theory of constructivism states that knowledge is created, not by transmission from tutor to learner, but by a learner constructing meaning for themselves. The theory proposes that learning happens as a result of using new information to construct knowledge, based on the information we already have.

Each learner constructs meaning from understanding, knowledge through experiences and then reflecting on those experiences. When a learner experiences something new, this has to be reconciled with previous knowledge and experience. It may result in changing what we believe or in rejecting the new information.

Constructivists believe that learners:

- ***Actively create their own meaning and knowledge from experiences.***
- ***Are the engine behind their own knowledge development, linking old information to new and then contextualising it.***
- ***Use their own personal and cultural experiences to contextualise new information.***

There are two ways that we incorporate new information:

- ***Assimilation:*** *Taking new information and including it into an existing schema.*
- ***Accommodation:*** *Using new information to update existing schemas or create new ones.*

Applying Constructivism

Learning and Development professionals can apply Constructivism concepts to build workplace learning programs which optimise learning for each individual. This is especially effective in very diverse organisations where employees come from unique backgrounds with very different life experiences.

Whilst constructivism may seem to be a simple concept, it offers a fundamentally new way of thinking about how people learn.

In the past the belief was that people learn by soaking up information like a sponge.

Knowledge isn't something that tutors can pour over learners like water. Learners build new knowledge in relation to the experience, knowledge, and beliefs they already have. A builder would have trouble adding the roof to a building without any walls and it is much harder for learners to add new information to their mental constructs if they don't have the appropriate prior knowledge to support it.

Knowledge can be considered highly personal and dependent on the foundation knowledge already held.

The content of a training course on how to complete an expenses claim, would be markedly different if planned for a cohort of accountants, compared to one for mechanics. The accountants are likely to already have a solid understanding of what expense claims are, what can be included, and the key detail needed. The training materials for the mechanics, on the other hand, may need to focus more on building the basic foundations before moving on to explanations of the claim process.

Learning happens best when the learner is actively involved

Learning is most effective when learners are able to assess their understanding by asking questions, engaging in discussion, and exploring alternatives. People can learn passively, but there is a much higher chance that some information may be lost or that the information received is constructed incorrectly.

When the learner is actively involved, receives feedback, and can evaluate their learning through trial and error, it is much more likely that they will be able to identify missed information and update their mental constructs.

Learners learn better when they are motivated

Learning is an active pursuit and motivation therefore plays a critical role in learning outcomes. Highly motivated learners are more likely to participate in the learning process and build meaningful connections to the knowledge they already have.

Motivating an individual to learn though, requires more than just sticks and carrots. Sternly worded emails or the promise of chocolate and wine can motivate employees to attend, but real motivation to learn comes from understanding how, why, and when the knowledge will be used.

If learners don't know the why they need to know something, their only motivation is to 'pass the test.' At which point, the learner will quickly forget everything they learned. This is why it is so easy to remember complex numbers like your National Insurance Number or your telephone number.
There are many elements to the theory of constructivism. The main points are listed below:

> ***Knowledge is constructed.*** Every learner begins the learning journey with some pre-existing knowledge and continues to build their understanding on top of that. They will choose which pieces of the experience to add.

This is why everyone's knowledge is unique.

> ***Learning is a social activity.*** Interaction with others is vital to constructing knowledge. Group activity, discussions, conversations, and interactions are all implicit in creating understanding.

Reflecting on past experiences reveals how the relationship with others is directly connected to the information learned.

> ***Learning is an active process.*** Actively engaging in discussions and activities with others is necessary to construct knowledge. It is not possible for learners to take a passive role and retain information.

In order to build meaningful ideas, there must be a sensory response.

Learning is contextual. Learning in isolation is not the best way to retain information. Learning occurs when connections are made between what is believed and the information already held. Learning also occurs in within the context of our lives, or alongside the rest of our understanding.

People reflect on their lives and classify the new information as it fits into their current perspective.

People learn to learn, as they learn. As each learner navigates the learning journey, they get better at selecting and organising information. They classify ideas and create more meaningful systems of thought. They also begin to recognise that they are learning multiple ideas simultaneously. When writing an essay on historical events, they are also learning elements of written grammar.

When learning about important dates, how to chronologically organise important information is also being learnt.

Learning exists in the mind. Hands-on activities and physical experience on their own are not enough to retain knowledge. Active engagement and reflection are critical to the learning journey.

In order to develop a thorough understanding, learners must experience activities mentally as well.

Knowledge is personal. Every learner's perspective is unique and so will the knowledge gained. Every individual enters into a learning activity with their own experiences and will take away different things as well.

The theory of constructivism is based entirely around each individual's own perspective and experiences.

Motivation is key to learning. Like active participation, motivation is key to making connections and creating understanding. Learners cannot develop knowledge if they are unwilling to reflect on pre-existing knowledge and apply their thought process.

It is crucial that tutors work to motivate students to be proactive in the learning journey.

Humanism Learning Theory

The Humanism Theory is a "learner-centric approach" in which the potential is the focus, rather than the method or materials. This theory is rooted in humanistic psychology. The key concept focusses on the fact that the learner is good at the core and that education should focus on rational ways to teach the "whole" person. The theory asserts that the learner is the expert on how they learn and that all their needs should be met, in order for them to learn effectively.

Recognising that people are inherently good, humanism focuses on creating an environment conducive to self-actualisation. In doing so, learner needs are met and they are then free to determine their own goals, while the tutor assists in meeting those learning goals.
The humanism theory utilises social skills, feelings, intellect, artistic skills, practical skills, and more as part of the education.

Self-esteem, goals, and full autonomy are key learning elements in the humanism theory.

The Humanist theory was developed by Abraham Maslow, Carl Rogers and James F. T. Bugental in the early 1900s' and was their response to the common educational theories at the time. These were behaviourism and psychoanalysis.

There are several important principles involved in the humanism theory which all lead to self-actualisation.

Self-actualisation is achieved when all needs are met, the individual has become the best they can and are fulfilled as a result.

Most humanists don't believe that people reach self-actualisation, but that they are always in search of it, and the closer they are, the more they can learn.

- ***Learner choice.*** *Choice is central to the humanism learning theory It is learner-centred, so learners are encouraged to take control over their own education. They make choices that can range from daily activities to future goals. They are encouraged to focus on a specific subject area of interest for an amount of time which they choose. Tutors who use humanism believe that it's crucial for learners to find motivation and engagement in their learning and that is more likely to happen when they are choosing to learn about something that they really want to know.*
- ***Fostering engagement to inspire learners to become self-motivated.*** *The effectiveness of this is based on learners feeling engaged and self-motivated so they want to learn. The humanistic learning relies on tutors working to engage students, encouraging them to find things they are passionate about so they become excited about learning.*
- ***The importance of self-evaluation.*** *Self-evaluation is the most creditworthy method to evaluate how learning is progressing Awarding grades to learners encourages them to only work to achieve a good grade, instead of doing things*

based on their own satisfaction and the excitement of learning. Routine testing does not lead to meaningful learning in this theory, and are therefore not encouraged. Tutors help students perform self-evaluations so they can see how the student feels about their progress.

- ***Feelings and knowledge are both important in the learning process.*** *Tutors acknowledge the association between knowledge and feelings in the learning process. Cognitive and effective learning are both important to humanistic learning. Lessons and activities will focus on the whole student, their intellect and feelings, not one or the other.*
- ***A safe learning environment.*** *Focussing on the entire learner, tutors understand that they need to create a safe environment so students can have as many of their needs met as possible. Learners need to feel safe physically, mentally, and emotionally in order to be able to focus on learning.*

A tutor using a Humanism Learning Theory will:

- ***Teach learning skills.*** *Tutors will focus on helping students develop learning skills. Students are responsible for learning choices, so helping them understand the best ways to learn is key to their success.*
- ***Provide motivation for classroom tasks.*** *Humanism focuses on engagement, so tutors need to provide motivation and exciting activities to help learners feel engaged about learning.*
- ***Provide choice in task/subject selection.*** *Choice is central to humanistic learning. Tutors have a role in helping learners to make choices about what to learn.*
- ***Create opportunities for group work.*** *As a facilitator in the classroom, tutors create group opportunities to help learners explore, observe, and self-evaluate. They can do this better as they interact with other learners who are learning simultaneously.*

Connectivism

Connectivism departs from constructivism by identifying and remediating gaps in knowledge.

Connectivism is a recent theory that suggests learners should combine thoughts, theories, and general information in a useful manner.

Connectivism encourages collaboration and discussion. This allows different viewpoints and perspectives to be presented when it comes to decision-making, problem-solving, and making sense of information.

It also promotes learning that happens outside of the individual. This can include social media, online networks, blogs, databases, etc.

Connectivism was first presented in 2005 by George Siemens and Stephen Downes. Their theories address the important role which technology plays in the learning process and how the digital age has increased the speed at which learners have access to information. Each has slightly different viewpoints. Siemens tends to focus on the social aspects of connectivism whilst Downes focuses on the non-human appliances and machine-based learning.

Connectivism builds on pre-existing theories. It proposes that technology today is changing what, how, and where we learn. In their research, Siemens and Downes identified eight principles of connectivism.

Those main principles of connectivism are:

- *Learning and knowledge rests in the diversity of opinions.*
- *Learning is a process of connecting.*
- *Learning may reside in non-human appliances.*
- *Learning is more critical than knowing.*
- *Nurturing and maintaining connections are needed for continual learning.*
- *The ability to identify connections between fields, ideas, and concepts is a core skill.*
- *Accurate and current knowledge is the aim of all connectivist learning.*
- *Decision-making is a learning process. What we know today might change tomorrow. Whilst there is a correct answer now, it could be wrong tomorrow, due to the constantly changing information climate.*

Before these principles were devised, many theories positioned learners solely as receivers of information. However, connectivism supports the theory that knowledge is distributed across networks where connections and the depth of connection informs learning.

Connectivism asserts that learning is more than the personal, internal, construction of knowledge, but what can be reached in external networks is also considered to be learning.

Two terms have been derived from this theory, nodes and links. These have been used to describe how we gain and connect information in a network.

In connectivism, learners are seen as “nodes” in a network. A node refers an object which in turn, can be connected to another object, like a book, webpage, person, etc.

Connectivism is based on the theory that we learn by making connections, or “links,” between various "nodes" of information, and we continue to make and maintain connections to form knowledge.

Using Connectivism

It's one thing to understand what connectivism is and another to actually incorporate it into learning activities.

In a connectivism viewpoint, the learning responsibilities shift from the tutor to the learner.

Unlike traditional teaching methods and other theories like constructivism or cognitivism, the tutor's job is to guide learners to become effective agents for their own learning and personal development. In other words, it's up to the learner to create their own learning experience, engage in decision making and enhance their learning networks.

Connectivism relies heavily on technology. The first step to creating a connectivist learning environment is to introduce the opportunity for digital learning – facilitating such things as online courses, webinars, social networks, and blogs.

Below are some ways to incorporate connectivism into the training room:

Social media

One-way tutors implement connectivism is through the use of social media. A group Twitter account can be used to share information, engage in discussion or announce homework tasks. This can help boost group engagement and open the lines of discussion among students and tutors.

Gamification

Gamification takes tasks and activities and embeds them into a competitive game to make learning more of an interactive experience.

There are many learning-based apps and instructional technologies teachers can use to add an element of gamification to the training room. Examples include: Brainscape, Virtual Reality House, and Gimkit, etc.

Simulations

Simulations engage learners in deep learning that empowers understanding as opposed to surface learning that only requires memorisation. They also add interest and fun. Electrician apprentices can create an electric circuit with an online program. Instead of being instructed via a book or lecture, they're learning about electricity by simulating an actual physical setup.

Incorporating some or all of these examples is a great way to allow students more control over the pacing and content of their learning. It also provides opportunities for individualised learning to match each student's unique needs and strengths.

Benefits of Connectivism

Both the learner and the educator can benefit from connectivism in the training room. When planning to adopt this theory in current or future teaching, consider the following benefits:

> ***It creates collaboration.***
> *Learning will occur when learners are connected and share opinions, viewpoints, and ideas through a collaborative process. Connectivism allows a community of people to legitimise what they're doing, so knowledge can be spread more quickly through multiple communities.*
>
> ***It empowers students and teachers.***
> *Connectivism shifts the learning responsibilities from the tutor to the learner. It's up to the learner to create their own learning experience. The tutor's purpose then becomes to "create learning ecologies, shape communities, and release learners into the environment" (Siemens, 2003).*
>
> ***It embraces diversity.***
> *Connectivism supports individual perspectives and the diversity of opinion. This, theoretically, should create no hierarchy in the value of knowledge.*

It's important to understand how different learning theories can benefit the training room and help learners find success.

Summary

Theory	*Explanation*	*Application*
Behaviourism	As Simply Psychology puts it: "Behaviourism is only concerned with observable stimulus-response behaviours, as they can be studied in a systematic and observable manner."	*Learning is based on a system of routines that "drill" information into a student's memory bank, as well as positive feedback from teachers and an educational institution itself. If students do an excellent job, they receive positive reinforcement and are singled out for recognition.*
Cognitivism	Learning relies on both external factors (like information or data) and the internal thought process.	*Developed in the 1950s, this theory moves away from behaviourism to focus on the mind's role in learning. According to the International Bureau of Education: "In cognitive psychology, learning is understood as the acquisition of knowledge: the learner is an information-processor who absorbs information, undertakes cognitive operations on it and stocks it in memory."*
Constructivism	The learner builds upon his or her previous experience and understanding to "construct" a new understanding.	*"The passive view of teaching views the learner as 'an empty vessel' to be filled with knowledge," explains Simply Psychology, "whereas constructivism states that learners construct meaning only through active engagement with the world (such as experiments or real-world problem solving)."*
Humanism	A "learner-centric approach" in which the potential is the focus rather than the method or materials.	*With the understanding that people are inherently good, humanism focuses on creating an environment conducive to self-actualization. In doing so, learners' needs are met and they are then free to determine their own goals while the teacher assists in meeting those learning goals.*
Connectivism	Informed by the digital age, connectivism departs from constructivism by identifying and remediating gaps in knowledge.	*Strongly influenced by technology, connectivism focuses on a learner's ability to frequently source and update accurate information. Knowing how and where to find the best information is as important as the information itself.*

Other Learning Theories

Cooperative Learning

Cooperative learning is a strategy used to improve the collective learning experience and understanding of the subject by a group of learners.

The strategy uses small group tasks and activities as the learning experience. Each group member is responsible for learning new information and skills and at the same time, assisting colleagues in their learning.

Cooperation among co-workers in an organisation will rarely occur naturally and it is up to the employer to try to bring employees together. Cooperative learning is divided into three types, with a different method of implementation for each.

1. ***Formal Cooperative Learning***
   Is the assignment of tasks and projects to a team by an employer. Team members have a clear structure of what is to be done and stay together until the project is complete. It can range from a few hours to several weeks.

2. ***Informal Cooperative Learning***
   This involves forming teams for short periods to complete a small defined task. There is no prior planning needed and has very little structure. They can help bring closure to a day's work or a small project.
3. ***Group-Based Learning***
   It is the most widely used form of cooperative learning used in organisations long-term groups are formed which can last for up to a year or more with group members giving each other support, encouragement, and assistance.
   It is effective when combining different departments in an organisation, with a group of people from each expected to make productive progress. It also works in long-term organisational projects.

The more frequently employees work cooperatively, the more productive the organisation becomes. The benefits of cooperative learning culture in an organisation are:

- ***Development and acquisition of necessary life skills***
- ***Sharing of information***
- ***Building a team that cooperates***
- ***Increases tolerance and acceptance of diversity***
- ***Improving output by employees***

Benefits of Cooperative Learning

Cooperative learning has a significant, positive, impact on employees and their working environment. It enhances productivity and improves employee knowledge. Below are some of the benefits of cooperative learning:

1. Gaining leadership and decision-making skills

To be successful, the individuals in the group need to show some leadership abilities. In every organisation, many tasks need someone to be in charge to run smoothly. Some of them are:

- *Delegating and organising work*
- *Ensuring the organisational targets are met*
- *Supporting team members*

Some people may turn out to be natural leaders but are not inclined to lead. The tutor can assign leadership roles to different members of the group. In a corporate setting, there are many decisions to be made among team members. The decision-making process should involve every member of the group expressing their opinion on the issue, but the final say, lies with the leader.

2. Acquiring conflict management skills

Conflict management focuses on positive results whilst minimising the negative ones. This process, by which disputes are solved, can impact an organisation positively when done correctly.

3. Increases employee work engagement

Employees become more satisfied as they have the opportunity to learn new skills. They will become eager to continue learning and growing. A growth in productive engagement is evident in work hence an increase in efficiency and output.

4. Enhancing communication skills

Group members need to learn how to engage productively with one another. Ethical commitment and communication keep the members on track and enhances efficient teamwork.

5. Personal responsibility

Cooperative learning increases the individual responsibility of employees. They know they have a specific task to perform in order for the entire team to succeed. They also become more accountable as they are aware of a possible backlash from team members if they fail to play their part.

6. Gaining confidence

Some employees find it more comfortable to speak up in small groups. They can express their ideas and ask questions, which enables them to gain confidence. This confidence improves from addressing a few people to a large crowd.

7. Positive attitude towards colleagues

In every organisation, there are those few employees that develop a dislike towards each other with or without reason. Cooperative learning creates an increasing positive attitude towards colleagues as they continue working together within a group.

Collaborative Learning

Collaborative learning is an educational approach which uses groups to enhance learning through working together. A group of two or more learners work to solve problems, complete tasks, or learn new concepts.

It actively engages learners to process and synthesise information and concepts, rather than using rote to memorise facts and figures. Learners work on projects, where they must collaborate to understand the concepts being presented to them.

By defending their own positions, reshaping their own ideas, listening to the ideas of others and presenting their own points, learners gain a more complete understanding as a group than they could individually.

Cooperative and Collaborative Learning are often confused. Cooperative learning is actually a form of Collaborative learning, which is why at first glance, the two might seem similar.

The difference between two is that, in cooperative learning, participants are responsible for a specific section of their own learning and success and also, that of the group as a whole. Learners must use their knowledge and resources to make sure all team members understand the concepts being learned. The roles and structure of cooperative learning are predefined. They may be likened to the cast and crew of a theatre production: the success of the show depends on all of the interconnected roles supporting each other, but there is a director overseeing the project closely.

Collaborative learning is evident in software development, a group of junior programmers are tasked to learn a new platform, then develop one part of a program whilst using it. Each programmer has their own piece of the program to write, but their section of code will only be successful if everyone else learns and performs their part properly. Even though each person has a separate role in the work, the entire group has a stake in the success of others.

The benefits of Collaborative learning

Every organisation can benefit from having an energised and informed workforce. There are many benefits to be derived from collaborative learning, both for the organisation and the individual.

Organisational benefits include:

1. Develops self-management and leadership skills
When individuals are tasked with working together to achieve a common goal, they also have the opportunity to develop high-level skills. By organising, assigning, and teaching, they are learning how to manage both themselves and others while leading in a productive manner.

2. Increases employee skills and knowledge
Not only will they strengthen existing skills by having to teach them to others, they will learn new skills from others. This reduces the need for formal training, whilst encouraging employees to continually upskill in known concepts and engage with new concepts.

3. Improves relationships across teams and departments
Collaborative learning forces individuals to develop new connections and find ways to work together when used across teams. This can be of particular benefit for organisations that depend on remote workers. Fostering strong connections among distant workers can be difficult but is enhanced with collaborative learning.

4. Improves knowledge acquisition and retention
Collaborative learning allows learners to achieve higher levels of thought and information is retained much longer than in a non-collaborative setting.

5. Improves employee retention and promotes workplace engagement
Employees that are given the opportunity to learn new skills tend to be more satisfied in their work and are less likely to seek out other opportunities. Satisfied employees are more productive and will engage in their work, leading to increased efficiency and output.

Benefits for the individual of collaborative learning

1. Turns learning into a truly active process
The learner must organise their thoughts, present a cohesive argument to demonstrate their point, defend that point to their peers, and convince others that their argument is correct. This active engagement causes the individual to learn and retain more knowledge.

2. Promotes learning from other's viewpoints
When a person is exposed to diverse viewpoints, especially from varied backgrounds, they learn more.

3. Teaches how to think critically and quickly
The learner must quickly formulate responses. If they find their argument is lacking, they must adjust their ideas on the fly. As a result, individuals learn how to think critically and quickly, whilst being exposed to new information and adjusting their viewpoint as new ideas are introduced.

4. Promotes listening to criticism and advice

The learner will listen to other's ideas, offering their thoughts for or against their arguments. This dynamic approach means learners gain a broader understanding of the topic, as they consider it from all angles.

5. Develops public speaking and active listening skills
Individuals learn how to speak in front of an audience, to listen pro-actively, to challenge the ideas of others and build a framework of ideas in association with others. This increased social ease helps both socially and at work.

6. Improves cooperation
When assigned a specific goal, learners are more likely to engage in thoughtful discussion with others, improving both their understanding of the subject and their esteem for each other.

Transformative (Transformational) Learning

Transformative learning concerns the ability to use learning to transform the way that the learner views the world. It was developed by Jack Mezirow in 1978

This theory proposes that by introducing new concepts, challenging assumptions, and disrupting perspectives, a learner:

- ***Can shift their world view in significant ways, resulting in a completely new frame of reference.***
- ***Experiences information that will challenge their perspective in such a fundamental manner that they rethink their existing viewpoint and use critical thinking to adjust their beliefs.***
- ***Will have an easier time remembering the concepts taught, as the transformation includes behaviour, thoughts, and beliefs.***

This type of learning is appropriate for learners who require personal or professional growth, learning about complex analytical processes or for teaching learners how to apply evaluation and analysis to various situations.

This type of learning will not always be relevant within an organisation, and has been criticised at valuing rationality over emotion, relationships and culture, as well as being blind to context.

Tutors should create an environment that supports the learners through authentic interactions, sincere and empathetic instruction and a supportive space where the learner is encouraged to question their beliefs without judgment.

Learners should be provided with material that explores different points of view and encourages them to engage with it deeply.

Learners who are debaters, rational thinkers or critical analysers will find this type of learning to be engaging.

Self-directed Learning

The Self-directed Learning theory is built on andragogy and was developed by D.R. Garrison.in 1997

It combines the concepts of how adults self-manage, creating a theory with the premise that the adult learner:

- ***takes the initiative to identify what they need to learn.*** *The learner sets learning goals, finds the resources they need, creates, and follows a learning plan, then they evaluate their own results.*
- ***will seek out help, including teachers, mentors, or peers.***
- ***will respond positively to being in control of their own learning journey, putting in the time to make informed decisions, and incorporate learning on a daily basis.***
- ***self-directed learning is well suited for those who respond well to technology-based learning as well as self-motivated learners.***

This type of learning works well with subjects that have concrete, black or white answers, rather than grey areas. A learner might identify a need to become proficient in a new language. Self-directed learning would be helpful in this instance, as they could seek out tools, books, or likeminded groups to help them learn. They are able to assess their own progress, and there will be clear feedback as to whether they are using the language correctly.
Learners need to be able to evaluate their own results to see how they are progressing with their learning and assess weaker areas they need to focus on.

While Self-directed learning can be a useful training tool, it is made much more useful by having a tutor to further facilitate the learning. The tutor can be on hand to assist the learner as they perform their self-assessment, work alongside them to help identify the proper starting point for the learning journey, as well as directing the learner to the resources that will be most appropriate for their needs.

In the facilitator role the tutor acts more as a guide and source of encouragement, being available to help, when necessary, but allowing the learner the space that they need to self-direct their learning.

The critics of self-directed learning highlight that it can be difficult for some learners, especially those who have less education, low literacy skills, or have low self-confidence.

The outcomes of self-directed learning may be different to the planned or desired outcomes. Learners may take more time to fully engage with the subject than those who have more controlled programs.

This type of learning can be a valuable part of a blended training program, especially in regard to upskilling.

Experiential Learning

Experiential learning was introduced in the 1970's by David Kolb. It focusses on hands-on learning and uses experiences to demonstrate concepts.

In experiential learning, the learner will:

- *Actively participate in the learning process.*
- *Reflect upon their experience after the participation stage, developing and firming the knowledge that they have gained.*
- *Consider the successes and failures of the learning process, in order to develop improvements for the next learning activity. In doing so, they will use abstract conceptualisation to use the new skills that they have learned during the process.*

This type of learning works well with learners who are eager to learn and in tasks that require systematic thinking or mechanical skills.

Some organisations use experiential learning to teach professionalism, customer service, or even supply chain management.

There are four elements in experiential learning:

- *Self-reflection*
- *Active involvement*
- *Conceptualising the experience*
- *Using the knowledge learned from it in real life.*

The critics of experiential learning have focused on the overemphasis on individual knowledge at the expense of social context.

An organisation can develop training programs that use experiential learning by setting up role-play exercises, bringing in people to share their experiences, or using virtual reality to simulate common situations that employees might face on the job.

A good tutor will encourage reflection and conceptualisation after the experiential aspect of the learning is complete and will prompt learners to contemplate how they can activate their new knowledge in their everyday roles.

Project-based Learning

This theory is based on the idea of learning by doing, usually as a group. It was developed by John Dewey in 1897.

The theory proposes that learners:

- *Acquire knowledge in a more holistic and deep fashion when they actively explore a real-world issue.*
- *Work on the problem for an extended period, investigating, developing, and testing potential solutions, while using tutors for feedback on a regular basis.*
- *Will understand the subject more completely as a result of having to actively apply it.*

Project-based learning is a great fit for organisations that want to develop the long-term project management skills of their management teams, improvement of processes, and research and development projects, especially in software and technology.

A criticism of project-based learning is that some members of the group may be tempted to take advantage of the collaborative nature of the group and allow others to do the work. If the tutor is not alert to the problem, some learners will take on more than their fair share, whilst other learners take the credit for the hard work someone else has completed.

To integrate this theory into a training program organisations should create an environment where groups can meet to solve real problems within the organisation. This could be as simple as learning new software or as complex as developing a new product concept. By providing tutors to function as guides and facilitators, groups can be primed to develop their knowledge with minimal interference and maximum ownership of the final product.

This theory shares many similarities with phenomenon-based learning, with the notable difference that phenomenon-based learning requires learners to approach problem-solving in a multi-disciplinary manner while using a global mindset

Action Learning

Developed by Reg Revans in 1982 Action Learning is concerned with solving problems while simplifying solutions, often in a group dynamic.

In Action learning theory, learners:

- *Analyse the problem to better understand it, reflect on what possible solutions might be, identify the best one, and then act.*
- *After acting, learners reflect again, questioning their process, the results, and how they could improve them.*
- *Build cohesion, gain collaborative skills and better understand group dynamics throughout the process.*

It is important with this type of learning that the group is given enough time to reflect on the process after the action has been taken. Without that time, the desired learning will not take place. A skilled tutor is necessary for these activities, primarily for keeping the participants on track, within time limits, and to make space for the reflection period.

Action learning can be implemented in training plans by gathering groups of learners to solve sample problems or even complex problems that the organisation is facing.

Using a facilitator, teams can be presented with the issue and then given the simple guidelines above. As they begin to work through the process, the facilitator will guide them, supplying knowledge where needed, but curating the environment needed for the learners.

Social Learning Theory

Developed by Albert Bandura in the 1970's, this theory combines behaviourism and cognitivism.

Learning takes place as a result of interaction with others in a social context. It includes the observation of others. The basis of learning is through communities of practice and situational learning, such as real-life project groups and action learning. It is used when developing behaviours through role modelling and interaction.

Social learning theory presumes that learners:

- *Will gain understanding by combining their personal experiences with observations of the rewards and punishments that others receive for their actions.*
- *Observe the response to behaviour within the workplace and gain understanding as to how they should act from that.*
- *Imitate the behaviour of those around them who they respect.*

This theory is useful in demonstrating appropriate workplace behaviour. Managers customarily act as role models. They demonstrate what is acceptable, rewarding those who follow their lead and correcting those who do not follow the modelled behaviour.

Tutors should be clear about what they are demonstrating and may use anecdotes, role-play, or training videos to reinforce the information. Successful programs use instructors who are well regarded within the organisation.
Social learning theory will not serve the organisation well if there is no uniformity. Learners will be quick to see if there are favourites, or if negative behaviour carries no consequences. Tutors should be careful to be even-handed and fair.

Many of these theories can be used alone or in blended training programs. Learners will differ in how they respond to training, and it is always helpful to have information presented in a few different ways so it can be ensured that the workforce is well-informed, competent, and safe.

Conscious Competence Learning Theory

The Conscious Competence Learning theory was first described by Martin Broadwell in 1969. The theory relates more closely to the development of skills rather than pure cognitive learning. Noel Burch then went on to develop the Conscious Competence Ladder in the 1970s'.

This learning theory focuses on two factors that are important when we are learning a new skill.

- *Awareness (consciousness)*
- *Skill level (competence)*

The model can help understand which of the four stages of competence if there is a desire or need to learn or improve a skill.

The four levels of competence, relate to the process of progressing from a state of incompetence to a state of competence in a skill.

These 4 stages of are called:

- *Unconscious Incompetence*
- *Conscious Incompetence*
- *Conscious Competence*
- *Unconscious Competence*

According to the Conscious Competence Model, the four stages of skills development can be organised into a matrix.

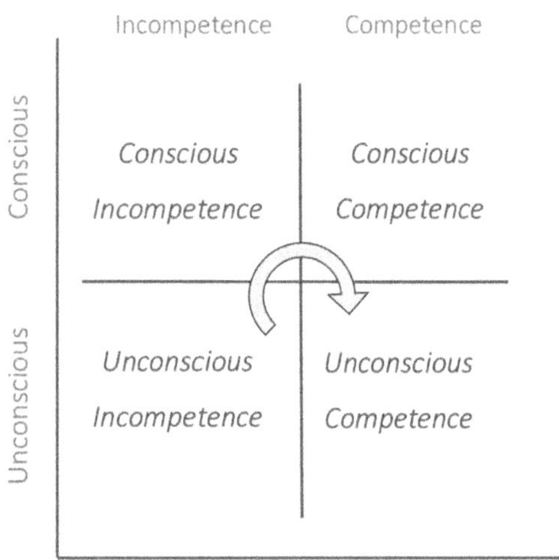

Stage 1: Unconscious Incompetence

At the unconscious incompetence stage, you don't know that you don't know! You don't give a certain skill any active thought because you're unaware that you may need it. That's why you don't see it as a relevant skill for now. You are unskilled, but it's not even on your radar.

You don't feel anything at this stage, as you are blissfully unaware of any issues.

Stage 2: Conscious Incompetence

At the conscious incompetence stage, you know that you are incompetent. Or to say it more politely: You know that you don't know.

You are aware that there is a gap and that this skill is useful. That's when you enrol to learn because you don't want to be unskilled anymore.

At this stage, it is common to feel self-conscious and lack confidence. You recognise that you still have a long way to go.

Stage 3: Conscious Competence

At stage three, you reach the conscious competence stage. Although you've learned the skill, it doesn't happen naturally yet. You have to concentrate to do it, and you practice, study, and repeat.

To do the task well, you need to make a conscious effort. With increased practice and hard work, you can achieve the next level. You start to feel more confident and more motivated. You realise how much you've learned and your progress is exciting.

Stage 4: Unconscious Competence

Unconscious competence is the final stage. This high-level skill is so embedded that you no longer use a conscious process. It is habitual.

The learning process to achieve this can be long and tedious, although you do it, you don't necessarily know how you do it.

This process will be much quicker if you already have certain skills or aptitudes.

At this stage, you feel completely confident.

Stage 5: ??

Although unconscious competence is the highest defined level of personal competence, there is, arguably, a fifth level of competence. At this stage, not only has the skill been mastered, but a level is reached where it is possible to teach students at the other learning stages how to develop that skill.

These stages are not set in stone. If skills are not practiced it is possible to fall back to previous stages – or you may never reach the final stage. It all depends on the difficulty of the skill and how well you know it.

You may still be able to wobble on a bike after 20 years... but it may be harder to play an instrument or speak a language you haven't used for some time.

Issues with Conscious Competence

Learning new skills is never easy. The process can create self-doubt, frustration, fear of failure and even overconfidence that be damaging too.

It is not uncommon for individuals to overestimate their skill levels. This is justified by the work of Dunning-Kruger.

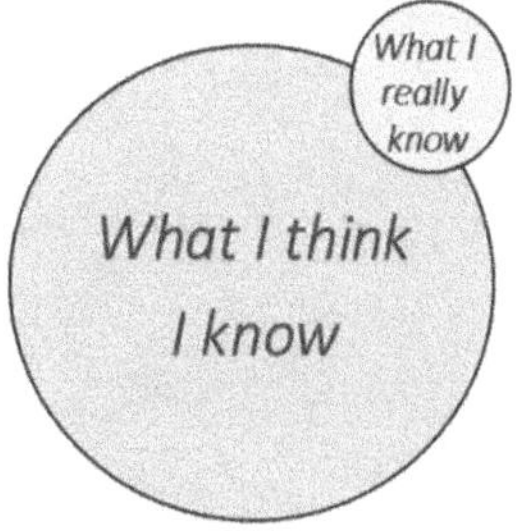

This is a typical problem at the unconscious competence level. There is a gap in their knowledge of which, they are unaware. Because of this lack of knowledge, they think they excel.

Think about a newly qualified driver, they have a pass certificate from a driving test and they believe they are now in the same league as a Formula One driver. It is only if they are lucky enough to extract themselves from the car, which is now wrapped round a tree, that they realise they lack the knowledge and skills that experience brings.

The driver may have achieved conscious competence in controlling a vehicle in controlled conditions, but they remain unconsciously incompetent to handle a vehicle in all conditions. It is an old saying but so true: You only start to learn to drive after you have passed your test.

The opposite of the Dunning-Kruger Effect is something called the Imposter Syndrome. In this case, learners obsess about their *lack* of knowledge and may underestimate how much experience and skills they actually have.

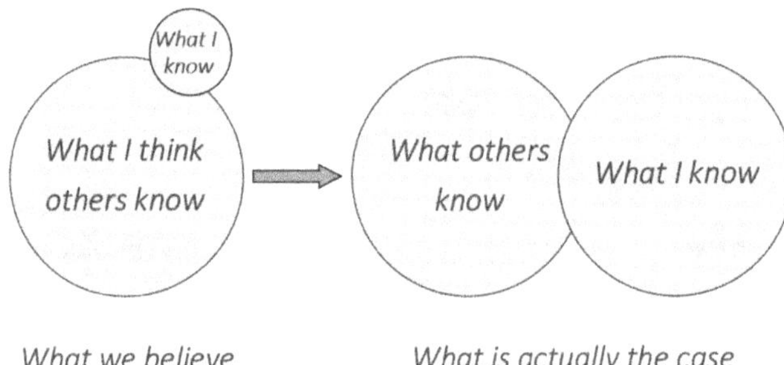

The imposter syndrome is most likely to appear around stages 2 and 3 of the conscious competence matrix. But even highly successful people suffer from it, too.

The Influence of Educational Theory

Educational theories influence learning in a variety of ways. For tutors, learning theory examples can impact their approach to instruction and training room management. Finding the right approach (even if it's combining two or more learning theories) can make the difference between an effective and inspiring training room experience and an ineffective one.

Applied learning theories directly impact on a training room experience in a variety of ways, such as:

- *Providing learners with structure and a comfortable, steady environment.*
- *Helping tutors, administrators and learners align on goals and outcomes.*
- *Empowering tutors to be, as Bates says, "in a better position to make choices about how to approach their teaching in ways that will best fit the perceived needs of their students."*
- *Impacting how and what a person learns.*
- *Helping outsiders (colleges, testing firms, etc.) determine what kind of education has been / is being delivered.*
- *Allowing learners a voice in determining how the group will be managed.*
- *Deciding if instruction will be mostly teacher-led or student-led.*
- *Determining how much collaboration will happen in a classroom.*

Applying Learning Theory

So, how do these learning theories apply in the real world?

Education is an evolving field with a complicated future. Roggeman states, the effects of applied educational theory can be long-lasting.

She explains:

> *"The learning theories experienced as a learner influence the type of work environment preferred as adults. If one experienced education, based heavily on social learning, during the latter school years 11 and 12, as an adult, one may be very comfortable in a highly collaborative work environment. Reflection on one's own educational history might serve as an insightful tool as to one's own fulfilment in the workplace as an adult."*

Educational theories have come a long way since the days of Socrates and even the pioneers of behaviourism and cognitivism. While learning theories will no doubt continue to evolve, tutors and learners alike can reap the benefits of this evolution as tutors continue to develop their understanding of how humans most effectively learn.

Adult Learning Principles

When implementing learning and development across an organisation, it is important to think about the learners who are to be developed. They will typically be adults and adults have specific needs when learning and these needs should be satisfied by recognising the adult learning theory.

It has been clearly evidenced that adults learn differently to children, and organisations that successfully implement adult learning principles will reap the benefits of a knowledgeable, competent, workforce.

The adult learning principles include:

- *Adults have a higher sense of self-direction and motivation*
- *Adults use their life experience to facilitate learning*
- *Adults are focused on achieving goals*
- *Adults need to know how/why the information is relevant*
- *Adults are practically minded*
- *Adults are looking for help and mentorship*
- *Adults are open for modern ways of learning*
- *Adults want to choose how they learn*

When planning any learning program for an organisation, these principles should be kept in mind, and learning resources should be developed which are suited to them.

1. Adults have an attuned sense of self-direction and motivation

Adult learners are much more self-directed and motivated than children.

Adults tend to learn because they want to or they see the direct benefit of learning, rather than because they are told to or are expected to. However, just because adults have a higher level of motivation, it doesn't mean that they will learn anything.

Adults have to see the benefit, value and purpose of learning.

Learning programs should clearly demonstrate how the learner benefits from their interaction, or they will be quick to disengage. Show the value of the content, and learners will be much more likely to engage with it.

Learners can be encouraged to identify their own learning needs, plan how to achieve their goals, find resources, then assess their own progress. Online learning is an ideal environment for this type of learning, and gives learners the ability to follow flexible learning paths, access to services that curate and recommend learning content to prevent skill gaps, and tools that are developed to deliver content tailored for each individual's needs.

Techniques:

- *Learning outcomes can be used to demonstrate the value and benefit of the learning material.*
- *Formulate learning paths that are tailored to the organisation, to better meet learners needs.*
- *Make accessing knowledge simple, to help learners get started.*

2. Adults use their life experience to facilitate learning

Adults have more life experience than children.

Adult learners rely heavily on their experiences when they engage in learning and they benefit from training programs that acknowledge this.

Delivering content that draws from real-world examples, relatable scenarios and builds on their experiences will lead to a more meaningful understanding of the subject.

Whilst using existing experience as a basis for new learning, there is a negative to this. The experience that learners base the new learning on may be outdated, incorrect, biased, or incomplete. Learners should be made aware of these challenges and guided towards new conclusions based on revising the misconceptions.

Learner may need support and guidance to search for resources, expert opinions, proven data and relevant publications to achieve this

Techniques:

- *Provide basic training, to help learners understand how to acquire new information that might be at odds with their previous experience.*
- *Training materials should focus on scenarios that learners will face in their day-to-day roles.*

3. Adults are focused on achieving goals

Adults enter the learning process are focused on results.

Adult learners need to know how the new learning will help them achieve their goals, whether personal or professional.

When designing learning programs, tutors need to keep this in mind and ensure the learner is given plenty of tools and information that will help them reach their goal.

The learner also plays an essential role in this. They need to set clear, achievable goals and be driven to engage with the content to reach their goals.

Adult learners will be energised and motivated once they understand how the content they are engaging with, will help them reach their goals. This energy can be harnessed and used to drive the learning process, leading to better results.

Project-based Learning can be used to take advantage of this need to reach goals. Giving a group of learners a recognisable, achievable goal in the form of a problem that they must solve, will encourage the development of knowledge, skills, and teamwork. This can be done in many formats, but an increasing number of organisations are turning to gamification in online training to encourage project-based learning. Learners are motivated to engage with leader boards, weekly goals and other ongoing challenges.

Other organisations use learning paths, which are made up of various stages, each with a goal that the learner must meet and an evaluation that must occur before the learner can progress to the next stage.

Techniques:

- *Use SMART objectives for goal setting*
- *Ensure that the information provided is relevant to the learner's current role and challenges.*
- *Clearly show the value of the information. When a learner can see this, they will apply it to real-life problems and they will learn faster.*

4. Adults need to know how the information is relevant

To properly engage a learner, the relevance of the information contained within the training program must be highlighted.

Both the short-term relevancy and the long-term benefits of engaging with the programme content should be highlighted in such a way that the learner will immediately dedicate themselves to learning.

A training program developed to upskill managers might focus on understanding core leadership principles in the short-term meaning they will become a more highly skilled leader which, in the long-term benefit is that they will be better able to reach departmental goals.

The short-term relevancy will demonstrate what they will learn in the course that is pertinent to their role. The longer-term benefit is how the knowledge gained, benefits them in their job role.

While some learners might enjoy learning for the sheer joy of knowing something new, adults are far more likely to engage with learning that shows a clear relevance for them, whether it is something related to their goals, role, job or hobbies.

Techniques:

- *All types of learning content should demonstrate both short and long-term benefit to learners.*
- *Provide a variety of content, allowing learners to engage with the types they feel most relevant for them.*
- *Materials used should be related to each role by tailoring the learning path.*

5. Adults are practical

Knowledge gained should be applied immediately.

Adults learn quickly and remember what they learn when they can turn around and apply that knowledge in their role.

Learning materials should be constructed with practical examples, using real-world scenarios and problem-solving that requires learners to access their experience and knowledge.

Allow learners to set their own pace, and allow them to forge their own path. Online learning is well suited for this type of learning, as learners can access learning content on their own schedule.

This type of knowledge acquisition will ensure that the learner remembers the content much more fully than with more static methods.

An organisation can create learning experiences cantered on the knowledge that they wish learners to gain in a variety of manners. Virtual reality training is fast gaining popularity in this area, as it can be much cheaper to develop experiential learning through virtual reality than setting up real-world simulations. Some companies prefer to develop role-playing games that lead individuals through the multitude of decisions that they need to make in their role every day, showing the consequences if a bad decision is made.

Techniques:

- *Focus should be on delivering knowledge that can be directly applied in the learner's day-to-day role.*
- *Set aside time after knowledge acquisition for learners to practice their new skills.*

6. Adults are looking for help and mentorship

Adult learners understand that looking to an experienced role model will help them in their learning journey.

When an organisation develops a training program, creating opportunities for mentorship can add value for both the mentor and mentee and has the added bonus of developing relationships within and across teams.

Learning by example is a powerful way of accessing new knowledge, allowing learners to quickly gain information and at the same time, avoid common mistakes.

Techniques:

- *Develop ways to connect learners with mentors within the organisation.*
- *Set up seminars, online or in person, to provide learning opportunities across departments.*
- *Create a culture of learning and knowledge sharing throughout the organisation.*

7. Adults are open for modern ways of learning

Adults are flexible when it comes to how they engage with knowledge.

Adults understand that knowledge can be gained in a variety of different ways, and are willing to try new formats.

By offering a variety of sources and options, an organisation can ensure that all learners have access to learning content that engages them.

When developing a training program, an organisation should provide many forms of content, such as online courses, blogs, videos, webinars, apps, and conferences. By offering a variety of learning paths, with different formats, the learner is able to acquire knowledge in a wide variety of manners and successfully contextualize it.

Techniques:

- ***Be flexible about learning, it doesn't only happen in a classroom! Look for new ways to transmit information.***
- ***Remember that people learn differently, and provide many ways to access knowledge.***

8. Adults want to choose how they learn

Adult learners respond positively to self-directed learning.

Being able to control how and when they learn means that adults are more likely to be fully engaged with the content, rather than simply going through the motions of learning. Organisations should build training programs in such a way that they give learners ownership of what they are learning. In doing so, the learners will invest more effort into exercises, offer relevant feedback, and will be active learners. This can be done by allowing learners to choose their learning path on an online training platform, or granting access to learning resources for learners to engage with at their own discretion.

The more that the learner is involved, from the planning stages to evaluation to feedback, the more onboard they will be with the entire process. Adult learners will respond negatively to being treated like a child, and with good reason.

Techniques:

- ***Build training programs that give learners a variety of options for engaging with information.***
- ***Allow learners to set their own pace and goals, and provide opportunities for them to give feedback about their experience.***

Summary

Understanding the principles of adult learning can improve the educational experience for adult learners. Adult learners can implement these techniques to improve their academic performance and these can take many different forms.

Given that adult learners tend to be internally motivated these principles are informed by the theory of andragogy and can help an organisation, training provider, or other type of educational organisation consolidate and conduct its educational mission.

Learning Styles

The notion that everyone has their own independent and, in some cases, unique learning style, gained popularity in the 1970s. It is an attractive thought: if we could identify one, "ideal" learning style for each learner, teachers, tutors and coaches could simply focus on that one style of delivery and be consistently successful!

For many years there have been countless theories relating to learning styles and these have been further interpreted and developed by other theorists, but in most instances, there has been very little viable evidence to prove the theories.

How we learn depends a great deal on what is being learnt.

Learning has changed forever

Today, learning takes place in markedly different ways to previous generations.

Instead of relying on face-to-face training and books for information, learners are turning to new information sources and mediums.

For years, people learned whilst sitting in a room, listening to a lecture, and perusing assigned readings in paper textbooks.

Today, the information and skill-acquisition paradigm has evolved to incorporate technology, and the resulting mountain of information and the variety of sources through which it is available, can leave learners feeling overwhelmed.

The immediacy of internet searches and the multitude of distracting advertisements which punctuate every paragraph, results in knowledge-driven consumers who struggle with patience and focus.

Educating the modern learner requires an understanding of how they interact with the World and their preferred avenues for accessing information.

Personal electronic devices are ubiquitous information-accessing tools, and their numbers are growing. If you have a device in your household, chances are that you have a second or third as well.

Studies show that 63 percent of the online adult population in the United Kingdom use two devices each day.

The number using a third device per day stands at around 20 percent!

Even more significant is the tendency for users to employ multiple devices for related purposes, such as acquiring information by reading text or watching a video with a cell phone and then demonstrating that knowledge via eLearning on a desktop computer.

Learning professionals must make their content compatible across devices without disregarding the impact of the smartphone.

Smartphones offer enormous benefit to learning, given the fact that they incorporate multiple tools to facilitate information gathering.

- *A book only provides written information and illustrations.*
- *A video player only allows you to view filmed content.*
- *A tutor can give oral instructions, answer questions, and manage discussions.*
- *A library houses reference material.*

On the other hand, a smartphone alone does all of these things and more. Add to the list the smartphone's capabilities of video recording, GPS integration, and app use, and you have an educational tool that has as much potential as the user can envision.

Seventy percent of modern learners use Smartphones to learn. Mobile devices with Touchscreen interfaces are increasing in number, whilst the market for home-based tech (such as desktop computers) is staying stable.

For many years it was argued that humans had "preferred" learning styles. These might typically be learning by looking at pictures, graphs, images, infograms, etc. This was known as a "Visual" learning style. This then led to further notions that people could not learn from a different method of learning delivery such as audio - listening to a lecture or audio book.

Serious doubts have arisen about some of the most popular learning style models – especially the ways in which they have been applied in education. There are also concerns that the "labels" they have initiated might actually limit the individual's learning.

These earlier theories are now generally discredited.

Discrediting Learning Styles

Neuroscientists now suggest the idea that we can be defined as purely visual, auditory or kinaesthetic learners is "nonsense."

They argue:

"Humans have evolved is such a way they build a picture of the world as a result of their senses working in unison"

A study by Massa and Mayer also found little difference in learning outcomes when they matched their test subjects' preferences (visual or verbal) to the learning materials they were given.

There are also arguments that learning styles will actually change, depending on the circumstances in which they find themselves. Eileen Carnell and Caroline Lodge stated in their book Effective Learning, "*an individual's learning method will be different in different situations, and likely change over time.*"

The Journal of Educational Psychology identified that there are big differences between people's assessed strengths, and how they actually tackle learning tasks in practice. A learner scoring a high mark in an assessment, after hearing the information, might still choose to learn by reading – simply because they enjoy that style of learning more.

Many people have been led to believe that students learn best when the teaching style is matched to their "preferred" learning styles. This is claimed to be one of the "50 Great Myths of Popular Psychology." By Scott O. Lilienfeld. He claims this encourages teachers to teach to students' intellectual strengths rather than their weaknesses, which, by default, limits their learning as a result.

Learning styles have been evaluated many times and to date there has been no rigorous evidence to support their use. They can be deconstructed to clearly show that they are not really a valid way of classifying learners.

Despite this discreditation, some of the ideas that underpin learning styles theories do still have value – especially the emphasis on metacognition:

"Thinking about thinking."

Metacognition

Metacognition is the awareness and understanding of our own thought processes. An alternative definition is:

"Learning to learn"

Metacognition is about the learner's ability to monitor, direct, and review their own learning.

Effective metacognitive strategies are designed to encourage learners to think about their own learning more explicitly. This is done by teaching them to set personal learning goals and monitor and evaluate their progress towards them.

Metacognition can improve learner outcomes by encouraging deeper thinking. It helps to develop and deepen subject knowledge. Metacognition enables learners to think more cohesively about the subject content, to make connections between content or apply old information in new contexts.

It also develops their ability to think critically, which is an essential skill in the 21st century. In an era contaminated with fake news and social media is infected with unreliable content, this is more important than ever!

Metacognition helps to develop transferable skills, such as reasoning, analysis and evaluation, which are critical skills for the 21st century.

In the future, the youth of today are likely to have the choice of numerous careers in jobs that don't even exist today, so cognitive agility and flexibility is a must for their future economic prosperity.

Unlike Learning Styles, metacognition has been shown to improve educational outcomes.

Analysing thinking can help plan learning strategies that work for us. It can help learners to become more organised in their study methodology. It will also prompt them to use their existing knowledge as the basis for their new learning to be built upon and to choose effective methods for different learning tasks.

By examining our strengths and weaknesses, we can make the most of many aspects of learning that "come naturally" and that we enjoy, while also working on the areas that might be holding us back.

Two Dimensions of Metacognition

Metacognition is often considered to have two dimensions:

- *metacognitive knowledge*
- *metacognitive regulation*

Metacognitive knowledge refers to what learners know about learning. This includes:

- ***the learner's knowledge of their cognitive abilities*** *(e.g. 'I have trouble remembering dates in history')*
- ***the learner's knowledge of particular tasks*** *(e.g. 'The ideas in this chapter that I'm going to read are complex')*
- ***the learner's knowledge of the range of strategies available to them and when they are appropriate to the task*** *(e.g. 'If I scan the text first it will help me to understand the overall meaning')*

Metacognitive regulation

This refers to what learners do about learning. It describes how they monitor and control their cognitive processes. If they identify that a particular strategy is not working as expected, they will elect to try a different strategy.

Phases of Metacognition

Planning

During the planning phase, learners think about the learning goal the tutor has set and consider how they will approach the task and which strategies they will use. At this stage, it is helpful for learners to ask themselves:

- ***What am I being asked to do?***
- ***Which strategies will I use?***
- ***Are there any strategies that I have used before that might be useful?***

Monitoring

At this stage, learners implement their plan and monitor the progress they are making towards their learning goal.

Learners might decide to amend the strategies they are using if these are not working. As learners work through the task, it will help them to ask themselves:

- *Is the strategy that I am using working?*
- *Do I need to try something different?*

Evaluation

During the evaluation phase, learners determine how successful the strategy they used was in helping them to achieve their learning goal. To promote evaluation, learners could consider:

- *How well did I do?*
- *What didn't go well?' 'What could I do differently next time?*
- *What went well?' 'What other types of problem can I use this strategy for?*

Reflection

Reflection is a fundamental part of the three-step process. Encouraging learners to question themselves throughout the process will support this reflection.

Research findings

Research into metacognition, has evidenced that the effective use of basic cognitive processes is a fundamental part of learning.

These processes include memory and attention, the activation of prior knowledge and the use of cognitive strategies to resolve a problem or complete a task.

For a learner to ensure that they are making best use of these basic cognitive processes, they need to have an awareness and an ability to monitor and adapt them.
A key challenge for tutors is to recognise how well their students understand their own learning processes.

David Perkins (1992) defined four levels of metacognitive learners. These level are useful when used as a framework upon which learners can be assessed.

- ***Tacit learners*** *are unaware of their metacognitive knowledge. They do not consider any particular strategies for learning and merely accept if they know something or not.*

- ***Aware learners*** *know and understand some of the types of thinking that they do, such as generating ideas, finding evidence etc. However, thinking is not intentional or planned.*

- ***Strategic learners*** *organise their thinking. They use problem-solving, grouping and classifying, evidence-seeking and decision-making etc. They know and apply strategies that help them learn.*

- ***Reflective learners*** *not only are they strategic about their thinking, but also reflect on their learning while it is happening. They consider the success of any strategies they are using and then revise them as appropriate.*

Once tutors have identified where their learners are on this continuum of 'tacit' to 'reflective' they can plan their support accordingly.

Benefits of Metacognition

Metacognition helps learners to become independent learners

Using metacognitive practice helps learners monitor their progress and take control of learning as they read, write and resolve problems in the training room.

Metacognition has a positive impact on learning

Metacognition delivers a unique contribution to learning over and above the influence of simple intellectual ability. Learners who use metacognitive strategies are likely to be able to achieve more. Research shows that improving metacognitive practices can compensate for any cognitive limitations a learner may have.

> *"Too often, we teach students what to think, but not how to think."*
>
> *- OECD Insights (2014)*

Metacognition is useful across a range of age and subject

Metacognitive practices are beneficial for all learners, from primary, upwards. Using metacognition improves learners academic achievement across learning domains. Metacognitive skills help learners to transfer what they have learnt from one context to another or from a previous task to a new task. This includes reading and text comprehension, writing, mathematics, reasoning and problem-solving, and memorising.

Metacognition is not expensive to implement

Implementing metacognition does not require expensive or specialist equipment or changes to the organisation's infrastructure. The only cost associated with the implementation of a metacognitive approach, is the cost of professional development.

Misconceptions about Metacognition

There are a number of misconceptions surrounding metacognition and the related construct 'self-regulated learning.'

Metacognition is simply 'thinking about thinking'
Although metacognition involves thinking about one's thinking, it is more complex than that. A significant part of metacognition is actively monitoring learning and then making changes to learning behaviours and strategies in use, based on this monitoring.

Any strategy which is used while performing a cognitive task is metacognitive
This is not always the true. Flavell (1981) defined a useful distinction between the two:

strategies used to make cognitive progress are 'cognitive strategies;'

strategies used to monitor cognitive progress are 'metacognitive strategies.'

A tutor plays no role in the learners' metacognitive practice
Metacognition usually focuses on allowing the learner to take control of their own learning; however, the tutor is still required to assist in the development of their metacognitive skills. The tutor must set clear learning objectives, demonstrate and monitor metacognitive strategies and prompt and encourage their learners.

Applying Metacognitive practice

A metacognitive approach typically involves learners applying metacognitive strategies to respond to clear and explicit learning goals which have either been set by the tutor or identified by the learner themselves. The learner uses their metacognitive strategies to plan, monitor and evaluate their own progress towards achieving the learning goals.

In order to apply a metacognitive approach, learners will need access to:

1. *A set of strategies to use.*
2. *A classroom environment that encourages the learners to use, explore and develop their metacognitive skills.*

1. Strategies

Clear learning goals are necessary for learners to effectively apply their metacognitive strategies. By clearly defined learning goals, learners can develop strategies that will help them to achieve the learning goals and will also help them to monitor their progress towards achieving these goals.

Learners can use strategies across different domains of the curriculum. For example, a strategy that they have applied in a previous session involving number might also be effective when studying another subject. Discussing strategies helps learners understand what strategies are available to them, how they impact on their learning and why the strategies work.

Below are five strategies that learners can apply across a variety of different subjects.

Mnemonics

Tutors are familiar with the use of mnemonics to help learners remember information that might otherwise be difficult to recall. There are different types of mnemonic.

Acronyms

In mnemonics, items in a list are arranged by their first letter to create a word or phrase.

The name 'McHale' can aid the recall of the different forms of energy:

Mechanical
Chemical
Heat
Atomic
Light
Electrical

Image

Image mnemonics use a visual reference to aid recall.

For example you can use your hands to recall how many days are in each month.

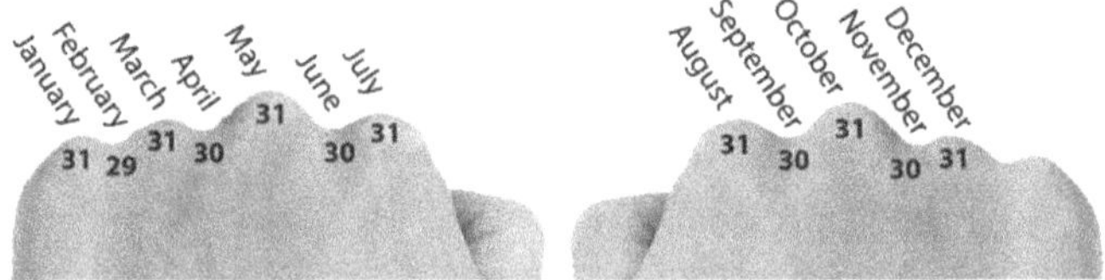

Mnemonics are limited in terms of supporting the development of higher order thinking skills, but they are useful in helping learners to swiftly recall information in order to move on with their learning.

Learning journals

Keeping a reflective learning journal can be a highly effective way for learners to develop their ability to plan, monitor and self-evaluate their learning.

A reflective learning journal is a powerful active learning tool that helps learners to reflect on how they think. It will also encourage learners to explore, question, connect ideas and continue with their learning.

The journal can be used in many ways including:

- *to record ideas from a lesson, film, presentation, etc.*
- *to make predictions about what will happen next*
- *to record questions*
- *to summarise and restate the main themes of a book, film, etc.*
- *to reflect upon and connect the ideas presented to other domains of knowledge.*

Reciprocal teaching

Working with small groups of learners, the tutor models the use of four key strategies that support comprehension:

- *questioning*
- *clarifying*
- *summarising*
- *predicting*

The learners are then asked to take on the role of tutor and teach these strategies to other learners.

Metacognitive talk

Metacognitive talk involves an individual speaking out loud what they are thinking while they are carrying out a task.

Learners speaking out loud is sometimes viewed by tutors as an annoyance or a distraction in a training room. Despite this, Metacognitive talk can be beneficial for learners to focus and monitor their cognitive processing, as well as helping them to develop a deeper understanding of their own thought processes.

1. *At the planning stage, the learner can ask themselves questions such as: 'What do I know about this topic?' 'Have I done a task like this before?' 'What strategies worked last time?'*

2. *While monitoring their progress, the learner can ask: 'How am I doing?' 'What should I do next?' 'Should I try a different strategy?'*
3. *When evaluating their performance, the learner can ask: 'How well did I do?' 'Did I get the results I expected?' 'Is there anything I still don't understand?' 'What could I do differently next time?'*

Learners, especially adults, may have become unused to talking aloud to themselves in the training room. To introduce this, the tutor can model metacognitive talk by working through a task or activity out loud. When tutors verbalise their inner thought processes, it helps learners to understand how more proficient thinkers solve problems. This can then be extended by encouraging the learners to think out loud, both with the tutor and among themselves.

Exam wrappers

Exam wrappers are simply worksheets which contain reflective questions that help learners review their performance in a test or exam.

Wrappers can be given to learners before and after they receive the results of the test and/or feedback.

Wrappers handed out before receiving feedback prompt the learner to reflect on how they prepared for the exam including the study strategies they used.

Wrappers presented after receiving the test feedback, may ask the learner to review the feedback and to categorise any errors made and discuss how they can prepare differently for the next assessment.

2. Creating a supportive environment

Modelling the strategy

Using a metacognitive strategy is a useful way of introducing a new strategy to learners. A step-by-step demonstration of the strategy gives learners a clearer understanding of what the strategy involves.

A metacognition checklist

If you are new to metacognition, it will help to ask yourself the following questions about your teaching practice.

1. Have I included clear learning objectives?

Learners need to understand what their learning objectives are so that they can plan how to achieve them. The process of planning should involve learners identifying which strategies they already know that could be applied in this new situation.

2. How am I going to encourage my students to monitor their learning?

Effective learners commonly use metacognitive strategies whenever they learn. However, they may fail to recognise which strategy is the most effective for a particular learning situation. Tutors can ask questions to prompt learners to monitor the strategies that they are using.

Before learners begin a task, ask them to identify where the task might go wrong and how they could prevent this from happening. Once the task starts, encourage them to focus on the learning objectives and get them to think about how they can maintain that focus. This will encourage learners to think more actively about where they are now, where they are going and how to get there.

3. How can I create opportunities for learners to practise new strategies?
When you introduce your learners to a new strategy, give them the opportunity to use it both with support and independently. It is important to monitor learner progress and provide them with feedback on the specific strategies they are using to help shape their learning process.

4. How can I allow time for learner self-reflection?
Self - reflection enables learners to critically analyse their performance in relation to a particular task and consider how they might act differently to improve their performance in future tasks. It is important tutors dedicate time for learners to reflect, and provide them with the tools to do so. One way of doing this is to use reflective learning journals as mentioned above.

5. Does the training room environment support metacognitive practices?
Tutors are instrumental in shaping the culture of learning in a training room. By establishing an appropriate environment which fosters metacognitive practices, these practices will become an integral part of the learning process. Ensure metacognitive practices are being modelled effectively. Giving learner plenty of opportunity to collaborate with their peers, encouraging reflection and evaluation of their progress.

Implementation

Here are two activities designed to encourage metacognition in the training room.

The KWL chart

KWL stands for:

> *What do I **know**?*
> *What do I **want** to know?*
> *What did I **learn**?*

The chart helps learners to organise information before during and after a lesson or unit of learning. A KWL chart will help to engage learners when starting a new topic, activate their prior knowledge and support them in monitoring their learning.

KWL Chart		
What do I know?	*What do I want to know?*	*What did I learn?*

1. Set the class a clear and explicit learning objective.

2. Ask learners to think about 'What do I know?'

3. Learners start by thinking about what they already know that could help them respond to the learning objective. They record their thoughts in the left column of the chart. However, learners do not have to be limited to working alone. They could share their ideas with others using techniques such as think-pair-share.

4. In addition to activating any prior knowledge, this first question can highlight any misconceptions in learners' current knowledge and understanding.

5. Ask learners to complete the middle column of the chart with their answers to the second question: 'What do I want to know?'

6. Monitor the class carefully. If learners are having difficulty producing ideas prompt them to think about questions beginning 'How...?,' 'When...?,' 'Why...?' etc.

7. This stage provides a good opportunity for you to see what learners are interested in and what they already know. You can use this information to shape future learning activities.

8. During the lesson or unit of learning encourage learners to monitor their own progress and to adjust the strategies they are using, as necessary. Prompt them to ask questions such as: 'How am I doing?' 'What should I do next?,' 'Should I try a different strategy?'

9. At the end of the lesson or unit of learning, ask learners to complete the final column 'What did I learn?'

10. At the same time ask learners to reflect on what they wrote in the 'What do I want to know?' column. Do they have any questions that remain unanswered. Do they have any questions that they would like to add? Make a note of these unanswered questions and use them to help plan future activities.

11. Reflect on their learning process.

12. Encourage learners to reflect on how effectively they discovered the answers to their 'What do I want to know?' questions. Support their discussions with questions that encourage reflection on their learning process:

    What strategies did I plan to use?
    What strategies did I actually use?
    What didn't work? What could I do differently next time?
    What did work? What should I do the same next time?
    Which other strategies could I use?

Levels of metacognitive learners

David Perkins (1992) identified four levels of metacognitive learners which can provide a useful framework for tutors.

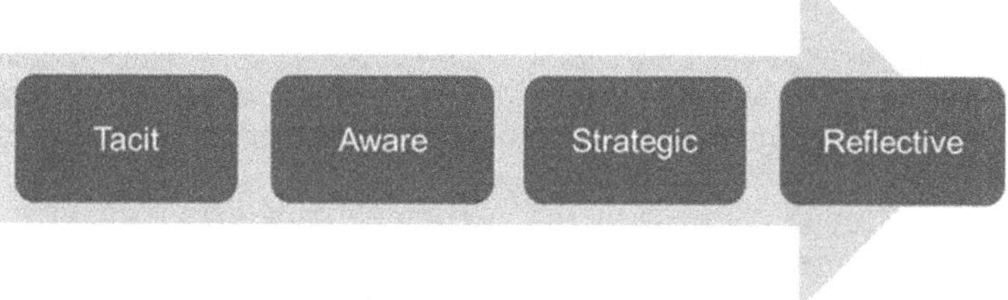

Challenges of adult learning

There can be many barriers to learning, especially for adults. Some of these barriers are listed below. This is by no means a definitive list, but may serve to help understand the challenges adult learners face.

Lack of time

Learners who are adults often have full-time jobs, and sometimes children or other dependents that are dependent upon them. This can make finding time to continue learning very difficult. It is important that every step is taken to remove these challenges.

Self-doubt

It is not uncommon for learners to feel that they are too old to continue their education. They may feel it is too late, and they have missed their chance. That's simply not true! You are never too old to pursue a new direction, it's never too late to follow the dream. Whether there are 5 years or 50 years left in the workforce, learners deserve to pursue a career that they're excited about.

Neuroplasticity

The human brain has an_element of plasticity, it can be re-shaped or changed to help us to learn and grow. Each time we think of something, we reinforce a neural pathway. When we learn something for the first time, we create a new pathway. The neural pathways in the brain are constantly changing, getting stronger or weaker, creating new pathways or strengthening older ones. Younger people have brains that are more plastic, so changes are easier for them. As we age, our brains become less plastic and we are more fixed in what we believe and know. His can be a struggle for learners who are trying to take on new concepts, forge new pathways, and more. Adult learners may have a harder time understanding new things simply because their brains are less plastic. While this is a difficulty, it isn't something that is insurmountable when it comes to adult learning.

Financial barriers

Younger learners may have parental help when it comes to accessing further and higher education. That's usually not the case for adult learners. Finances can get in the way of learners pursuing their dream of earning a degree.

Contradiction

Some of the things adult learners will learn in their education may be different to what they thought they knew or learned before. This can be difficult for adult learners to comprehend. Their previous knowledge base may have to change to make room for new things, and that takes some mental power.

Lack of support

It can be overwhelming to try and tackle new learning without support. Learners may find they don't have the support system they need in place to be able to tackle the difficulty of classes and learning.

Reflective Practice

Reflective practice is simply thinking about or reflecting on what we do. It is closely linked to the concept of experiential learning. Remembering what we did or what happened when previously performing a task will influence how it would be done differently next time, is part of our normal behaviour.

Reflecting is a natural part of human behaviour. The difference between normal 'thinking' and 'reflective practice' is that, reflective practice requires a conscious effort to think about events which have taken place.

Once reflective practice becomes habitual it will be useful both at work and at home.

Reflective Practice might also be called other names:

- *Personal reflection*
- *Self-review*
- *Self-awareness*
- *Self-criticism or self-critique*
- *Self-appraisal*
- *Self-assessment*
- *Intra-personal awareness*
- *Personal cognisance/cognisance*
- *Reflective dialogue*
- *Critical evaluation*
- *Self-analysis of our thoughts, feelings, actions, performance, etc*

Reflective Practice is a valuable tool for using insights and learning from past experience to:

- *Assess where we are now*
- *Improve our present and future*

Reflective Practice offers benefits far beyond professional learning and development, extending but not limited to,

- *Human relationships - workplace, romance, parenting, etc*
- *Rehabilitation*
- *Reconciliation*
- *Mediation*

- *Stress-reduction and management*
- *All sorts of teaching, training, coaching, counselling, etc*
- *Parenting*
- *Coping with change and trauma*

Benefits of Reflective Practice

Reflective practice is beneficial for increasing self-awareness. It is also a key component of emotional intelligence and helps to develop a better understanding of others. Reflective practice can also help develop creative thinking skills and encourage active engagement in work processes.

Reflective Practice can be used for self-development and/or to help others develop. It can be used in parallel with many other concepts for training, learning, personal development, and self-improvement.

Reflective Practice as a Skill

Various academics have referenced reflective practice and experiential learning over the years. There is common consensus that Reflective Practice is a skill, which can be learned and improved with practice.

> ***Reflective practice is an active, dynamic and ethical set of skills, placed in real time and dealing with real, complex and difficult situations.*** Moon, J. (1999)

Experts tend to agree that reflective practice helps bridge the gap between the 'high ground' of theory and the 'low ground' of practice. It helps to explore theories and to apply them to experience in a more structured way. These can be formal theories from academic research, or personal ideas. It also encourages the exploration of our own beliefs and assumptions and to find solutions to problems.

Reflective Learning

Reflective learning is an acquired process that requires time and practice. It is an Active process: involving thinking through the issues yourself, asking questions and seeking out relevant information to aid your understanding.

Reflective learning works best when applied before, during and after a learning experience. Reflective learning is therefore not only about recognising something new, but also about seeing reality in a new way.

Reflection is an important skill to develop and requires you to think about how you are personally relating to what is happening in the workshop or in your work.

The Reflective Learning Process
Identify a situation you encountered in your work or personal life that you believe could have been dealt with more effectively.
Describe the experience
What happened? When and where did the situation occur? Any other thoughts you have about the situation?
Reflection
How did you behave? What thoughts did you have? How did it make you feel? Were there other factors that influenced the situation? What have you learned from the experience?
Theorising
How did the experience match with your preformed ideas, i.e., was the outcome expected or unexpected? How does it relate to any formal theories that you know? What behaviours do you think might have changed the outcome?
Experimentation
Is there anything you could do or say now to change the outcome? What action(s) can you take to change similar reactions in the future? What behaviours might you try out?

Developing and Using Reflective Practice

How can the critical, constructive and creative thinking that is necessary for reflective practice be developed?

It is suggested that there are six steps:

> ***Read*** - *around the subject being studied and develop understanding and theories*
> ***Ask*** - *others about the way they do things and why*
> ***Watch*** - *what is going on around you*
> ***Feel*** - *pay attention to your emotions, what prompts them, and how you deal with negative ones*
> ***Talk*** - *share your views and experiences with others in your organisation*
> ***Think*** - *learn to value time the spent thinking about your work*

In other words, it is not just the thinking that is important. It is equally important to develop an understanding of the theory and others' practice as well and explore ideas with others.

Reflective practice can be a shared activity: it does not have to be done alone.

Some social psychologists have suggested that learning only occurs when thought is put into language, either written or spoken. This could explain why we may announce a particular insight out loud. We may even do this when alone! As a consequence, it may also have implications for reflective practice, in that thoughts not clearly articulated may not endure.

It can be difficult to find the opportunity for shared reflective practice in a busy workplace. There are some obvious ones, such as appraisal interviews, or reviews of events, but they do not happen every day. Other ways need to be found to put insights into words.

Although it can feel a bit contrived, it can be helpful, especially at first, to keep a reflective learning journal. This involves taking everyday activities and events, and writing down what happened, then reflecting on them to consider what has been learned and what could or should have been done differently. It is not just about changing: a reflective learning journal can also highlight when you have done something well.

Keeping a Reflective Learning Journal

This is a simply a collection of notes, observations, thoughts and other relevant materials, built-up over a period of time. It may be the result of study, learning and/or working experience.

The purpose of the reflective learning journal is to enhance learning through the process of writing and thinking about the learning experiences. The learning journal is personal and will reflect personality, preferences and experiences.

Why use a reflective learning journal?

- *To provide a "live" picture of your growing understanding of a subject experience*
- *To demonstrate how your learning is developing*
- *To keep a record of your thoughts and ideas throughout your experiences*
- *To help you identify your strengths, areas for improvement and preferences in learning*

A reflective learning journal helps reflection about learning. A reflective learning journal should not be a purely descriptive account of what has been done, but an opportunity to communicate thinking process: how and why you did what you did, and what you know think about what you did.

Structuring a reflective learning journal

The reflective learning journal may be called by a variety of names: a learning log, a Field-work diary or personal development planner. Different subject areas may ask you to focus on different aspects of your experience and may have different formats.

A reflective learning journal could be a notebook, an electronic document or sometimes recorded verbally on tape. Choose a method that works best for you!

Content of a reflective learning journal

A reflective learning journal should focus on personal responses, reactions, thoughts and reflections towards new ideas or new ways of thinking about a subject that might have been introduced through:

- *Workshops, seminars, training sessions*
- *Research and reading including any visual research including television, film and internet*
- *Conversations and discussions with other participants, your Manager, Mentor, Coach and other colleagues*
- *Significant experiences in the workplace*

Process of Reflective Learning

- *What do I think about this Issue/topic/ experience?*
- *Explore my understanding, perceptions and ideas*
- *Question my assumptions*
- *Identify anything confusing or difficult to understand*
- *What more do I need to know to help my understanding?*
- *Develop and refine my ideas and beliefs*
- *Identify, locate and interpret relevant Information and resources.*
- *How can I use this experience to improve my learning, thinking and working?*
- *e.g., What would I do Differently next time?*

Thoughts about issues discussed at the learning event.

- *Any flashes of inspiration you had*
- *What you understand so far*
- *What you find puzzling, difficult or contradictory*
- *How can you reach a better understanding?*
- *What do you need to know more about, and how can you go about finding out more?*

- *What resources have helped you to understand and/or been interesting to use*

How do you feel about the way you have approached the subject/topic so far?

What new knowledge, skills or understanding have you gained during the process of writing your journal?

Regarding your long-term development.

- *Have you changed your opinions or values during the process/experience?*
- *How can you improve your learning, thinking and working in the future?*

Models of Reflective Practice

It is not easy to produce a reflective learning journal. Part of completing it is an inner sense of discomfort (in fact the first stage of reflection as described by Boyd & Fales 1983) so it is no wonder many people put it off and may even try to get by without it, or conduct token reflections just to comply with CPD or course requirements.

To begin with, reflecting on your actions is something that requires conscious effort after the event but eventually, according to Johns (2000), it will become an automatic thought process even when you are in the middle of experiencing the event.

Below is a brief guide to the different models of reflection out there, and towards which situations they are best geared.

Gibbs reflective cycle (1988)

Graham Gibbs developed his Reflective Cycle in 1988. It gives structure to learning derived from experiences.

Gibbs cycle provides a framework for examining experiences. Its cyclical nature lends itself well to repeated experiences, allowing learning and planning to develop from things that either went well or did not go well.

It covers six stages:

- *Description of the experience*
- *Feelings and thoughts about the experience*
- *Evaluation of the experience, both good and bad*
- *Analysis to make sense of the situation*
- *Conclusions about what was learned and what could have been done differently.*

- ***Planning for how a similar situations in the future might be dealt with in the future, or general changes which might be appropriate***

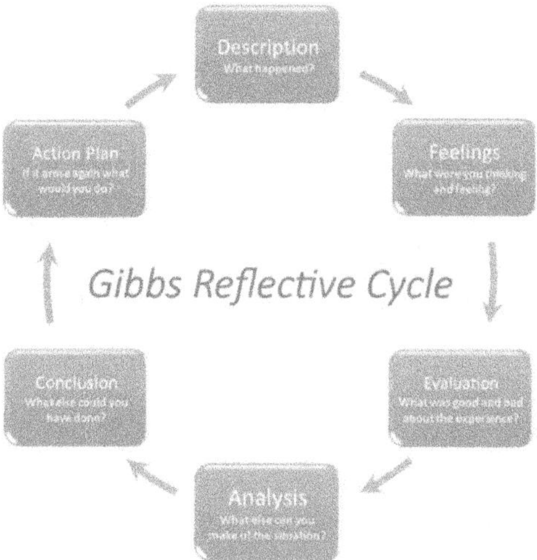

Advantages: A basic, good starting point, six distinctive stages. Makes you aware of all the stages you go through when experiencing an event.

Disadvantages: superficial reflection- no referral to critical thinking/analysis/assumptions or viewing it from a different perspective (Atkins & Murphy 1993). Lacks the number or depth of probing questions as other models.

Kolb Reflective Cycle (1984)

Kolb's reflective cycle is referred to as "experiential learning." The basis for this model is a personal experience, which is then reviewed, analysed and evaluated systematically in three stages. Once one cycle has been completed, the new experiences will form the starting point for the next cycle.

Concrete experience:

A situation is consciously and physically experienced. This prompts the learner reflect systematically about the experience in order to learn something new or improve on existing skill and practice. At this stage make a note of the specific situation and describe what you see, how you feel and what you think.

Reflective observation:

Based on the description of the experience, it is time to reflect more deeply on what has happened in that situation. The questions to ask are: what worked? what failed? why did the situation arise?, why did others and I behave the way we did?

Abstract conceptualisation:
This stage follows on from the questions in the reflective observation stage: what could have been done better or differently? how can I improve? Initially, try to find different ways for dealing with the situations and think up strategies for when a similar situation recurs. This is also the stage where colleagues and literature should be consulted in order to gain a better understanding and further ideas.

Active experimentation:
This stage practices the newly acquired theoretical knowledge. Take the learning from the reflections and thoughts about improvements, as well as the theories and put it back into personal practice and try out the new strategies. Some of them will work, others will not. This is then becomes the basis for a next cycle, as the experiences within the active experimentation stage become the new "concrete experience."

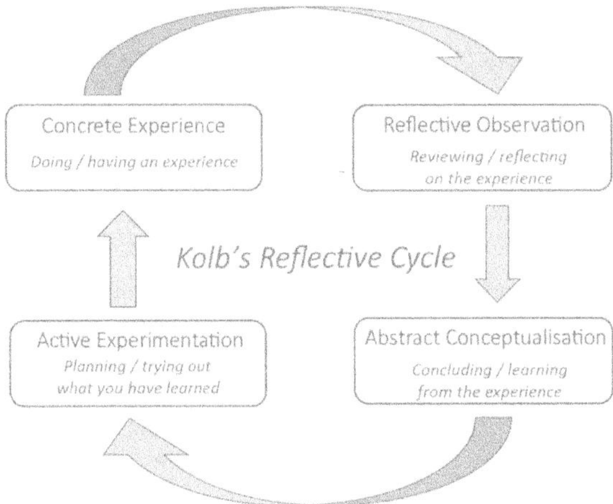

Advantages: The reflective cycle. Consists of doing, asking how/why, making judgement, testing out.

Disadvantages: Superficial reflection- no referral to critical thinking/analysis/assumptions or viewing it from a different perspective (Atkins & Murphy 1993). Lacks the number or depth of probing questions as other models.

Schön model (1991)

The Schön (1991) model strives to distinguish between reflection-on-action and reflection-in-action. Effectively it is a reflection held in the present and past tense.

Reflection-**in**-action is concerned with critically assessing what is happening in real time. A personal trainer might be working with a client on an exercise programme and is making decisions about the suitability of particular exercises, which exercise to do next and judging the success of each exercise at the same time as they are conducting the activity.

Reflection-**on**-action occurs after the activity has taken place. When the personal trainer is thinking about what they (and the client) did, judging how successful they were and whether any changes to what they did could have resulted in a different outcome. This is usually the type of reflection which might be included as part of a Reflective Learning Journal.

Reflecting on academic or professional practice in this way should make personal beliefs, expectations and biases more evident. This personal understanding should help to improve performance as it increases awareness of the assumptions which might be made automatically or uncritically as a result of a perceived view of the world.

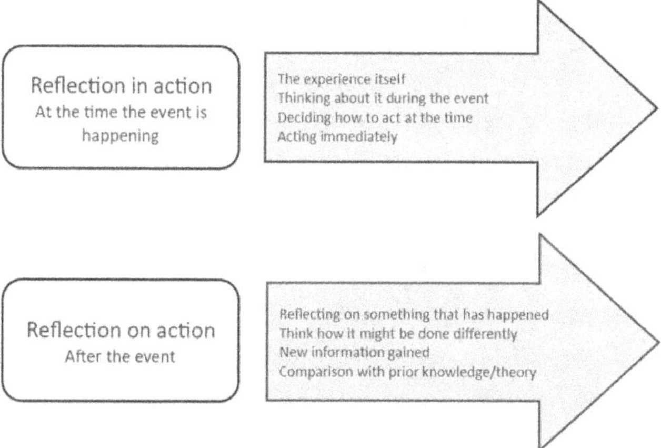

Driscoll model (1994)

This model focuses on three stem questions: "What?" "So what?" and "Now what?" Matching these questions to an experiential learning cycle and adding trigger questions which can be used to promote the learning experience and reflect on what was learnt.

Below is a list of questions that you may choose to answer in response to the three elements.

What. (returning to the event)

- *is the purpose of returning to the event?*
- *happened?*
- *did you see? did you do?*
- *was your reaction?*
- *did other people do?*
- *do you see as key aspects of this situation?*

So, what. (understanding the context)

- *how did you feel at the time?*
- *how do you feel now? are there any differences? why?*
- *were the effects of your actions?*
- *are the positive aspects?*
- *troubles you? if anything?*
- *were your experiences in comparison to your colleagues etc.?*
- *are the main reasons for feeling differently from your colleagues etc.?*

Now what. (adjusting future outcomes)

- *are the implications for you, your colleagues, customers etc.?*
- *needs to happen?*
- *are you going to do about it?*
- *happens if you decide not to do anything?*
- *might you do differently if faced with a similar experience?*
- *information / skills do you need to face a similar experience?*
- *are your key learning points from this experience and reflection?*

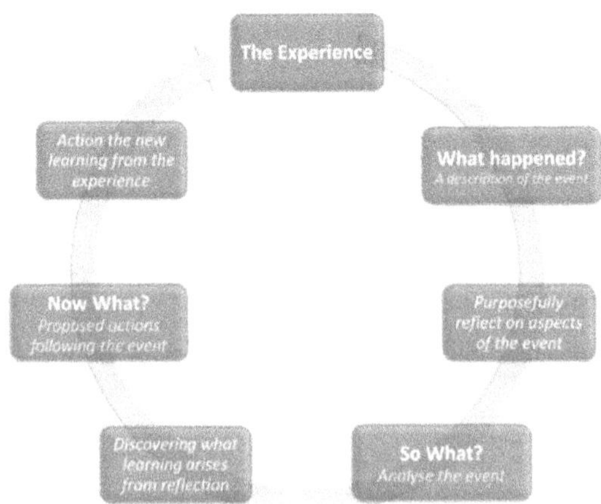

Advantages: Organisational model. Easy to follow cued questions. Easy to remember when you're out and about using the simple "What? So what? Now what?"

Disadvantages: It does not lead to deeper reflection about yourself, only the situation.

Johns' Model for Structured Reflection (2006)

Johns model is based on five questions which prompt and enable you to break down your experience and reflect on the process and outcomes. John used the seminal work by Carper (1978) as the basis for his model, exploring aesthetics, personal knowledge, ethics and empirics and then encouraging the reflective practitioner to explore how this has changed and improved their practice.

Description of the experience
Describe the experience and what were the significant factors?

Reflection
What was I trying to achieve and what are the consequences?

Influencing factors
What factors like internal/external/knowledge affected my decision making?

Could I have dealt with it better?
What other choices did I have and what were those consequences?

Learning
What will change because of this experience and how did I feel about the experience?

How has this experience changed my ways of knowing?

- ***Empirics*** – *scientific*
- ***Ethics*** – *moral knowledge*
- ***Personal*** – *self awareness*
- ***Aesthetics*** – *the art of what we do, our own experiences*

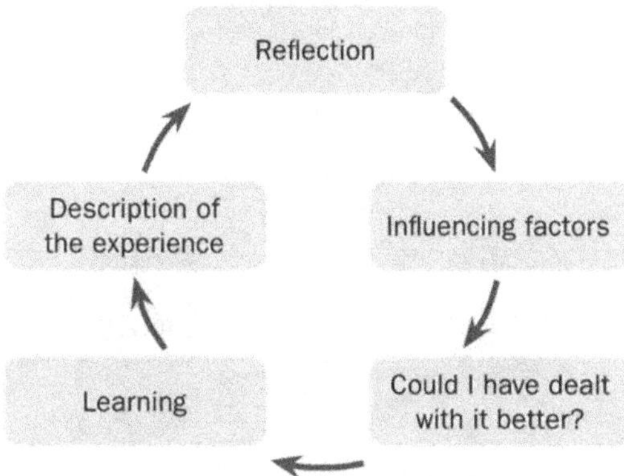

Advantages: Organisational model, examines situations in context of the environment. Provides prompt questions that are easy to follow and can be used in any order (although they follow a natural progression). Can be used by individuals or groups.

Disadvantages: The prompt questions are not rigidly structured which could be confusing for someone inexperienced to know which ones could be omitted and which are salient for their particular reflection. The number of questions means it could be time consuming.

Atkins & Murphy model [1993]

Created by Atkins and Murphy in 1994, the model was created with the intention of studying an individual's experience, in order to identify points for improvement, also referred to as reflective practice.

It is frequently used by professionals who want to continually learn. It is believed that a proactive attitude towards reflective practice will help improve professional competencies and abilities because it forces people to look at discomforts and next to learn from these experiences.

According to Atkins and Murphy model of reflection, discomforts are essential to make improvements.

However, individuals avoid confronting previous behaviours and actions because it is an uncomfortable practice. It requires a proactive attitude to assess things that did not go well, and therefore, reflective practice is preferably avoided. It is however suggested by various researchers who have studied reflective practice models that it will become easier for individuals to perform reflective practice when they continual think about discomforts.

The utilisation of this model has shown that by performing reflective practice, a learning effect occurs. As a result, it will become easier for reflective practitioners to reflect on past discomforts.

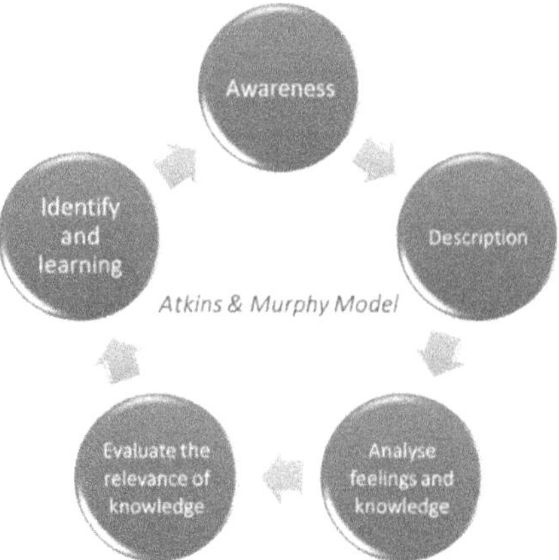

Atkins and Murphy model of reflection components

1. Awareness

In the first step it is essential to gain knowledge or awareness about the triggers that have caused discomfort. This step is not yet concerned with the whole situation - this will be described in the next stage. Identify thoughts and emotions that have resulted from the experience. The individual must be open and honest to identify the discomforts. Analysing personal feelings and thoughts in this way improves developments. Discomfort can also be a result of new experiences. This could include a discomfort caused by switching roles if a new job must be learned.

Key questions to ask in this step could be for example:

- *What happened?*
- *What influenced my emotions?*
- *What were my emotions after the situation occurred?*
- *What was I thinking?*
- *What am now thinking looking back at the situation?*

2. Describe

In this step, the subject must analyse the situation and key events that have occurred critically. For example, a particular environmental setting may have caused a trigger for an individual to experience discomfort, but it could be that a different environmental setting has prevented the discomfort from happening. For this reason, it is important to analyse and describe the situation. A better understanding of why a discomfort occurred, and it will be easier to learn from this discomfort.
The following question could lead as an example to analyse the situation:

- *What was the event?*
- *Where was the event?*
- *When did it happen?*
- *What was my involvement during the event?*
- *What did other people do?*
- *What were the key observations?*

3. Analyse

This step analyses the assumptions that have been made. Before a situation occurred, the individual might have thoughts about the event. It is essential to determine whether the assumptions were correct or false. More importantly, the subject must explore alternatives. This means they must analyse how the behaviour would have been different in a different setting.

Various questions could be asked to analyse this part of Atkins and Murphy model of reflection such as:

- *What did I already know about the situation?*
- *What were my assumptions about the situation?*
- *How did the reality reflect my assumptions?*
- *What were the differences?*
- *How would I react if something else happened?*
- *In what type of scenarios would the discomfort not occur?*

4. Evaluate

This step is concerned with personally assessing how the knowledge gained in the previous step is relevant for improvement. The relevance of knowledge is therefore concerned with identifying if it helps to explain the problem or discomfort. It also deals with assessing how the problem could be solved.

The following could be asked to assess the relevance of knowledge:

- *How does it help to explain the situation?*
- *How does analysing different scenarios influence your thoughts?*
- *How complete was your use of knowledge?*
- *How can your knowledge next time be useful?*

5. Identify

At this point the model has assessed the emotions, situations, assumptions, and knowledge of the subject. By assimilating all elements, the subject can easily state what has been learnt and make use of it in future situations.

Potential questions to ask in this step:

- *What have I learned?*
- *How can my learnings be used in future situations?*
- *How to use Atkins and Murphy model of reflection?*

By using reflective practice theories and models such as the Atkins and Murphy model of reflection, participants of reflective practice create self-awareness and conduct a critical analysis of situations and the related personal emotions and behaviours. However, the Atkins and Murphy model of reflection assumes that development is realised by facing the discomforts. Analysing discomforts can demand some practice because it requires honesty, motivation, and commitment. One must learn to be comfortable with analysing discomforts.

Advantages: Deeper reflections, building on your previous experience. It encourages you to consider assumptions

Disadvantages: It may not be suitable for quick reflections on-the-go or for beginners.

Mezirow model of transformative learning [1981]

Developed by Jack Mezirow in the late 1900s', Transformative Learning Theory relates to deep, useful and constructive learning. This way of learning is far more than simply acquiring knowledge. It offers constructive and critical ways for learners to consciously give meaning to what they do.

When used, this type of learning often causes a fundamental change of the learners world view. This is as a result of a reassessment of current knowledge and understanding into a deliberate, reflective type of learning which supports real change.

Mezirow defines transformative learning as:

> *the critical awareness of unconscious suppositions or expectations and the evaluation of their relevance for making an interpretation.*

Transformative learning often leads to a deep change the thoughts, feelings, perspectives, convictions or behaviour of an individual.
This is caused by the fact that Transformative learning facilitates a radical change of consciousness that permanently changes people's view. In learners, it also leads to a life changing shift that has direct impact on their future experiences. An example of this is a learner who suddenly discovers they have a hitherto unknown talent.

Mezirow identifies two types of learning in the theory:

1. ***Communicative learning***
   Communicative learning aims to improve students' communicative skills. Here, students learn how to communicate their wishes, needs and emotions.

2. ***Instrumental learning***
   Instrumental learning concerns task-oriented or problem-oriented learning. This could be in a classroom setting, but also online. Students are set the task of identifying cause-effect relationships of certain events or cases.

Writing a Reflective Learning Journal

There is an old saying that "you can't teach an old dog new tricks" and it is certainly true when the "old dog" has a mind which is closed to new learning and experiences. A "old dog" with an open mind will analyse their experiences and use that analysis to influence their reaction and behaviour should the experience occur again.

You will hear the term 'reflective writing' many times as part of your apprenticeship and indeed, it is an integral part of every successful apprenticeship. Without reflecting on something, how will you know whether to do the same thing again or maybe manage a situation differently next time? How will you know when something has gone well, but more importantly, why it went well?

You should update your journal every time you undertake some activity relating to your apprenticeship or PDP. Your reflection may be of a general nature, a reflective conversation with yourself or, alternatively, it could be a structured review of your experience over a period of time. Ideally you should follow a structure like the one below.

- ***What have you learned or experienced that is new?*** *(Knowledge)*
- ***Where did you learn this?***
- ***How did you learn it?***
- ***How have you, or could you, introduce this into your working life?*** *(Skills)*
- ***How might this affect the workplace?***
- ***How might this affect you in the longer term?***
- ***How might others in the workplace be affected?***
- ***How will, or could this affect the way in which you work and how might others be affected by it?*** *(Behaviours)*
- ***What have you done differently?***
- ***How will others be affected by this change?***
- ***Will others benefit from the change?***
- ***Will some in the workplace be disadvantaged by the change?***

This is not a definitive list and not everything in the list needs to be addressed every time, but you should feel free to expand and add to this list as you see fit.

You should also keep a record of activities which take place around you which are not "normal." You should think about the actions and behaviour of others and reflect on how their activities affected others and the organisation as a whole. Reflect on how it was dealt with and what the outcomes were. Where possible and/or appropriate, ask those who were dealing with the matter why the particular outcome was chosen, what considerations had they made to make the decision – did they reflect on the matter before making the decision?

Be mindful of other workplace issues too. You have a responsibility for staff welfare, safeguarding, PREVENT, Equality and Diversity. Any issue arising under these headings should also be included in your reflective journal whether you were directly affected or involved. What you experience and your views and thoughts upon that experience are likely to affect and influence you in the event it should ever occur, in which case it is important that you have reflected on the experience.

Warning!

Reflective practice is one of the easiest things to drop when the pressure is on, yet it is one of the things that you can least afford to drop, especially under pressure circumstances. Time spent on reflective practice will ensure focus is on the things that really matter, both to you, your employer or family.

Chapter 6: Learning Needs Analysis and Designing Learning

The Training Cycle

Depending on which page your search engine lands when asked to search for the training cycle, you may find it has between three and as many as nine or ten stages! Different theorists tend to have different ideas and each postulates their own and yes – you guessed, we will postulate our own training cycle, but will justify its content at each stage.

For the purposes of most qualifications, a six-stage model is the best one to use to ensure that each step is explained and justified and when applied, forces consideration on the actions being taken at each stage.

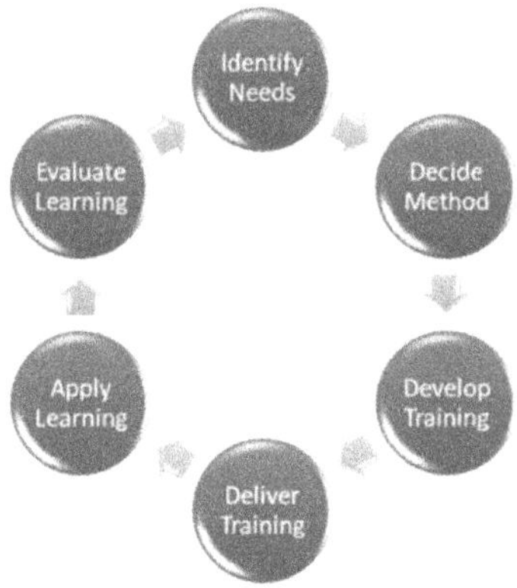

These six stages follow the logical sequence of developmental activity. This can be used when planning development activity, but it can also be applied to a programme of continuous improvement.

Identify Needs

Without an accurate knowledge and understanding of what development is necessary, it is exceedingly difficult to plan and deliver development which resolves the identified problems. If the development needs are not identified correctly it could lead to unnecessary and ineffective training being delivered which is an unwarranted cost and will not correct the problem. Exactly the same outcome will be achieved if too much developmental activity is deployed. Learners will become disengaged and the development they do need, will not be committed to long term memory because of the distractions caused by the unnecessary activity. Additional and unnecessary costs will also be incurred for development which is not needed. It is for this reason that a detailed assessment of the training needs should be performed before and development planning takes place.

Decide Method

Once the development need has been identified, many unskilled an unprofessional operators will launch PowerPoint and roll up their sleeves to get started. This is not appropriate.

The next step is to decide how to deliver the development based on the development needed. Is it knowledge, a skill, or a behaviour which needs to be developed? Each type of need will require a different method of delivery to ensure success. The range of delivery methods is wide, but key methods include:

- *Tutor Led Learning*
- *Virtual Tutor Led Learning*
- *On the Job Learning/shadowing*
- *eLearning*
- *Blended Learning*

The delivery method chosen will be directed by the subject which is to be developed. The development need must be broken down into its constituent elements. Some development might be delivered in the classroom, some may be delivered by eLearning and some may be based in a practical situation in a simulated environment or in the workplace itself.

The learning outcomes derived from each element of the development need will be significantly influenced the method of delivery – you cannot teach someone to drive a car in a classroom. You can teach the knowledge and understanding of the Highway Code and the principles of how a car engine works, but the only way to teach someone to drive it, is by allowing them to get behind the wheel and operate it!

Develop Activity

Once the method of delivery has been decided, the activity for each developmental method can start to be developed. The development need, having been broken down into its constituent elements, simplifies this process. There will be a need for resources for classroom-based learning. eLearning resources will be needed and there will be a need for access to workplace resources to facilitate the practical activities. The practitioner who will deliver the development should also be identified and briefed as to what the development need is and what element of that need, they will be responsible for. It is often the case that one person will deal with the training room delivery, another will be responsible for the development of eLearning resources and another practitioner may be used to deliver and monitor the practical element. Within each of these activities, the learning must be designed to meet the need exactly and not include unnecessary or superfluous activity which may confuse the key learning aim. Finally, the desired outcome at each stage must be identified as this information will be required later.

Deliver Training

Having planned the delivery of each element of the developmental activity and having designed and developed the supporting materials and resources to be used, the delivery of the learning becomes more straightforward. The practitioners for each stage have been identified and they have been briefed as to how It will be delivered in a planned, logical order and their role within that. They will also have been informed what the expected outcome of the development is. The delivery should then be appropriately facilitated in each instance.

Apply Learning

Having received the developmental activity, the learners will then apply the new knowledge, skill or behaviour into their normal working routine. It is rare that there is an immediate and measurable impact on performance and results, however, as they become more accustomed to the new ways of working, so the development will take effect. They should be encouraged to reflect on the implementation of this learning and how it impacts on the task and them personally. This reflection can provide valuable feedback for measuring the success of the development as well as for the planning of future activity.

Evaluate Learning

Having had time to settle into the new method of working, evaluation of the development can take place. The most important question is has the development worked? It is not enough to assess the change only qualitatively in knowledge, skills or behaviour. Earlier in the learning cycle the desired outcomes were set which detailed what changes in business performance was desired as a result of the development. It is these metrics against which the developed performance should now be measured. Without the evaluation of learning, there will be no feedback upon which to develop the learning further, to streamline it by removing unnecessary elements or shifting the focus on areas which have been less well achieved from those where there has been a high level of achievement.

Learning and Development Needs Analysis

A Learning and Development Needs Analysis is sometimes also referred to as a Training Needs Analysis. The two are exactly the same in purpose and application. Unfortunately, not all development needs can be resolved with training which is why Learning and Development Needs Analysis has become a preferred name in most environments.

The world of work is changing rapidly and so are the skills needs of the workforce. The availability of suitably qualified and skilled employees is diminishing and organisations have realised that in order to stay ahead in the skills shortage, they must develop the employees they already have.

Lifelong learning has been part of the education system for many years. Previously it tended to be a generic term for all personal and professional development, today it has become a necessity for employees and employers alike to continually develop knowledge and skills.

Definition:

A Learning and Development Needs Analysis is the systematic process of identifying what development is required and subsequently identifying and implementing appropriate solutions to remediate it.

When applied, a Learning and Development Needs Analysis (LNA) helps an organisation identify the gap in terms of skills and training in their existing employees to perform the current and upcoming Jobs efficiently.

It can also be described as a management tool which is used to identify the new skills, knowledge, and attitudes that employees need to acquire in order to improve their performance and/or that of the organisation.

The Learning and Development Team will use a LNA to identify exactly which skills and competences need to be developed before then identifying appropriate and viable solutions.

The role of the Learning Needs Analysis

Every organisation needs their employees to perform at the very highest level. The organisation's strategy will define what the organisation hopes to achieve and the direction it intends to take. This may include the development of new products or

methods of operation. For the organisation to be able to achieve this, employees must have the necessary skills, competences and capabilities to facilitate this.
The role of the LNA is to identify the gap between the current skill levels and those which will be needed as the organisation moves forward.

The LNA will strive to answer the following questions:

- *Who needs development?*
- *What type of development is required?*
- *What solutions might be available?*
- *What the expected impact will be?*
- *What is the cost of the development activity?*

Learning and Development Needs Analysis process

The Learning Needs Analysis process will vary depending on the job role for which the analysis is being undertaken. The analysis of developmental needs for a group of managers will be different to the one used for a group from a shop floor.

It is important that the correct process is used in each case to avoid the learning being over ambitious, but equally, not too insignificant as to not deliver any benefit. The following methods can be used depending on the job role being studied.

Observation – *Employees are observed in their role. The observation is seeking to find skills gaps where the employee is not performing to standard and also the behavioural aspects of their role.*

Interview – *Employees might be interviewed about their performance, either as part of an appraisal system or simply as an information gathering exercise.*

Focus groups – *Using a brainstorming approach, the focus group strives to identify the skills gaps. They may do this by forming the focus group from a wide selection of employees across the organisation who must be well informed about current performance levels and the plans for the future.*

Assessments and Surveys – *These are quick and easy ways to identify weaknesses in performance across a department or even the whole organisation. A carefully planned survey can be issued with both open and closed questions, allowing the collection of both quantitative and qualitative responses. Such types of survey should be completed on a confidential basis and the responses should be anonymous*

Customer feedback – *Feedback from customers can also be used to inform a TNA, however, it should be noted that if the customer has been affected by poor capability, the problem may be more serious than anticipated.*

***Other** – other sources could include consultation with individuals in key positions within the organisation or external consultants. Internal reports will often identify areas of development need along with physical samples of work completed.*

Minimum Expectation of a Learning Needs Analysis

As mentioned above, there are different process used in a LNA depending on the type and grade of role being analysed. Whilst the content of the process may vary, there is a standard process which must be met by all LNA, regardless of the job role and type of organisation being studied. This four-step process is detailed below:

1. ***Identify the gap** - between the current performance and the desired performance.*

2. ***Analyse the root cause** – the root cause is typically identified in one of five distinct categories, these are:*
    - ***Skills***
    - ***Resources***
    - ***Incentives***
    - ***Motivation***
    - ***Information***

3. ***Needs Analysis** – identifies the appropriate solution to the problem. The information gained from the Root Cause Analysis can be used to help identify the optimum solution. The needs analysis will also consider, who needs the training and this will include:*
    - ***Job analysis***
    - ***Task Analysis***
    - ***Environment analysis***
    - ***Cost benefit analysis***

4. ***Presentation of solutions** – having conducted the in-depth analysis if the training need the information is then analysed to identify the optimum training solution.*

Components of Learning Needs Analysis

McGhee and Thayer's Three Level Analysis is widely used to gain an understanding of the overall view of learning and development within an organisation.

The model identifies three areas of analysis which should be completed in order to identify the development needs of the organisation.

1. Organisational Level

Providing any development for employees which is not aligned with the strategy or the short to medium term goals of the organisation is nothing more than a waste of time effort and money.

If the development to be provided does not deliver a tangible, measurable, outcomes, then it should not be delivered. All development must be focussed on the true need.

For the overarching development need across the organisation, the following questions must be answered:

- *Is the organisation meeting its defined performance targets?*
- *Is there new legislation or regulation which must be informed?*
- *Have the organisations objectives or goals changed?*
- *Is new technology being introduced?*
- *Are limits set to be imposed on resources?*
- *Are there issues related to staff turnover or recruitment problems?*
- *Which department is in most urgent need of development ?*
- *Which type of development program will resolve the issues?*
- *Information from SWOT and PESTLE analyses*

At this level, there must be, clear and measurable outcomes defined which must be met for the development to be successful.

2. Operational Level

At an operational level, it is a job analysis which will be used to determine the development needed to improve performance.

It will identify the knowledge and skill needed to perform the tasks efficiently. The target levels can be drawn from:

- *the work performance standards*
- *job descriptions*
- *job specifications*
- *consultation with Stakeholders*
- *analysis of operational issues.*

At the operational level of LNA the following questions should be answered:

- *What is the expected standard of performance for the job?*

- *Do skill levels need to be raised to meet to meet objectives?*
- *Could health and safety, legal or compliance issues arise without the development?*
- *Are operational best practices in place?*
- *How should the employee execute the task to meet the set expected standards?*
- *What type of development might be appropriate to improve the deficit?*

3. Individual Level

At the individual level, the LNA will analyse the way employees actually performs their duty. The gap between the expected and actual performance is the development need for that employee.

Analysis of performance at this level will use data from:

- *performance appraisals*
- *assessment of employee skills*
- *psychometric tests*
- *interviews and questionnaires*
- *customer surveys*
- *work samples*

At this level of analysis the following questions must be answered:

- *Does the employee have the necessary skills and knowledge?*
- *Have team members requested development?*
- *Are people the taking the next step in their natural development?*
- *What barriers are preventing satisfactory performance?*
- *What is the most appropriate development solution to resolve the problem?*

Needs Analysis Process

There are notionally ten steps in the process of conducting a learning needs analysis. This is one of the reasons why they cannot be conducted ad hoc and must be carefully planned. This is also the reason why the cost of such activity can be high, especially if the outcome is inaccurate or the identified solution does not resolve the problem.

1. *Which part of the organisational strategy needs to be satisfied with the developmental activity?*
2. *What are the expected outcomes from the development and how will these meet the strategic objective?*
3. *What do the subjects for the development need to do to deliver the outcomes required?*
4. *What ability do the subjects need in order to be able to do what is required?*
5. *How do the current levels of capability compare to the identified need?*
6. *Based on the gap between actual and desired behaviour, what do the subjects need to learn?*
7. *How will the development be delivered?*
8. *How would the development be delivered to the subjects?*
9. *How will the development be evaluated? What metrics will be used to identify success or failure?*
10. *What are the benefits to be derived from the developmental activity compared to the cost of delivery?*

The results of the analysis can be reported in many ways and this will often be dictated by the scale and scope of the analysis. A small-scale analysis could easily be reported in a simple table or matrix. There are many of these templates available on the internet and very often it is as much about how to fit the information onto the paper as it the design.

Analysing the Analysis

Even for a modest skills gap analysis there will be a considerable amount of data generated which must be analysed carefully to ensure that the needs identified are real and that any proposed solution will correct the gap.

The best way to begin to analyse this is by following the three levels of assessment described above.

Organisational Analysis

The first analysis should be conducted at an organisational level. Key members of the team should be assembled along with the line management for that department.

A meeting should be convened with key stakeholders and leaders and they should work to answer the following questions:

- *Are there any changes anticipated in organisational strategy?*
- *What development might be needed to meet any such strategic change?*
- *Are there plans to change production or processes?*
- *Is there a forecast change in the business environment?*
- *Are there differences between desired and actual performance?*
- *What common themes tend to appear in appraisal reports and development plans?*

Task/Skills Analysis

The second step is to analyse the results derived from the team or department.

- *What are the teams/departments key tasks?*
- *What training has been provided to date?*
- *Was this training successful?*
- *What type of development will be most effective in resolving the need?*

Individual Level

The last step is to analyse the data at an individual level or, where teams are small, the team could be brought together to answer the following questions.

- *What gaps in performance exist?*
- *What development do individuals need?*
- *What development do the subjects think they need?*
- *What development are they interested in?*
- *How important are the skills gaps to the he performance of the subjects?*
- *How can the development be best delivered?*

Once this analysis has been completed, there should now be some clear signposts as to what development is needed at all three levels.

The identified needs should be listed alongside those who are to undertake the development. Once this has been completed each development need should be prioritised by the degree of urgency and importance of the work being completed and dates should not only be set for the commencement of the development, but also dates for the completion of the development.

Variations of Learning Need Analysis

Another way in which a LNA might be applied in a business is to look at the developmental need at three different stages in the work cycle.

New starters

The induction programme is a key part of the new starters integration process into the organisation. Too often these induction programmes are far too intense and do not address the immediate needs of the new start. They go into detail about booking holidays and what to do if unwell, but sometimes they omit to include simple welfare issues such as where to get a coffee, what to do on a break.

Promotion and New Roles

Development will be needed when people change job roles or are promoted for one level to the next. This is especially important as people move from the shop floor to management roles. This type of organic progression should be easy to anticipate and employees can be groomed for the role over a period of time before the promotion actually takes place. Unfortunately in organisations with a high turnover, this is not always possible and people need to be promoted quickly and will need urgent developmental support to help them adapt and adjust to the new role.

Long Standing Employees

The third group under consideration are those who have been in their job roles for a period of time for whom there is no desire or scope for promotion or role change. They too will need ongoing development to ensure that their competence is maintained and that their knowledge is current and up to date. They will also require development when systems, processes or technology are planned for change. This particular group of subjects can often present the greatest opposition to development, as they are happy with the way things are and cannot see the need for change. As a result, unless there is a well-planned change management programme in place, there is every possibility they will work against the change and even go as far as to try and sabotage it!

Advantages and disadvantages of Learning Needs Analysis

All process have advantages and disadvantages depending on which perspective they are being viewed.

Advantages

- *It identifies those most in need of development.*
- *It determines the type of development needed to improve skills, knowledge, and behaviour*
- *Enables the assignment of resources to where they will be most beneficial.*
- *Improve productivity and performance.*

- *Improves quality which in turn improves customer satisfaction.*

Disadvantages

- *A learning needs analysis can be a time-consuming and expensive process*
- *Poor response rate from employees can hide underlying problems.*
- *Timescales can be protracted, meaning the training is not valid by the time it is delivered.*

The role of Data in a Learning Needs Analysis

As identified earlier, providing developmental activities can be a costly and time-consuming exercise for every organisation. It is therefore important that very careful consideration is given to who needs the development and who should attend.

A common source of referral for development is via the appraisal system and/or line manager feedback. The problem with this strategy is that it tends to be reactive rather than proactive. It is vital that organisations develop a more holistic approach to the identification of development needs and data can become an essential part of that process.

Development may be required at an organisational, departmental/job or individual level. The use of data will ensure that the correct solutions are identified. This can be drawn from a variety of sources, not limited to:

- *Job descriptions*
- *Work sampling*
- *Problem analysis*
- *Organisational efficiency reports*
- *Management requests*
- *Etc.*
- *Performance standards*
- *Job specifications*
- *Employee skills audits*
- *Sector climate*
- *Exit interviews.*

By drawing data from a range of these possible sources, the identification of the developmental need becomes far more accurate and as a result the solutions to be created become much more effective and targeted at those who really need it.

This is not necessarily the end of the process though. There must also be analysis at an individual level. An employee who already has undertaken training in one area may well not require development in another given the skills they already have and those which have already been developed. Placing this employee on a training programme would be of no benefit to the organisation or the individual, but would still incur significant cost to the organisation.

The use of data can define both what and who in terms of development and by using data as an integral part of the TNA process, far great benefit and cost efficiency can be derived.

Planning Development

Having identified the gap between current capability and the level of performance desired, the development needed to close the gap is now more clearly defined.

It is most important at this stage to remember only the development needed to close the gap should be included. The temptation is to add additional content or use a standard development programme, however, as identified earlier, this "additional" development will not be actively remembered, because it is not relevant and, in some instances, could actually have a detrimental effect as it causes additional "noise" over and above the development which is actually needed.

When planning development it is best to consider the 5Ws' and an H – also known as five bums on a Rugby post!

Why?
What?
Who?
Where?
When?
How?

These simple questions are key to the development of effective interventions.

Why?

Asking why the development is needed is a question which is usually forgotten when planning development. The training needs analysis should have considered the strategic goals of the organisation in its identification of need, but it does not always ask why. The first question those identified as needing development will ask is why do I need it? If the reason for the development is established at the planning stage, it then becomes easy to incorporate the reason why into every subsequent element of the development programme.

What?

The second question –What development is needed? This will be answered and defined by the Needs Analysis. It is also important to know what type of development is actually needed.

Is the development needed to improve knowledge, develop skills or change behaviours?

The method of delivery and the approach taken will change, depending on the nature of the development required.

Who?

The third question is to establish who needs the development? There is no point putting people forward for development if there is no need for it – if the learner cannot see the benefit, they will not engage with it. Only those who need the development in order to meet the organisations strategic goals should be considered for training. Whilst it may seem financially prudent to include as many as possible on an expensive development activity – in fact, it is counterproductive because those who do not need the development will distract those who want to be engaged reduce the outcomes and benefits of the training for all.

Where?

Where is the best place to provide the development. This could be on the shop floor, it could be in a training room, online or in a hotel function suite. The choice depends on many factors and these must be considered carefully before a decision on where the development will take place is made. Delivering on site training for management is usually foolhardy as the session may be punctuated with calls or queries which not only distracts the individual involved, but also the rest of the group and the tutor too. Off site where mobile telephones can be switched off and computers left in the boot of the car provide a much more suitable environment for learning.

When?

The question when to deliver development is another one which requires careful thought and planning. It should not be planned at the end of a shift and it should not be planned at the very start of a shift. Holiday periods are a notoriously difficult time to get people together for a series of development sessions. Work volumes are another factor which needs to be considered.

How?

This question asks how it will be delivered. Will this be an in-house development activity? Will it be delivered by outside providers or will it be a programme of development in association with a local college or University?

When answered, these simple questions will clearly define the development which is needed, who should engage with it and how, when and where it should be delivered.

Types of Developmental Intervention

The scope of the development need will dictate the type of intervention needed. If the decision is taken to generally improve all learners IT capabilities, this will need a significant intervention which might include the development of curriculum of study.

The term curriculum is often used by Training Organisations to describe the "package" of courses or learning programmes they have on offer. On a smaller scale it typically refers to all of the learning undertaken by a learner in a particular area of study and is used interchangeably with the term "Scheme of Work". Whichever term, the purpose and function in an L&D environment is basically the same.

As a consequence we may find that a training solution could require a substantial, sequential, programme of study when needed organisation wide, or it could be a one-off intervention to correct knowledge, skills or behaviours on a selective basis.

A third type of intervention should also be included and that is a spontaneous response to an identified need. For example, an employee, as part of their role, is required to update a spreadsheet with live data. If that employee does not know how to do enter data, there will be a need for immediate development to take place, however, unlike coaching, this intervention will need to be planned.

The level of prior or existing knowledge will need to be established so the new knowledge can be built on this foundation. Where a structured programme exists for developing IT skills, a section relating to developing Excel skills could be extracted and tailored for use, however, its fitness for purpose should be checked against the training need identified. No development should take place until the need has been very clearly identified in full and a solution developed which fully satisfies the need.

Whichever type of intervention is needed, the design process will be the same – it is only the scale which will change.

Methods of Delivery

What is important to consider is the suitability of the subject when planning a method of delivery. Some subjects, especially those which revolve around corporate culture, technical skills, communication skills, executive development and sensitive issues such as sexual harassment are all far more suited to a closed training room environment where people can speak openly and freely and express their views without fear of reprisal.

Tutor led Delivery.

Training room delivery has been at the core of developmental learning for many years and continues to be the primary method of delivery in compulsory education. The impact of technology and the COVID pandemic opened the doors to development via different channels and given that around 40% of all development activity during the pandemic was still conducted on a face-to-face basis with a further 29% being delivered online. Technology is therefore clearly unlikely to signal the death knell for classroom development in the workplace, but it does open up new avenues which offer more cost effective and arguably more powerful development tools.

The disadvantages of face-to-face training room development include the time taken out of the working day and it may certainly not be the best delivery method for some subjects. The cost of travel, hospitality and accommodation costs along with the cost of hiring a venue if the organisation does not have the resources. It is because of these additional costs that Virtual Tutor Led Training is becoming an increasingly popular option.

Virtual Tutor Led Training

In many ways this type of delivery is the same as training room delivery but without the physical interaction which is highly valued by learners and tutors alike. Because the deliver is live, learners undertake the learning at the same time using platforms such as Teams or Zoom. These can be used alongside other resources such as virtual whiteboards and other collaborative tools. The big advantage of this type of learning is its accessibility form anywhere with a connection to the internet. The benefit of a live tutor to respond to questions and queries is also highly beneficial as these can be resolved immediately. The greatest disadvantage is the loss of physical interaction. The inability of the tutor to read body language and gauge learner involvement and also for the learners, it can be difficult to have that personal one to one opportunity with the tutor which they might be able to take during a coffee break or over lunch.

On the job training and shadowing

These methods will obviously be conducted outside the training room and typically in the workplace or on the shop floor. On the job training as implied by the name, provides learners with the opportunity to practice new techniques or methods whilst under the supervision of a more experienced employee. A significant benefit is the fact that this is usually a one-to-one interaction where the inexperienced individual can ask questions openly and freely of the more experienced employee which they might not have asked in a group situation due to embarrassment. Too often this type of development delivery is limited to one employee showing the ropes to another employee before abandoning them to their destiny. This can often lead to failure because the novice has not fully developed their knowledge and understanding. This type of delivery should be supported with additional learning in the form of videos, online learning and structured assessments to evidence progress. Another benefit of this type of learning is that it delivers exactly what the learner needs to know and builds on existing knowledge from the first step. A disadvantage is that all too often the people providing the development are not tutors or competent trainers and therefore the development they provide could include acquired practices and behaviours which may not be wholly appropriate in every situation. This is a practical form of Chinese Whispers and can lead to declining standards in quality and performance.

Job shadowing is similar to on-the-job training except the learner tends to watch a more experienced individual do their job and then ask questions along the way. This is often called "watching Nellie"! It is a good development tool when someone is thinking about a promotion or a change of role. The developmental benefits in terms of changing behaviours, knowledge or performance is limited.

eLearning

eLearning is an impersonal developmental methodology which eliminates human contact and interaction completely from the activity. Well designed and carefully planned eLearning resources are rare, but for those which are, they offer excellent development opportunities which increases retention, engagement and reinforcement in a far more personalised way than other methods. The disadvantage though is that good eLearning resources are hard to find and poor-quality resources will have exactly the opposite effect.

Most people engaged in a Learning and Development role have experienced "death by PowerPoint" at some point in their career – endless slides scrolling up the screen with thousands of words on every screen. There can be few more dispiriting experiences in education. However, we have also experienced PowerPoint presentations with interactive elements, seamlessly slipping into a video or animation before returning to a quiz or other activity. We remember it – because it was enjoyable and we remember what we learnt!!

Given that a tool as common and easily used as PowerPoint can be used to provide development in an eLearning format, it can be used for a wide variety of subjects across many levels and is cheap to deploy, easy to develop and can be used across organisations, globally. The use of eLearning as a developmental tool should not be underestimated when planned and prepared properly.

Blended Learning

Blended Learning, as its name suggests is a combination of delivery methods used in conjunction with each other to deliver the desired outcome. Face to face learning can be used to start the development process and then subsequently eLearning, On the Job and further face to face development can be planned to deliver development in a manner appropriate to the subject, at the appropriate time. There is no secret recipe for Blended Learning, it needs to be built and designed around the training needs identified and the objectives which it needs to meet.

For the most part, learners can work at their own pace and with tutorial access with the tutor, they have on demand access to support if they find some areas challenging.

Designing Learning

Having identified the method of delivery to be used, it becomes easier to decide the structure and content of the activity. As part of the Learning Needs Analysis the specific development needs were identified.

Improving customer satisfaction is a common theme in many development programmes, typically prompted by customer complaints. As a result, development solutions are often considered to be additional training for customer service representatives on how to manage calls and how to soothe irate customers so the aggrieved customer is less inclined to complain further. An effective LNA will identify there is nothing wrong with the Customer Service team, but rather, the problem lies on the factory floor where inferior quality goods are being produced.

As a result, the customer service training manual can be set to one side and a deeper study of where the true problems lie on the factory floor will be needed.

It might be established from customer feedback that the product breaks easily or is not durable in use. Once again, this is a production problem rather than a development need. If goods being made are being assembled incorrectly then this may warrant a developmental solution. Employees may need developmental training on quality standards or the correct production processes.

Whatever the identified need, implicit in this is the desired outcome. This is also known as the learning objective.

The learning objective must be satisfied at the end of the development activity. To ensure clarity in each objective each one is typically preceded by the words...

At the end of the development activity the learner will..........

These learning objectives are critical to the design, development, delivery and ultimately the success of the development activity. If the learning objectives are not met the development has not been successful and those engaged on the programme will not display the required knowledge, skills or behaviours with the result that the entire process needs to be repeated.

It is therefore essential that the learning objectives are very clearly defined and that all development activity is targeted at achieving those objectives.

Poorly performing development activities will often have vague learning objectives or none at all. The practitioner delivering the development needs to know what the expected objectives are, the learners need to know what they are expected to achieve and they will form the metrics for assessing the success of the development.

When designing training, consideration must also be given to the audience who will receive the development activity. This will not only influence the decision regarding the person appointed to deliver the development activity but also how it is to be delivered.

Planning the Development

Providing developmental activity is a very costly exercise. Not only is the cost of the provider and materials a factor, but also the cost of the employees attending the programme who are still earning a salary, but not generating any income for the business. As a consequence, the design of the course is about cost efficiency as well as effectivity. A well-designed intervention will minimise time spent attending the intervention and focus on only the new knowledge, skills and behaviours desired.

There are two elements to consider when considering the overall planning:

- ***An efficient process***
    - *Consideration must be given to variables such as prior knowledge and planned method of delivery.*
    - *Planning development which optimises progression.*
- ***Effective Outcomes***
    - *Aligning elements of the programme so they integrate and build on each other.*
    - *Use research-based learning practice which supports independent learning.*

Every effort should be made to ensure these two simple criteria are met in every planned developmental intervention.

Planning the Intervention

When planning development or designing the development activity, there are three elements in this process:

- ***Learning Outcomes*** – *What the learners should know by the end of the intervention.*
- ***Assessments*** – *Evidence which demonstrates the learner has met the outcome*
- ***Activities*** – *the opportunities provided for learners to achieve the outcomes.*

The delivery of development activities must be based on a structured plan. The aims of each session must be clearly defined and from that the learning objectives which must be achieved in that session can be defined. This may seem a backward approach to planning – and your assessment is quite correct!

The planning of developmental activity should be a backward process!

By starting the planning with the desired outcome, planning how to achieve it becomes more straightforward and there is less tendency to prevaricate and add unnecessary content which could cause confusion and prevent learning from taking place.

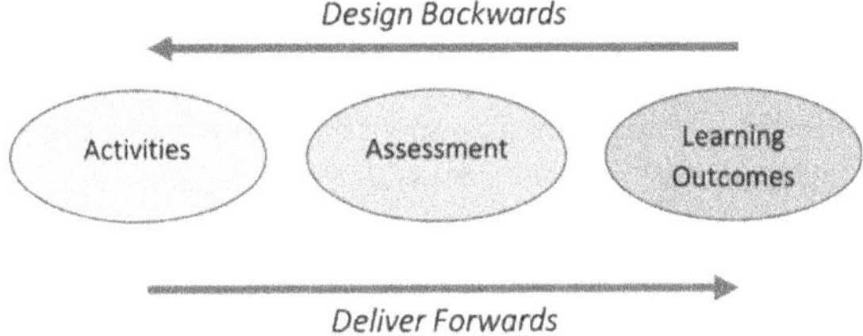

The learning outcomes – the desired change in knowledge, skills and behaviour have been identified in the Learning Needs Analysis. This prompts the question:

"How will we know when they have met the outcome".

The answer to this question will help to define how the success or failure of the developmental intervention will be measured. This will create the method of assessment. The assessment will provide the evidence that the outcome has been met.

Once the assessment methods have been defined, it then becomes much easier to design the learning and the method of delivery to meet the assessment requirements. In other words, it asks the question:

"What needs to be learnt to ensure the assessment requirements can be met".

Once this is known, the actual learning content can then be designed and developed.

What is also clear from this type of planning, is that the delivery of the development activity simply follows the same path - but forward!

Designing the Delivery

There are two main methods of delivering learning at this level and these are:

- *Tutor Centred*
- *Student Centred*

There are few situations where either should be used in exclusivity. A combination of the two, weighted either way as necessary or a 50:50 split will deliver the best outcomes in most cases. The approaches chosen will impact heavily on the learners experience and well as their ability to understand new concepts and transfer knowledge.

	Tutor Centred	*Student Centred*
Definition	*Tutor provides the information to the learner*	*Student builds knowledge and understanding with tutor guidance*
Theoretical Support	***Behaviourism:*** *Learning consists of inputs (information) and outputs (behaviours) measured by assessment*	***Constructivism****: Learners build knowledge and understanding building on prior knowledge and new experiences*
Focus	***Singular****: Tutor actions and content coverage*	***Shared:*** *Learner activity and tutor facilitation*
Tutor Role	*Delivery of information, assess outcomes, reinforce behaviours through process and rules*	*Provide experiences and guide understanding of meaning*
Learner Role	*Passive learning – simply absorb information*	*Active learning by constructing and developing understanding*
Method	***Direct Instruction:*** • *Modelling* • *Explanation* • *Elaboration* • *Lecturing* • *Demonstration* • *Thinking aloud through processes* • *Recapping or summarising information*	***Coaching and Facilitating:*** • *Interactive lectures* • *Asking questions* • *Guiding student thinking* • *Prompting and cueing* • *Scaffolding learning and information* • *Thinking collaboratively with students* • *Incorporating formative assessment*
Role of assessment	*Sorts learners by performance*	*Guides learners on progress*

Each method has merits and demerits and often these may also be a factor in deciding which approach to take.

	Tutor Centred	*Student Centred*
Advantage	*Control and order* *Coverage ensured* *Efficient delivery: one-to-many*	*Engaging and interesting* *Communication and collaboration skills* *More self-directed learning*
Disadvantage	*Exhaust attention* *Less communication or collaboration* *Less opportunity for self-direction and guidance*	*Noisy and chaotic* *Coverage not ensured* *Large numbers difficult*

The design of an intervention will always be influenced by many factors and most of these will be situational factors. These factors may apply constraints to the planned delivery or there may be opportunities which can be exploited to benefit the programme.

- ***Constraints:*** *Factors which cannot be controlled or changed and the intervention must be designed around them. For example, number of learners, availability of resources, room size and duration of the session.*
- ***Opportunities:*** *Factors which can be changed to improve the intervention. For example, developing own knowledge of teaching strategies to improve performance.*

Fink (2013) identified the following groups as being the situational factors which require consideration.

- ***Context of learning*** *– includes information about the intervention such as the duration, time and delivery mode. Additionally, it may include general information about the learners.*
- ***Expectations of the organisation*** *– includes expectations of learner performance in the field or program from stakeholders such as senior management, the organisation, colleagues and accreditation requirements.*
- ***The subject*** *– includes content, delivery approaches, application of skills, complexity of learning.*
- ***Characteristics of the learners*** *– includes the diversity of learners, previous knowledge or experience, their attitudes towards the subject as well as their personal and professional lives.*
- ***Characteristics of the tutor*** *– Includes the tutor's prior experience, knowledge, skills and attitudes toward both the subject area and the art of teaching. It might also include challenges in course design and delivery.*
- ***Special challenges*** *– Includes specific requirements, accreditations, curriculum, and/or standards that are unique to the intervention, program or environment.*

If there are any concerns about the situational factors or there is a desire to identify them for a particular developmental intervention, use these three simple steps to identify any which may affect the delivery of the planned intervention.

1. ***For each factor consider your situation and note any implications which are important to the design of the intervention***
2. ***For factors that are identified as constraints:***
    a. *Note the resources necessary and how these can be accommodated into the design of the intervention.*
    b. *For those that need to be prioritised, create an action plan. This can be a simple statement such as, "I will assess a large number of learners with rubrics."*
3. ***As the course develops, refer back to the factors for which it is possible to design opportunities into the programme.***

Writing the Learning Objectives

When designing learning it is essential that the development activity is broken down into its constituent parts.
This will ensure that all aspects of the learning aim have been addressed and assessed.

- *The learning aim will identify the general subject to be covered by the session.*
- *The learning outcome will define the capability at the conclusion of the development activity*
- *The learning objective will specify the elements of learning which must take place and provide a metric to measure the outcome*

Like all objectives a learning objective should be SMART.

S - *They should be Specific to the element of learning they define*
M - *They should be Measurable*
A - *They should be Achievable*
R – *They should be Relevant to the subject*
T – *They should be introduced in a Timely manner*

Writing learning objectives is clearly rather more challenging than might be reasonably expected!

The learning outcomes will define what the learner must know at the end of the session, but this is an umbrella statement rather than a step by step specific.

The learning objective breaks the outcome down further into its elements.

A learning outcome may state that the learner will be able to "make a sandwich" at the end of the developmental session. The learning objective will break this down into its fundamental stages. These may include types of bread, types of spread, types of sandwich fillings and how the sandwich is to be presented.

It is immediately clear that without careful thought, important elements could be omitted, meaning the learner will still have areas of weakness at the end of the session.

By breaking down the learning outcome into SMART objectives it also highlights the volume or amount of learning which will take place during the session. It is very important to limit the number of objectives in each session to allow the learners time to fully understand the development they are being given. This also allows the order of the planned delivery of the objectives to be changed and reordered if the situation dictates (Timely). If learning objectives are met in the wrong order, it is unlikely that the development will be effective.

The use of learning objectives is also highly beneficial when ensuring that the learning aims and outcomes are fully met.

SMART Learning objectives also provide a metric for measuring whether or not the learning has taken place. Learning objectives typically begin with the words:

At the end of the session the learner will........................

This immediately provides the test (Measure) of whether the learner has gained the desired knowledge or skill. Looking back to the sandwich above, examples of learning objectives could include:

At the end of the session the learner will......

> *Identify different types of bread suitable for a sandwich.*
> *Name the common types of spread used when making sandwiches.*
> *List a variety of fillings suitable for use in a sandwich.*
> *Etc...*

It is now immediately clear that the assessment of whether the learner has fully understood the training can be easily tested.

> *Can they identify different types of bread?*
> *Can they name the common types of spread?*
> *Can they list a variety of fillings?*

It then becomes easy to design a method of assessment to check learning. The learner could be asked to write a list of bread types, identify the type of bread from samples or photographs, by selecting correct examples from a range etc.

The language used.

The way in which the objective is written is also important. It has already been established that each objective will be preceded by the words; "At the end of the session the learner will......", the words which follow this must be succinct and precise. They must define exactly what the leaner must be able to do (Specific). Do they need to know something, do something or behave in a prescribed manner? The way in which the learning objective is worded will significantly affect the way it might be interpreted by another person if it is not clearly defined.

The verbs used in learning objectives were initially defined in Blooms Taxonomy and have been further developed by Simpson who approached it from a psychomotor perspective, though detailed knowledge of these is not necessary here. An example of verbs which might be used in learning objectives for different activities are listed in the table below.

Knowledge	*Skills*	*Behaviour*
Compare	*Actuate*	*Advocate*
Define	*Adjust*	*Accept*
Describe	*Administer*	*Agree*
Designate	*Align*	*Allow*
Discover	*Alter*	*Analyse*
Distinguish	*Assemble*	*Approve*
Explain	*Build*	*Assess*
Identify	*Calibrate*	*Believe*
Itemise	*Change*	*Choose*
Label	*Copy*	*Collaborate*
List	*Demonstrate*	*Comply*
Name	*Design*	*Conform*
Recite	*Develop*	*Convince*
Recognise	*Draft*	*Cooperate*
Recount	*Execute*	*Decide to*
Relate	*Form*	*Defend*
Retell	*Handle*	*Endorse*
Specify	*Manipulate*	*Evaluate*
State	*Measure*	*Pick*
Tell	*Mend*	*Recommend*
Write	*Perform*	*Select*
	Prepare	*Support*
	Process	*Tolerate*
	Record	*Volunteer*
	Regulate	
	Remove	
	Repair	
	Replace	
	Set	
	Service	

Finalising the Development Planning

Once the Learning Aims, Learning Outcomes and the Learning Objectives have been defined for each element of the development activity, they can be assembled into a sequential format and presented in a format which can then be passed to the individuals who will be tasked with delivering the learning.

There is no “prescribed! format for this and is often limited by the word-processing skills of the person creating it!

A simple tabular layout of three columns is a simple way of dealing with this in a spreadsheet such as Excel.

Thinking about the sandwich again – below is an example of how a development activity might be planned to improve the quality and presentation of sandwiches.

As can be seen below, a relatively simple learning aim can result in at least three learning outcomes and an absolute minimum of nine learning objectives being necessary!

An additional fourth column could be used for the person defining the development or the tutor to add additional prompts to emphasise the specifics which must be covered and reinforced during the delivery.

The use of this level of planning means the person/s receiving the training can be tested against the learning objectives to check that learning has taken place and the organisation can use the learning outcomes as metrics for assessing whether the development activity has produced the desired results.

Learning Aim	*Learning Outcome*	*Learning Objective*	*Tutor notes*
To improve the quality and presentation of sandwiches	Effectively respond to customer needs	State the variety of breads available	*NB: Animal products in wholemeal bread*
		State the variety of fillings	*Identify vegan / vegetarian options*
		Know the nutritional content of each filling	*Identify those high in fat* *Identify those which contain allergens*
		Know the Vegetarian / Vegan status of each filling	*Identify all fillings which contain animal products*
	Improve the distribution of fillings	State the appropriate quantity to use of each filling	*50g for meat products* *60g for Fish products* *70g for vegetable-based fillings*
		State why it is important to ensure an even distribution of filling	*Filling should cover the bread in an even thickness*
	Present the finished item in an attractive way	Know the correct type of crockery to be used for each type of sandwich	*Round plates for rolls* *Square plates for cut sandwiches*
		Know the correct cut for each type of sandwich	*Quarter triangles for afternoon tea* *Half triangles for lunch*
		State the appropriate garnishes for each filling	*Lemon with fish* *Peas shoots with Meat*

Chapter 7: Planning the Delivery of Learning

Delivery of Learning

Learning Cycle

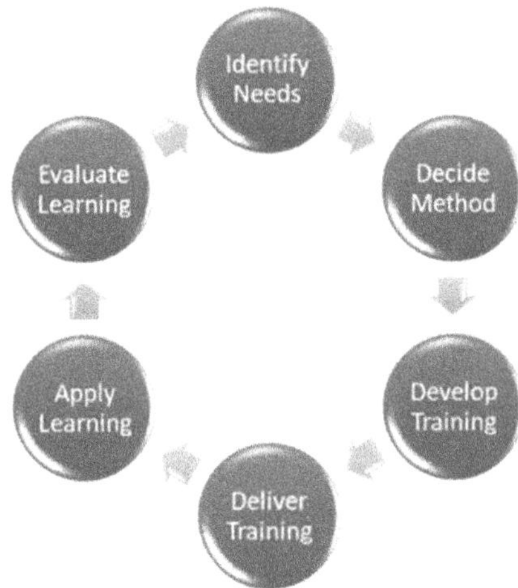

Think back to the Learning Cycle introduced earlier, the planning stage is the next step in the process, although the results of the planning stage will also be involved in the subsequent stages. It cannot be emphasised enough how important this stage in the learning cycle actually is.

Fail to plan – Plan to fail!

The first question which needs to be asked is are we planning learning or planning for learning?

Planning learning is a practice used many years ago when sessions were broken down into one- or two-hour blocks and the whole event was planned around time. If you were teaching learners about Einstein's Theory of Relativity, it could be trimmed and curtailed to fit into a two-hour session and every minute of the two hours would be meticulously timed and planned. If the session was reduced to one hour rather than two, further trimming and condensing of content would be applied until it conveniently fitted into what would probably be a dizzying, breathless sixty minutes. Fantastic – great job done by all and a big tick next to the Relativity theory on the scheme of work. Except that not one of the learners in either session has the faintest clue about what the entire session was about. The entire exercise was quite futile because "The plan" was designed around time slot and not the learners needs.

For many years, teachers, tutors and trainers were required to produced highly detailed session plans for all of the delivery they undertook. These documents took hours to produce and considered every aspect of the session from the capability of the learners to the detailed timing of every element, which had to be adhered to rigorously.

Thankfully, those days are now gone and OfSTED has decreed that individual lesson plans and historic plans are no longer a requirement in their inspections. This prompts the question – So, why are we reading this then?

There is very good reason for including this section. You would not set off on long journey with a map or a sat nav and likewise it is imprudent to even contemplate the delivery of learning without meticulous preparation and planning.

On a personal level, there is nothing worse than walking into a training room full of keen learners and experiencing a mind block. You struggle to remember your name, never mind what you were meant to be delivering! Believe me – it happens! Furthermore, without planning and preparation it is a realistic probability that you will omit a significant element of learning which disadvantages the learners and incurs additional cost when the problem has to be subsequently corrected at a later date.

A session plan is a tutors comfort blanket!

It doesn't matter how the information is recorded on a piece of paper or a flip chart or on a computer screen. It doesn't matter how it is laid out and it doesn't matter whether it is written in jargon, text speak or whatever else you may prefer. This is a document personal to the individual who will deliver the learning and will not be assessed or reviewed by anyone else.

What is important is that you have taken time to think about what you are going to do and you have recorded in a format which you can read, understand and use.

Training rooms are unpredictable places and a session plan can significantly help a tutor maintain a little more control when they find themselves succumbing to nerves.

The key here is to remember that you are Planning FOR Learning rather than simply planning learning. One small three letter word makes an enormous difference to what we do and how we do it.

Planning Delivery

The first decision which has to be made is how the learning is to be delivered.

There are commonly five methods used to deliver learning and these will be considered in turn.

Virtual Learning

Virtual learning has become commonplace since the pandemic in 2020. It allows learners and a tutor to meet online though Teams or Zoom meetings and whilst the participants may be scattered across the country – or even the World, it allows the active participation in the learning process by all.

Presentations can be delivered through PowerPoint or Nearpod and they can be split into breakout rooms to undertake a group activity before returning to the main room and sharing their ideas, thoughts and findings.

Given that participants can be spread across the globe and the number of participants which are visible at any one time is limited, it can be difficult to notice when learners start to become distracted. A good workaround is to introduce short activities such as tests, polls, quizzes, etc. all of which engage learners and keep them focussed on learning. All such activities should relate directly to the learning objectives which are being covered at the time.

Advantages
Familiarity – *Most learners are used to video conferencing so there should be few challenges in adapting*
Feedback – *Although the number of learners visible is limited, it is possible to see them and ask their opinions and ask for ideas and suggestions from them. Because this is a "live" interaction, you can also address any questions they may have immediately*
Community – *Because everyone is meeting at the same time in the same virtual space, it allows a sense of community to develop which encourages connection between participants*

Disadvantages
Technology – *Internet connections can be unstable and cameras and speakers can unexpectedly fail.*
Communication - *Although learners can see the tutor and others in the virtual room, the lack of proximity can result in the loss of context and nuance and the absence of non-verbal communication except facial expression can also increase this problem.*
Distractions – *Virtual learning tends to place from home rather than the workplace and if the tutor or learner does not have a dedicated office to work in, the session can be punctuated by family members, dogs barking, deliveries, calls from work and telephone interruptions, all of which can significantly affect the quality of the training.*

E-Learning

E-learning involves the use of digital devices which are loaded with software and apps to deliver the learning.

There are immediate cost savings with e-learning because a tutor is not needed to facilitate the learning. Initial costs of developing software solutions can be high and this is a common are where attempts are mad to reduce costs resulting in less than effective solutions which are poorly received by learners and fail to fulfil their purpose.

Well written and carefully developed software solutions can increase product knowledge and improve and develop soft skills.

E-learning solutions tend to comprise interactive quizzes, videos, screencasts, podcasts and e-books all based around a slide based presentation which learners can access and use on PCs, laptops, tablets and mobile phones.

Advantages
Accessibility – *Available to learners 24/7 and is especially useful for remote teams*
Self-paced – *The learner can decide how quickly they want to undertake the course and also the sequence could be at their discretion*
Tracking – *The software will capture data on learner progress, scores, duration, number of attempts and common errors which could indicate a need for remediation in the course itself*
Engagement – *Younger learners are skilled at interacting with digital platforms and simulations, characters, multimedia and virtual or augmented reality are all new tools in the toolbox to engage learners and make learning enjoyable for them*
Repetition – *the resources can be used repeatedly and can be developed incrementally to include new technology, subject matter, etc.*

Disadvantages
Technical – *Learners who are not IT literate may struggle with the technology*
Bespoke software – *The software used will need to be bespoke to the needs of the organisation and there will be a significant cost incurred as part of the initial development, however, this will be recovered over time*
Communication – *There is little if any contact between tutor and learner or between learners themselves*
Feedback – *Given the lack of direct communication, spontaneous feedback is limited to that provided by the software or app.*

Mobile Learning (m-learning)

Mobile learning utilises mobile, portable devices to deliver online learning. The content is digital, but is converted into HTML5 Format which is used in websites. This allows the learning material to automatically reformat to fit a variety of screen sizes and types. M-Learning is delivered in much smaller chunks than e-learning. It is designed to provide an on-demand format to learning so employees can quickly find the topic of interest and acquaint themselves with it spontaneously. These small courses can be downloaded to the mobile device and stored there to allow them to be used when there is no connection to the internet available and whilst on flights, trains, etc. This allows organisation to provide product updates, industry regulations, product features, company policies, etc at any time, any place.

Advantages
Convenience – *m-learning content is designed to be task oriented and delivered in chinks or bite sized portions.*
Engaging – *Given the capability for high interactivity, learners tend to regard this in much the same way as the regard social media. They can interact directly with the application itself.*
Evolution – *Smart phones and tablets are becoming an integral part of life and have an increasing life span. As a result m-learning has an excellent future and it is unlikely that investment made today will become obsolete in the near to medium future.*

Disadvantages
Distraction – *the fact that the mobile device is used for multiple tasks means that learners can become distracted by other activity on the mobile device*
Reliability – *The quality of the mobile device will directly affect the learning outcome. Cheap and inferior devices will not have adequate storage capacity and processor speeds may make using the software arduous*
Connection – *If the mobile device has limited storage, there will be far greater dependency on an internet connection. Where this is poor, access to the learning resources may be difficult if not impossible.*

Blended Learning

Blended learning combines training room learning with online learning. It allows learners to undertake online learning in their own time, at their own pace, but this is underpinned by face-to-face meetings for discussions, group activities, seminars, and mentoring session.

In many ways this offers the best of both learning worlds. Learners can work independently in a planned and regulated structure but tutors can take back control at key stages and milestones through the learning programme.

Blended learning is best suited to situations where learners can develop their own knowledge, but there is a need to retain some control. It is especially useful to help learners understand theory before being introduced to the application in practical situation.

Advantages
Cost effective – *allows costs to be managed by reducing delivery costs by using e-learning*
Flexibility – *allows the selective use of both e-learning and face to face to optimise learning*
Comprehensive – *addresses a number of different learning styles within one structure*

Disadvantages
Technology dependent – *requires a good IT infrastructure and good quality software solutions*
Stability – *The dependence on internet connectivity limits the stability of this as a solution until access to the internet improves*
Set up costs – *initial costs are high. Not only does the solution require a robust IT system, but also the cost of software design and development must be considered*

Face to Face Learning

Face to face learning is where it all began. From the first days in nursery school to the last days at high school or university, the face-to-face interaction between learner and tutor is the one in which everyone feels most comfortable.

Face to face learning has a huge role to play in any training programme. With new technology today, it no longer needs to be the only learning method in common use. Learning and Development departments now have the freedom to make best use of a number of delivery methods and can stylise these to meet the individual learning need, A welder can develop their knowledge of a new type of welding online, but there is no substitute for the face to face interaction and watching a demonstration by an expert, before putting all that new knowledge into practice.

Not only does the learner gain the hands on experience under expert supervision, but also the tutor has the opportunity to observe the learner perform the task and exercise judgement as to whether they have reached a level of competence or whether additional development is necessary.

Advantages
Direct – *ideal for a group of learners to undertake a specific development activity with a fixed time frame*
Interaction – *Learners can interact directly with the tutor and vice versa*
Perception – *The tutor is able to read the feeling amongst the group and manage motivation, engagement etc.*
Eye contact – *Eye contact is one of the strongest tools a tutor has to establish whether to learner has understood*

Role Modelling *– The tutor is able to model how task should be completed or model the behaviours expected.*

Disadvantages

Limited *– There are constraints on the number of people who can be taught and accommodated*

Consistency *– It is difficult for tutors to deliver the same course in the same way again and again*

Subjective *– The quality and content of training is dependent on the skills of the tutor*

Cost *– The operational costs of delivering face to face training is higher than other methods of delivery.*

Summary

	eLearning	*Face-to-face training*	*Virtual classrooms*	*Blended learning*	*m-Learning*
Driver	*Online courses and quizzes Video tutorials Dialogue simulations*	*In-person, instructor-led training in a physical setting*	*In-person, instructor-led training in a virtual space*	*Face-to-face sessions Online learning*	*Mobile learners Portable devices*
Main task	*Provide unified, consistent, replicable training across an organisation*	*Share hands-on experience and exchange ideas*	*Keep the lively nature of F2F training, but make it available to remote participants*	*Bridge the necessary instructor-led training and more scalable online learning*	*Make learning accessible anywhere and anytime, even on the go*
Main challenge	*Maintain engagement*	*Scale training*	*Hold attention and maintain engagement*	*Needs both technologies and instructors*	*Fight distractions caused by smartphones*
Facilities needed	*Authoring software Learning management system (LMS)*	*Dedicated training venue Printed materials Whiteboard Transport and accommodation for participants*	*Video Conferencing tools Virtual classroom software*	*Authoring software LMS Webinar platform Video conferencing tools Training venues*	*Smartphones or tablets*

Clearly the last methodology is the key one for practitioners who are developing learning for delivery to people within the organisation. The technology-based methods will require a markedly different skill set, including the ability to use software packages to produce the online learning packages. Virtual learning, however, is much the same as face to face at the planning stage.

Planning the Delivery of Learning

When planning for learning the process focusses on delivering the development needed by the learners in a way which is effective efficient and carefully considered. The learning must be centred on the needs of the learner and the organisation and every step op ensure success must be taken.

By planning learning rather than planning sessions, learning can take place at its natural pace. Somethings will be snapped up in a few minutes whilst other, seemingly straightforward elements, may take an hour or more. There is no point trying to move on until the objective is understood because all subsequent learning will not be adopted or understood.

Instead of planning a session, plan all of the learning which must be completed and then approach it step by step at the natural speed of the learners, the more they begin to learn, the faster the learning will take place and the more complex and challenging tasks which can be set will result in far greater engagement and motivation for learners.

Content of a Session Plan

The Session content will already have been defined in the curriculum or the scheme of work so the subject which is to be delivered is already known. The learning aim/s will have already been defined so these should be included at the top of the session plan. The learning outcomes which are required at the end of the session will also be defined and can be included onto the plan.

Depending on the organisation, the Learning objectives may or may not have been defined. If not, then planning starts here. The learning objectives must be written for every element of development needed.

Learning objectives must be SMART and should be listed in the order in which they will be covered. This now provides a route map for the entire session. A turn-by-turn guide how to negotiate the delivery of the learning aim.

Once the learning objectives have been defined and listed in order, the process of planning how each on should be met can begin.

This simple step by step process helps to focus your thoughts on how you will deliver the learning and will begin to give some ideas how the learning will be presented and the resources which may be needed.

The following considerations should always be made when beginning to plan learning:

Prior Learning

Prior learning includes a number of elements, not least your own thoughts and experiences from having delivered the same or similar session previously. Are there elements which learners find especially difficult or are there elements which require little input? It should also link to the development the learners have undertaken previously. It is important to remember that learning needs to be built element by element in much the same wall a wall is built with bricks. One by one, layer upon layer. It is important that new learning is linked and integrated to prior learning. Think about trying to teach a learner how to use Excel when they have little Maths knowledge and no prior experience of using a computer!

Having considered prior learning, you can use this at the start of the session to remind learners of previous knowledge and explain how the new session will link to the previous sessions.

Aim

The aim will define what will be learned in the session. There are a number of terms which are inexorably linked to this, but for now, it is important to define and explain the aim so learners are aware of what they will be covering during the session and also why they need to know it. This frames the session and provides clarity for all concerned.

Outcomes

The outcome will break down the session into relevant, realistic chunks of learning which will be delivered one after the other. It is important to keep these quite small to ensure learners are able to understand what is being presented to them and then link it to what they have learned previously as well as being able to begin to envision how it relates to the learning aim. Once again, this process helps the tutor to begin to plan the actual delivery, structuring ideas and concepts into a format which follows seamlessly from one outcome to the next.

Objectives

The objectives are the real focus of all learning delivery. There may be a number of objectives for each outcome and they must be delivered in the correct sequence with checks for comprehension being made along the way. These should be listed in delivery order. These are the learning steps along the route to meeting the Outcome and ultimately the Aim and each one must be addressed and measured.

Location

The detail of the session will also be influenced by the method of delivery and the location.

Delivering learning about the braking system on cars in a workshop would be an ideal location to deliver practical learning on fixing brakes, but it would be far from ideal for the delivery of the associated theory. It is often the case that a tutor has to make best use of facilities available to them.

Resources

Every session will need resources of some kind and arriving for a session without the planned resources not only causes acute embarrassment, but also reflects badly on the practitioner. The development of materials and resources are an implicit part of the planning process.

Depending on the subject, they may be as simple as a flip chart and pens or may include a variety of resources which may need to be procured ahead of the session. The use of flash cards, group activities, individual tasks, research activities, etc, require a great deal of thought and planning, but all make for a far more engaging learning experience than being bored to death by a never-ending PowerPoint show. The planned resources should be included in the plan to ensure they are all in place ahead of the session.

Planning the Session

Once the learning aims, outcomes and objectives have been identified and sequenced, it is time to actually begin to plan the delivery of the learning.

The questions which need to be asked will be similar if not the same for each objective:

- *What do they already know?*
- *Do they all know the same thing?*
- *What is the development need – Knowledge, Skill or Behaviour?*
- *Does it need to be contextualised?*
- *What key terminology or vocabulary does the learner need to understand?*
- *Are there any technical terms or specialist knowledge about which you need to be reminded?*
- *What delivery method will be best?*
- *What resources will be needed?*
- *Are there any learners who may need additional support?*
- *Are there learners who are very competent and will need additional work?*
- *How will learning be measured?*
- *How will the learners demonstrate their learning?*

It is the answers to these question which will begin to from the plan of how you will deliver the learning. Whether or not you intend to record the answers to these questions on the plan, they still need to be asked and answered.

Reflecting on the sandwiches considered in the previous section, the Aims, Outcomes and Objectives were placed into a tabular form which allowed specific content to be identified and added. This should not be confused with a session plan. An example of a session plan is shown below:

Session Plan				
Department:	Sandwich Production		*Plan:*	12324
Subject:	Product Quality:			
Session Rationale:	There has been a decline in customer satisfaction with the quality, content and presentation of sandwiches being provided for sale. This is further underpinned by the change in gross margin being achieved due to incorrect/excessive use of commodities and increased levels of wastage due to production errors.			
Learning Aim:	To improve the quality and presentation of sandwiches			
Learning Outcome:	Effectively respond to customer needs			
By the end of the session the learner will......				
Learning Objectives:	1	State the variety of breads available		
	Notes	*NB: Animal products in wholemeal bread*		
	2	State the variety of fillings		
	Notes	*Identify vegan / vegetarian options*		
	3	Know the nutritional content of each filling		
	Notes	*Identify those high in fat* *Identify those which contain allergens*		
	4	Know the Vegetarian / Vegan status of each filling		
	Notes	*Identify all fillings which contain animal products*		
	5			
	Notes			
Assessment:	Q&A using pictures to help with identification and also examples in the room			
Learning Outcome:	Improve the distribution of fillings			
By the end of the session the learner will......				
Learning Objectives	1	State the appropriate quantity to use of each filling		
	Notes	*50g for meat products* *60g for Fish products* *70g for vegetable based fillings*		
	2	State why it is important to ensure an even distribution of filling		
	Notes	*Filling should cover the bread in an even thickness*		
	3			
	Notes			
	4			
	Notes			
	5			
	Notes			
Assessment:	Short Test / Q&A / Discussion / Demonstration			

It should be further emphasised that the design, layout, structure and content of these documents should be defined by the need and situation. This is purely an exemplar for the purpose of this exercise.

Benefits of Planning

Effective planning contributes to the successful achievement of learning outcomes for learners in several ways. A well-designed lesson plan:

- *Helps learners and tutors understand the goals of a developmental activity*
- *Allows the tutor to translate the development need into learning activities*
- *Aligns the delivery content and materials with the assessment need*
- *Aligns the assessment with the learning objectives, outcomes and aims*
- *Helps ensure that any necessary resource and materials are available*
- *Enables the tutor to consciously address the individual learning needs of the learners*

Effective session planning can also contribute to the tutor's own success and well-being. Tutors teach because they want to support learners, and effective session planning can contribute to job satisfaction when a session is successful or a learner does well on an assessment. Having a carefully-planned session can also make teaching more pleasurable because it increases tutor confidence and allows them focus more on interaction with the learners rather than dwelling on what is supposed to happen next.

Good planning can save time by avoiding last-minute efforts to buy supplies or create materials needed for a day in the training room. Tutors can use that reclaimed time for themselves or other parts of their lives, increasing work-life balance.

Blooms Taxonomy

It is all well and good to have planned a development session but at this point the needs of the organisation have been considered in detail and the developmental needs of the learners have been identified, however, no consideration has been given to the learners themselves.

A group of three or more learners will have diverse backgrounds, differing levels of knowledge and understanding to say nothing of experience and desire to develop.

It is always prudent to always check what learners already know and therefore establish what they need to develop.

Benjamin Bloom, an educational psychologist presented his Model of Learning in 1956, It was revised in 2001 and remains a seminal model of how learning works and how it can be improved.

Bloom defined three models which explore three different aspect of learning. He called these the three domains.

- ***Cognitive*** – *knowledge-based learning*
- ***Affective*** – *emotional learning which considers feeling and attitudes*
- ***Sensory*** – *physical learning – moving, sensing, manipulating*

All three domains are necessary for development, however, it is the Cognitive domain which is of greater importance and is widely referred to as Blooms Taxonomy.

Bloom originally defined 12 types of knowledge but the revision in 2001 reduced this to four types. These are:

- ***Factual*** – *information which provides the building blocks for learning.*
- ***Conceptual*** – *includes categories, structures and theories*
- ***Procedural*** – *how to use specific techniques and methods*
- ***Metacognitive*** – *strategy decisions, self – knowledge and "thinking about thinking"*

Bloom argues that people will start at the lowest level and progress through each level. This means that the higher levels are unachievable unless the lower level are achieved first.

What Bloom is suggesting is that all learners will have achieved a level of knowledge in a subject and that level of knowledge will fall into one of these domains

> A child has knowledge of a car – they may know it has two doors or four, that it has four wheels and a bonnet and a boot. This type of knowledge is in the Factual Domain
>
> A teenager will know that the size of the engine is important in a car. That it may be two- or four-wheel drive and that there is a range of safety features which may or may not be fitted to the vehicle. This knowledge in in the Conceptual Domain.
>
> A young adult will learn how to drive the vehicle safely and will begin to test the performance of the vehicle. Its top speed, its handling and stopping capabilities. This knowledge is in the Procedural Domain.
>
> An adult with years of driving experience behind them will be able to envisage the difference between driving a normal family saloon car compared to a very high-powered sports car, even though they may never have driven a super car. They are able to envision the experience and consider whether they would find it desirable or not.. This knowledge is in the Metacognitive Domain.

It is clearly impossible for anyone to jump from the Factual Domain to the Metacognitive Domain unless they have progressed through the conceptual and procedural domains first.

Bloom also defined six levels of learning. This is known as Blooms Taxonomy Verbs. This was also changed slight with the revision in 2001. The verbs used originally have been changed slight to reflect what learners must do to attain that level and the last two have been switched over. These are presented as a pyramid, the lower levels being wider than those above, because more people remain at the lower levels of knowledge.

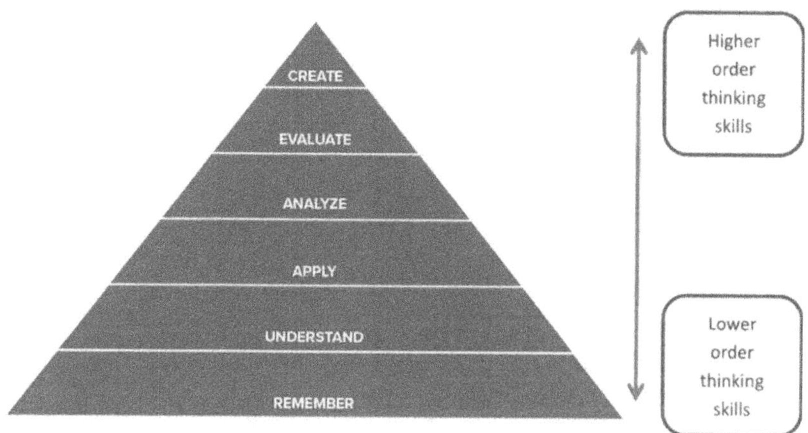

The levels are defined as follows:

- ***Remember*** – *Learning at its most basic, although the information may be complex. People will know key terminology for a subject and know relevant facts, statistics and theories developed by others.*
- ***Understand*** – *The individual knows what the information actually means. They can organise, compare and interpret the information.*
- ***Apply*** - *The knowledge which is held and has been interpreted is now used to solve more complex problems.*
- ***Analyse*** - *Breaking information down into its constituents part to analyse the individually to establish the relationship with each other.*
- ***Evaluate*** -*The learner may a judgement on what they have discovered so far which allows them to make recommendation and suggest innovative solutions.*
- ***Create*** - *The learner is able to reorganise the information they have, or combine it with information from other sources, to create new possibilities*

Learners who know about a subject and understand what that knowledge means, would be at the Understand Level. They can only improve their knowledge and understanding by beginning to apply their knowledge and understanding, at which point they will have reached the Apply Level.

As a tutor any attempt to develop others will fail if the starting point is not identified before the development begins. Learners cannot begin to understand something unless they have a basic knowledge of the subject first. Similarly a learner who has reached the Apply level will continue to be able to effectively apply their knowledge and understanding to a problem, but will not develop until they stop to look and analyse the results of what they have applied . It is only when they have done this that they will move up to the next level.

If delivering new types of knowledge it needs to be done gently and with high levels of support. Where there is existing knowledge, the process can be a little quicker and with greater complexity. This type of analysis is also beneficial in deciding how far to go in each session and the degree of challenge which the learning and the resources will demand. Asking someone to apply something before they have the fundamental knowledge is clearly doomed to fail. Establishing these levels will ensure that the content and quality of both materials and assessment will be appropriate to the needs of the learner and the level of learning assessment which will be desired.

Level	*Learners can...*	*Examples for making an omelette in a cookery session*
Creating	Use elements to form an original product.	*Construct a new recipe influenced by the ingredients of a specified country.*
Evaluating	Make judgments based on criteria.	*Argue for how a recipe might be improved.*
Analysing	Determine parts, their purpose and their relation to each other and the whole.	*Compare two different omelette recipes and predict how they will turn out.*
Applying	Carry out a procedure in a given situation.	*Demonstrate how to cook an omelette.*
Understanding	Determine meaning.	*Describe how each ingredient contributes to an omelette.*
Remembering	Retrieve knowledge.	*Remember ingredients for French Omelette.*

Active Learning

Active learning is a process which is learner centric. Active learning focusses not just on what they learn, but how they learn. Learners are encouraged to "think hard", rather than simply sit back and passively receive information from a tutor.

Learners cannot be taught by simply telling then what they need to know

Tutors must challenge learners thinking. Active learning creates opportunities for the learner to learn.

Active learning is based on the theory of constructivism in which learners construct or build their own knowledge and understanding. Using their existing knowledge, learners build on this with the new knowledge they receive and as a result they develop a greater and deeper understanding of the subject.

Blooms taxonomy defines the higher order skills such as analyse, synthesise and evaluation. These are ethe deeper levels of understanding which can be achieved by providing opportunity, interactions, tasks and instruction that creates these.

Active Learning encourages learners to become life-long learners. Because they take responsibility for their own learning they continue to develop and build on their founding knowledge.

Active learning also encourages success. Once learners realise they can use their knowledge to process and synthesise solutions to other problems, learning becomes easier and they are able to achieve far more. As a result, active learning is often referred to as being engaging and intellectually exciting – not a term commonly used for learning and development activities! The reason being that learners find it enjoyable, rewarding and learners remain focussed on their learning for longer.

Planning Process

What is being developed?

The next consideration is to establish what is being delivered. Is it Knowledge, a Skill or a Behaviour? Each will require a distinct method of approach. Knowledge will need to be taught, Skills will need to be developed and Behaviours will need to be conditioned.

> *Knowledge will need to be taught in a training room environment which is supported by resources such as projectors, screens, flip charts, whiteboards, etc. The availability of these resources will also directly influence how the session will be planned and delivered. The absence of a projector may prevent the use of a PowerPoint presentation, the absence of flip chart may limit the opportunities for group participation.*

Skills development will require a practical element in the delivery which allows the learner to practice what they have been taught or shown. A learner who is developing their welding skills will need to develop their knowledge of the theory behind welding but will be unable to practice welding as a skill until it has been demonstrated to them and they have the opportunity for hands on practice themselves. Access to live equipment, materials and other resources will be necessary in order to develop skills

Behaviours may also require a practical element; however, it may be possible to simulate this outside a live working environment. Conditioning behaviours is about identifying not only the good parts of a certain behaviour, but also identifying the negative elements and eradicating them. This can often be done using simulation. A simulated scenario can be created in a training room and the learners allowed to practice a particular element of behaviour and identify the positive and negative elements on display.

By identifying exactly what is being developed, the tutor can identify the best environment for the session and also plan and obtain the necessary resources and develop materials accordingly.

Deciding the method of delivery

Having identified what is being taught, the method of delivery will become much clearer. Knowledge can be developed as easily through a video meeting as in a face-to-face classroom session. The learner can be given research tasks to undertake to further develop their knowledge outside of the training room too. Skills development requires practice and, in many instances, that practice cannot be achieved through a classroom session, it requires a practical environment with tools materials and resource with which to work and develop those skills. Practical demonstration by the tutor is the first step or observing an expert whilst the tutor provides a commentary on the key elements the learner should identify. That does not mean that handouts, pictures, posters and PowerPoint presentations will not be required. These can be invaluable support tools to allow learners to practice and experiment independently. The use of video can help a learner move through a process step by step independently of the tutor who may be providing support to another learner.

The development of behaviours can usually be successfully developed in training room in some instances, in some instances it may be more appropriate to use a simulated realistic working environment, however, this is no substitute for a real live working environment. Depending on the behaviour being developed, live practice of behaviours is by far the most effective, however, the discreet observation of other's behaviour can be almost as effective. Care needs to be taken to ensure that the learner is not likely to become self-conscious in a live environment as this can result in the loss of all confidence which can be far more difficult to remediate.

Identifying resources needed for delivery

Having decided on the method of delivery, the resources which will be needed must then be identified. Very often, in a corporate environment, these resources will need to be pre-booked to ensure that the IT department, stores, or the administrators of workshops, etc. can make the necessary arrangements for the resources to be made available. When these cannot be made available, the tutor must decide whether they can proceed with the session as planned, change the method of delivery or deliver an alternative activity until the resources are available.

How much is being delivered?

There are many constraints of development activity, but one of the most important is time. Every development activity is constrained by time in some way. As a result, there is an inclination to deliver as much learning in one session as possible to cover the leaning outcomes as quickly as possible and reduce the high costs of providing the learning. Unfortunately, this actually has the opposite effect on the learning which takes place. Cognitivism looks at how we learn and embedded in that theory is the constraint that the human brain can only deal with a certain amount of information in one session. Once that limit is reached, all further information which is provided will not be absorbed and will not be retained in long term memory.
The ability of the brain to absorb and retain information through experience, senses, and thought is known as cognition.

Cognitive learning is an active style of learning that focuses on striving to maximise the brain's true potential. It makes it easier to connect new information with existing knowledge, thereby deepening memory and retention capacity.

Cognitive Load Theory is based upon the Information Processing Model proposed by Richard Atkinson and Richard Shiffrin in 1968.

It models the process as having three main parts:

- *sensory memory*
- *working memory*
- *long-term memory.*

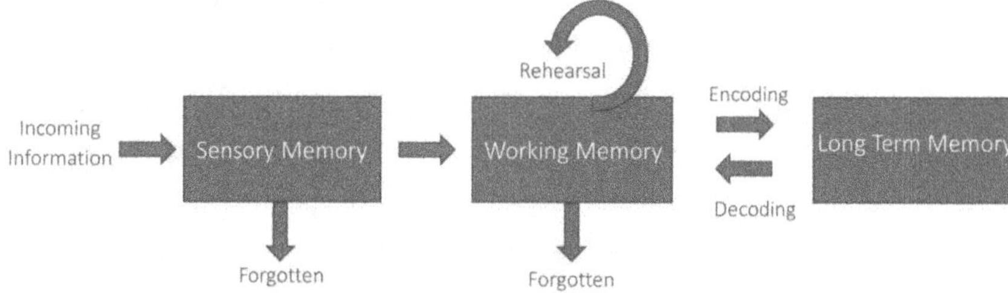

Every day, we are continuously bombarded with sensory information. Filters will remove most of this information, but they allow an impression of the most important items to remain for long enough for them to pass into working memory.

> *When travelling on a train, sensory memory discards information about people in other seats, general conversation and the smells we commonly experience and focus on the book being read or the movie being watched.*

The filtered information gathered in the sensory memory then passes into the working memory, where it is either processed or discarded.

The Working memory, typically, can hold between five and nine items (or pieces) of information at any one time.

This is central to Cognitive Load Theory

As the brain processes information, it classifies that information and moves it into long-term memory, where it is stored in knowledge structures called "schemas." These schemas organise information according to how it is used in much the same way we might organise a filing cabinet. It will create schemas for different themes such as car, bike, bus, vehicle, transport, etc.

During learning, information must be held in working memory until it has been processed sufficiently to pass into your long-term memory.

The brain will also form schemas for behaviours too. Actions such as sawing wood, slicing meat, throwing snowballs will be categorised into schemas. The more these behaviours or actions are practised, so they become more effortless to perform – we become highly skilled in completing these actions and the behaviour becomes and automated response.

Cognitive Load Theory was developed from the work of Atkinson and Shiffrin by John Sweller in 1988.

"Cognitive load" is the term used to quantify the amount of information that working memory can hold at one time.

The working memory's capacity is very limited.

Sweller postulated that, given working memory has a limited capacity, the teaching method used should avoid overloading it with all additional activities that don't directly contribute to learning.

A labelled diagram will place a lesser demand on working memory than a diagram which has the labels listed to one side.

Look again at the diagram above when it is presented with the labels below it.

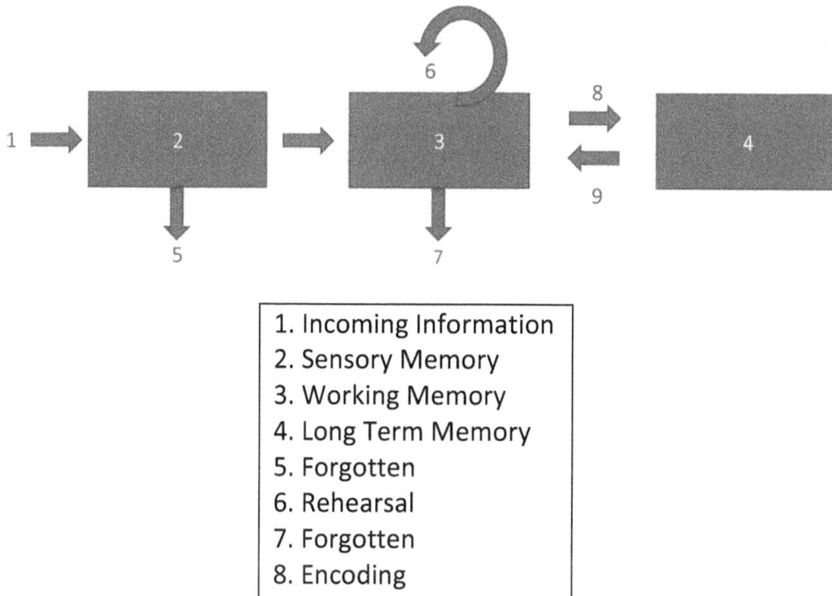

Cognitive Load Theory also shows that working memory can be extended in two ways.

The brain processes visual and auditory information separately.

Auditory items in working memory do not compete with visual items in the same way that two visual items, a picture and some text, compete with one another. This is known as the "Modality Effect."

Explanations of detail have less impact on working memory if it is narrated, rather than being added in a table to an already complex diagram.

Secondly, working memory treats an existing schema as a single item, and a much practiced schema, the use of which has become "automated",. barely counts at all. As a result, learning activities that draw upon existing knowledge effectively expand the capacity of your working memory.

This suggests that providing basic knowledge to gain understanding before introducing more complex elements will help to establish schemas which will extend working memory; allowing more difficult information and concepts to be understood and learned.

When too much information is presented at once, the working memory becomes overwhelmed and much of that information is lost.

Clearly, it is vitally important not to overload learners with too much information in one session. It is also important to try to link the new learning to pre-existing knowledge and allow understanding to develop naturally.

As a guide, try not to address more than 5 or 6 learning objectives in one block, without there being time for a break and a period of consolidation which could include a test, a discussion, a Q&A discussion, practice, watching a video, etc. It is this changing method of presentation and delivery which helps with the embedding of new information with existing knowledge which makes learning more effective and significantly improves recall.

Creating the materials needed for delivery

The materials used in delivery are separate to the resources. Resources might include flip charts, projectors, etc. Whilst materials are the things needed to practically support the learner. These could include PowerPoint presentations, handouts, videos, pictures, pieces of equipment, tools or samples.

The quality and content of these materials will have a direct influence on the learners engagement and retention of information.

The production of material requires the same level of planning as the session itself.

The fundamental expectation is that the spelling and grammar will all be correct, that the items are appropriately branded in line with the organisations expectations, that there is no copyright infringement and any personal information relating to any person living or dead are erased or redacted. Beside this basic expectation, the content must also be very carefully planned and considered.

It is important to ensure there is variety in the resources. A pile of handouts might cover many of the learning aims, but will they be read? Will they ever make it into a file – more likely, they will end up in a bin on the way out of the building.

Try to make the materials engaging and be selective in the materials you select. Avoid the temptation to recycle previously used materials. Always check that the content is still current and directly relevant to the learning outcome for which it is chosen.

Good materials might include:

- ***Case Studies*** *- as the basis for group discussion*
- ***Job aids*** *– a pocket guide designed to be used as a point of reference*
- *Handouts*
- *Video clips*
- *E-books*
- *Voting apps*
- *Video games*

- *PowerPoint Presentations*
- *Games and Quizzes*
- *Pictures*
- *Templates*

It cannot be reiterated enough that any materials must be specific to the learning objective and/or aim, anything which is not relevant to the this is a distraction which may limit the learning as a result.

Applying Cognitive Load Theory

Cognitive Load Theory helps in the design of training and learning materials which reduce the demands on learner's working memory, meaning they learn more effectively.

The concept of cognitive load can be applied in several ways.

1. Measure Expertise and Adapt Presentation Accordingly

The greater the level of expertise held in a particular area, the greater the amount of information available in the relevant schemas.

It doesn't matter how complex a schema is – it counts as a single item in working memory.

The level of learning being delivered should reflect the level of expertise of the learners being taught.

A simple question and answer session with the learners will help to establish how familiar they are with the topic.
Once this the level has been established, it will help to ensure that the information being presented is at the right level for the learners – what seems obvious to you may not be at all obvious to them!

2. Reduce the Learning Gap

The Learning Gap is the gap between the current level of knowledge and the desired level. If this gap is too broad, the learner's working memory will become overloaded.

This is common with complex problems, which require the learner to work backwards from the goal to the present state. Doing this means they will have to hold a great of information in their working memory. Focusing on the goal also distracts attention away from the information being learned, making learning less effective.

It is better to break the problem down into smaller parts. This reduces the learning gap, lightens the cognitive load and therefore makes learning more effective.

Other ways to reduce the Learning Gap include providing exemplars and partially completed tasks for the learner to complete. These approaches are particularly useful because they demonstrate strong problem-solving strategies in practice.

3. Reduce Divided-Attention Effect

Multiple sources of visual information, such as diagrams, labels and explanatory text, causes attention to be divided between them. This further adds to the cognitive load, making it more difficult for the brain to create new schemas.

This effect is reduced when you integrate visual information.

Labels can be incorporated into diagrams as discussed above. When this is not possible, allow the learners to focus on one element before moving on to the second before assimilating the two together.

The same effect also applies to multiple sources of auditory information. Think how hard it can be to concentrate on a conversation if there is a TV on and music playing all at the same time. When speaking to learners on a specific topic, remove any extraneous sources of noise, such as other people talking or music playing in the background.

4. Combine Auditory and Visual Channels in Working Memory

It is possible to reduce the cognitive load by replacing some of the visual information with auditory information and vice-versa. This reduces the cognitive load on people's working memory by also using both memory spaces at the same time.

In a study it was shown that students were found to learn most effectively when they were shown an animation that was accompanied by narration, rather than using the animation with added on-screen text.
This can be easily replicated by directing learner’s attention to parts of a diagram while talking about it.

Planning for Assessment

There are two types of assessment which are commonly used. The first is formative assessment.

Formative assessment is the assessment which takes place at each stage in the session. This could be the assessment of each learning objective to ensure learning has taken place, or it could be the assessment of the learning outcome for that part of the session. The decision as to how to assess and what to assess will depend on the learning content. Simple knowledge can be tested with a quiz or Q&A whilst more complex issues will inevitably require more complex assessment methods.

The second type of assessment is summative assessment. This is the assessment which takes place at the end of a development activity and measures learning across all learning objectives. This type of assessment may come at the end of a session, at the end of a programme or on completion of module or unit of study.

> ***"When the chef tastes the soup, that's formative. When the guests taste the soup, that's summative."*** *Robert E. Stake*

As discussed early the planning for assessment begins at the outset of planning. When learning aims are being defined, the learning outcomes and learning objectives provide the metrics for measuring the success of the development when it is complete.

A well-planned session will therefore already have the metrics for assessing learning defined in the session plan, the only decision which needs to be made is how the development will be measured. This decision will be addressed later in the book.

Planning for Learning Summary

1. Profile your target audience

What educational background, work commitments and resoures do they have? How many students are in the group?

2. Write your learning outcomes

What do you want learners to know and be able to do by the end of the lesson or module?

3. Content and activities

What features can you include to make the activity engaging, in alignment with the learning outcomes? What resources do you need? Provide a short description and timing for each activity.

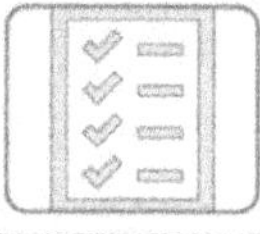

4. Design formative assessment tasks

What types of assessments can you inlcude that are linked to the outcomes, and emphasise students' learning needs?

5. Summary

What are your key 2-3 take home messages?

Chapter 8: Delivering Learning

Delivering Learning

Having identified the development needed and carefully planned the content, the time comes to actually deliver the learning.

Learning delivery is the actual process of communicating knowledge, skills or behaviours to the learner.

Tutors should always ensure they allow sufficient time before the arrival of the learners and the start of the session, to prepare both themselves and the room.

Preparation

Depending on the nature of the delivery method, the pre delivery checks will vary. Technology can usually be relied upon to be troublesome, so a check of all technology which will be used should be completed before delivery begins. Ensure any WiFi passwords have been obtained and access is available. Make sure that any PowerPoint presentations are loaded and working. Check that the audio systems are working for any video or sound resources which may be planned and that the volume is appropriate.

Where the development will take place face to face, there should be a thorough check of the room to check for any Health and Safety hazards such a trip hazards from trailing wires, slip hazards from wet floor or leaking pipes, damaged furniture, etc. It may be that the furniture in the room may need rearranging to allow group work or maybe a lecture style might be more appropriate. Walk around the room and check that learners will be able to see the screen, flip chart, whiteboard, etc form all positions. Make sure there is nothing in the room which may distract learners from participating. Ensure that the room is accessible to all and make sure there is easy access to toilets.

Checks should be made as to the escape routes from the building in the event of an evacuation being required and learners should be informed of this at the start of the session. A check should also be made as to whether there is a planned Fire alarm test or practice due to be conducted that day.

The environment should also be considered. Is the area too hot or cold? Is there bright sunshine streaming into the room which may be distracting or make seeing screens, and whiteboards difficult. Are there any distracting noises or unpleasant smells? All of these issues can cause a distraction for learners and affect the learning which is planned to take place.

Having ensured the safety and wellbeing of learners, it is time to check and organise resources or materials, before the learners arrive. There is nothing worse than having to shuffle through paperwork trying to find materials in front of a group of learners!

For virtual training sessions – the required etiquette for online sessions should be issued to all participants ahead of the session, to ensure they are fully aware of the expectations placed upon them in terms of dress code, appearance, behaviour, cameras on mics off, etc. By setting thee expectations ahead of the session, there are less likely to be issues once the session begins.

Starting the session

On arrival, the candidates should be welcomed and directed towards any refreshments or invited to take a seat. Try to have a conversation with each learner, however brief, which will help break the ice and make everyone feel more comfortable and engaged.

The opening of the session should be to cover the domestic issues. Welcome the learners collectively and explain the plan in the event of a fire evacuation, the location of fire exits, extinguishers, etc. Provide directions to the bathrooms and rest areas. Detail when coffee breaks will be and the time and duration of a meal break if applicable. Always ask if anyone has any questions or queries about these arrangements.

The "Rules of the Room" should then be addressed, tell the learners to turn off mobile phones (not silenced), turn off computers or tablets and make it very clear that bullying, harassment and discriminatory or derogatory comments will not be tolerated under any circumstances. Some organisations will address this through a Learner Charter to avoid the need for this to be repeated at each session, which they are asked to read and sign at induction.

In order to ensure all learners feel comfortable in expressing their thoughts and views, it is important to emphasise that Chatham House rules apply, where appropriate, in the training room. State that anything which is said by a participant in the room must never be repeated outside of the room. This does not legitimise unacceptable language or the inappropriate expression of personal views, but does allow participants to speak freely about their own experiences in life, a workplace or behaviours they have encountered, without fear of this becoming public knowledge or shared with other parties.

If this is the first in a series of sessions and/or when learners do not know each other, plan an introduction activity which will allow them to get to know the rest of the group. There are numerous activities which can be used to facilitate this, the objective being to encourage all learners to speak and interact with the rest of the group, as well as providing the tutor with an opportunity to get to know the learners a little better and gain an insight into their role and background.

Introducing the Learning

When introducing the session, it is important to link the session to what has been developed before. Linking the current session to what was learned on a previous session will help the learners to contextualise the new learning and enable the learner to understand the relevance of the new learning to them and their role.

It is also important to explain to the learners why the new learning is important them and why they need to learn it. If learners cannot see the relevance to them and their role, they are far less likely to engage with the learning and the planned development will not be achieved.

The session plan which has been prepared will detail the planned learning aims, outcomes and objectives for the session. These should be explained to the learners and often this can be presented by adding them to the opening slide of the presentation. This will prompt discussion which helps with the justification for the learning.

Having shown them the "menu" it is not time to whet their appetite! Try to grab their attention by showing a video clip or telling an anecdote which engages them. Try to shock or surprise them or move them emotionally – this will capture their attention and they will listen far more intently to what they are being told.

Delivering the Learning

It is now time to return to the session plan and pick up the first learning outcome and its associated objectives. Whilst it is unnecessary to set exacting time limits on the delivery of each element of the learning, it is a good idea to have in mind how much of the planned learning will take place in the first session up to the coffee break and what will be addressed after coffee and before lunch, etc. This will allow the learning to be delivered in a measured and controlled manner.

Every learner loves it when a session finishes earlier than planned, but none enjoy a session which extends beyond the planned end time.

When a session is running late, learners will be distracted thinking about rush hour traffic, collecting children, etc with the result that learning will simply not take place.

It is important to try and maintain a consistent rhythm and pace to the delivery, avoiding digression and keeping on track throughout. The session plan is structured in such a way that it guides the tutor from topic to topic in a coherent and logical manner. Irrelevant anecdotes may provide a little humour into what could be a dull session, but are they learning the joke or the subject in hand?

The whole purpose of the session plan is to structure and guide learning

A good way of managing time during delivery is to add time for discussion and reflection at the end of the session which can then be cut or extended as necessary to remain within timings.

Mehrabian contended that only 7% of communication is achieved using words the rest is through the tone of voice and body language. This, however, was only in defined contexts. It is more realistic to say that approximately 35% of communication is through the words used in general conversation meaning that around 65% of communication is through tone of voice and body language, including expressions and gestures. With this in mind, it is vital that the tutor conveys their own enthusiasm for the subject matter. By doing this the learners will connect on a personal level and are much more likely to remember what has been discussed. Anecdotal support can also help with developing this connection at a personal level providing it is relevant to the subject.

Checking for Learning

It is vital that checks are made throughout the session to ensure that learning is taking place. Tutors should use questioning to explore the understanding of learners. Being selective in who is asked can also be a very effective tool for managing engagement. If a learner appears distracted or is apparently not listening, ask them a question. This brings their attention back to the subject. Don't allow them to be embarrassed by being unable to answer the question, if they are unsure of the answer because they have not been listening, help them out or ask others to help them. The result will be the learning check will be completed, but the person questioned is now much more likely to concentrate and focus to avoid being put in that situation again.

It is important that the tutor is also constantly monitoring facial expression and the body language of learners to establish whether the learner is engaged and the new learning is being understood. Maintaining eye contact with learners is another tool which can be used. If a learner is not making eye contact, it is likely that learning is not taking place.

Effective Questioning

Asking effective questions is productive, positive, creative, and can provide what we require!

Most people accept this and yet they still don't ask enough good questions. One of the reasons for this, is that effective questioning requires it be combined with effective listening.

Effective questions help you:

- *Connect with your team in a more meaningful way*
- *Better and more fully understand your team's problem*
- *Have employees experience you as an understanding, competent manager*
- *Work with your staff more effectively*
- *Help your staff take responsibility for their actions and solve problems within the workplace more easily*
- *Cross examine more effectively*
- *Gather better information*
- *Do more solution-oriented problem solving*

- *Improve your negotiating skills*
- *Reduce mistakes*
- *Take the sting out of feedback*
- *Defuse volatile situations*
- *Get cooperation*
- *Plant your own ideas*
- *Persuade people*

Effective Questions

Effective questions are questions that are powerful and thought provoking. Effective questions are open-ended and not leading questions. They are not "why" questions, but rather "what" or "how" questions.

"Why" questions are good for obtaining information, but can make people defensive so be thoughtful in the use of them. When asking effective questions, wait for the answer and not pre-empt or provide the answer.

When working with people to solve a problem, it is not enough to tell them what the problem is. They need to find out or understand it for themselves. You help them do this by asking them thought provoking questions. Rather than make assumptions find out what the person you are talking to knows about the problem.

Example:

"What do you think the problem is?"

Effective questioning also includes the ability to listen to the answer and suspend judgment. This means being intent on understanding what the person who is talking is really saying. What is behind their words? Let go of your opinions so that they do not block you from learning more information. Pay attention to your gut for additional information.

Powerful Questions

The following are examples of typical questions. These questions can help you improve your communication and understanding of the client or staff member.

Identification of issue:

These questions can be used in staff interviews and meetings, settlement negotiations and to work with others in solving problems.

What seems to be the trouble?
What do you make of_________?

How do you feel about _____________?
What concerns you the most about _____________?
What seems to be the problem?
What seems to be your main obstacle?
What is holding you back from _________________?
What do you think about doing X this way?

Further information:

These questions can be used to find out what someone has already done to resolve a work problem.

What do you mean by __________?
Tell me more about _______________
What else?
What other ways did you try so far?
What will you have to do to get the job done?

Outcomes:

These questions can be used in settlement negotiations or while working with staff to plan how to do something.

How do you want ____________ to turn out?
What do you want?
What is your desired outcome?
What benefits would you like to get out of X?
What do you propose?
What is your plan?
If you do this, how will it affect ________?
What else do you need to consider?

Taking Action:

These questions can be used in working with staff.

What will you do? When will you do it?
How will I know you did it?
What are your next steps?

Listening as Part of Effective Questioning

When staff are listened to, they feel understood and are more trusting of you. Effective listening is a skill that requires nurturing and needs development. Since managers are "smart", the temptation is to get by with listening at a minimal level. To connect with your staff and have them experience you as an effective manager requires you to maintain superior listening skills along with asking effective questions.

Consider the following different levels of listening:

Level 1 Listening:
When we are listening at level 1 our focus or attention is on how the words the other person is saying affect ourselves with minimal concern for the person talking. We listen for the words of the other person to see how they affect us. The attention is on me - what are my thoughts, judgments, issues, conclusions and feelings. There is no room to let in the feelings of the person being "listened" to. When listening at level 1 our opinions and judgments arise. Level 1 listening is appropriate when you are gathering information for yourself like getting directions or ordering in a restaurant or a store.

Level 2 Listening:
When we listen at level 2, there is a deeper focus on the person being listened to. This often means not even being aware of the context. Our awareness is totally on the other person. We notice what they say as well as how they say it and what they do not say. We listen for what they value and what is important to them. We listen for what gives them energy or sadness or resignation. We let go of judgment. We are no longer planning what we are going to say next. We respond to what we actually hear.

Level 3 Listening:
When we listen more deeply than the two levels described above, in addition to the conversation we take in all information that surrounds the conversation. We are aware of the context and the impact of the context on all parties. We include all our senses, in particular our intuition. We consider what is not being said and we notice the energy in the room and in the person we are listening to. We use that information to ask more effective questions.

Listening Skills as part of Effective Questioning include:

Articulating
Attention and awareness result in articulation and succinctly describing what we have learned from the employee. Sharing our observation clearly but without judgment does this. We can repeat back to our employee just what they said. We can expand on this by articulating back to them what we believe they mean. This helps a person feel heard. For example: "What I hear you saying is . . ."

Clarifying

Clarifying is a combination of asking and clearly repeating our understanding of what we have heard. By asking questions the employee knows we are listening and filling in the gaps. When the employee is being vague, it is important for us to clarify the circumstances. We can assist them to see what they cannot see themselves by making a suggestion. For example: "Here's what I hear you saying. Is that right? "

Being Curious

Do not assume you know the answer or what the employee is going to tell you. Wait and be curious about what brings them to see you. What motivates them? What is really behind the meeting? Use your curiosity so that your next question can go deeper.

Silence

Giving the person we are listening to time to answer questions is an important aspect of listening. Waiting for the employee to talk rather than talking for them is imperative for an effective listener.

Types of Question

There are countless reasons for asking questions, however, the information we receive back (the answer) is dependent upon the type of question we ask.

At a basic level questions, can either be open or closed - this section also details many other question types and when it could be appropriate to use them, to improve understanding.

Closed Questions

Closed questions invite a concise, focused, answer- the answers to closed questions are often (but not always) either right or wrong. Closed questions are typically easy to answer. they can be used effectively early in a conversation to encourage participation and can be very useful in fact-finding scenarios such as research.

Closed questions are used to force a brief, often one-word answer.

- ***Closed questions can simply require a 'Yes' or 'No' answer,*** *for example: 'Do you smoke?', 'Did you feed the cat?', 'Would you like a cup of tea?'*
- ***Closed questions can require that a choice be made from a list of possible options,*** *for example: 'Would you like beef, chicken or the vegetarian option?', 'Did you travel by train or car today?'*
- ***Closed questions can be asked to identify a certain piece of information, again with a limited set of answers,*** *for example: 'What is your name?', 'What time does the supermarket open?', 'Where did you go to University?'*

Open Questions

In contrast, open questions allow for much longer, detailed, responses and therefore potentially more creativity and information.

There are lots of different types of open question; some are more closed than others!

Open questions prompt a conversation because they cannot be answered with a one-word answer. An example is: "Where do you want to be in five years?" The answer to this question varies from person to person but can only be answered with a unique perspective that prompts a longer conversation.

Open questions prompt the beginning of a longer conversation by asking questions starting with "why," "who," "where." "how," and "what if?"

Closed questions can be answered with single-word answers, such as "yes" or "no."

Asking Open Questions

If at the end of the session, you ask a learner, "Did you find this session helpful?" that's a closed question and they can only answer "yes" or "no."

While it is good to know that they found the session helpful, unless they volunteer some elaboration to their answer, you do not know in what ways they found it helpful. Maybe they are just being polite.

On the other hand, you could ask, "We've been through a bit of a process to get to this point, can you tell me what you have learned by going through this process?"

The learner now has to explain their perception of the process, which helps you to get an even clearer picture of the outcome. In addition, asking the learner about value, it actually helps them reinforce it in their own minds. The net result is you become more preferable to them and reinforce your position in their mind.

Tell, Explain and Describe (TED) Questions

When using probing questions, TED can become your best friend. TED stands for three simple words that will help you get the answers you are looking for: Tell, Explain and Describe.

Some examples could include:

Tell me, how will that affect you?
Tell me, has this happened before?

Tell me, what was your main motivation for calling?
Explain to me, what impact has this had on your...?
Explain to me, how did this situation begin?
Explain to me, what difficulties did you face when you tried to...?
Describe how you felt about that
Describe how it looks
Describe your ideal outcome

TED questions should be used at any moment when you feel as though you have heard something that they would like some more information on. They are used best interjected between open and closed questions."

These probing TED questions help to pinpoint the relevant insight from an employee's open response. The style of wording helps to prompt the employee into giving you all the relevant information in regard to your query.

By starting a question with one of these words, you are essentially demanding an answer from the customer without letting them know that you are.

However, the key point Is listening - There is absolutely no point asking questions if we are not prepared to listen.

Leading or 'Loaded' Questions

A leading question subtly, points the response in a certain direction.

Asking a learner, 'How are you getting on with the new operating system?' prompts the person to query how they are managing with a new operating system. In a very subtle way, it raises the prospect that maybe they are not finding the new system quite so good.

'Tell me how you're getting on with the new operating system' is a less leading question – the question does not require any judgement to be made and therefore does not imply that there may be something wrong with the new system.

Children are particularly susceptible to leading questions and are more likely to take the lead for an answer from an adult. Something simple like, 'Did you have a good day at school?' points the child towards thinking about good things that happened at school. By asking, 'How was school today?' you are not asking for any judgement about how good or bad the day has been, and you are more likely to get a more balanced, accurate answer.

This can shape the rest of the conversation, the next question may be, 'What did you do at school?' - the answer to this may vary based on the first question you asked – good things or just things.

Recall and Process Questions

Questions can also be classified into 'recall' – requiring something to be remembered or recalled, or 'process' – requiring deeper thought and/or analysis.

A simple recall question is, 'What is your mother's maiden name?'. This requires the recall of information from memory, a fact.

A tutor may ask recall questions of their learners, 'What is the highest mountain?' Process questions require more thought and analysis and/or a sharing of opinion. Examples include, 'What skills can you bring to this organisation that the other applicants cannot?' or 'What are the advantages and disadvantages of asking leading questions to children?'

Rhetorical Questions

Rhetorical questions are often humorous and do not require an answer.

'If you set out to fail and then succeed have you failed or succeeded?'

Rhetorical questions are often used by tutors to get the learners to think – rhetorical questions are, by design, used to promote thought.

Politicians, lecturers, tutors and others may use rhetorical questions when speaking to large audiences to help keep their attention. 'Who would not hope to stay healthy into old age?', is not a question that requires an answer, but our brains are programmed to think about it thus keeping us more engaged with the speaker.

Funnelling

Questioning can be used to funnel the respondent's answers –asking a series of questions that become more (or less) restrictive at each step, starting with open questions and ending with closed questions or vice-versa.

For example:

- *"Tell me about your most recent holiday."*
- *"What did you see while you were there?"*
- *"Were there any good restaurants?"*
- *"Did you try some local delicacies?"*
- *"Did you try the Clam Chowder?"*

The questions become more restrictive, starting with open questions which allow for very broad answers, but at each step, the questions become more focused and the answers become more restrictive.

Funnelling can also work the other way around, starting with closed questions and working up to more open questions.

A counsellor or interrogator might use these funnelling techniques to find out the maximum amount of information, by beginning with open questions and then working towards more closed questions. In contrast, when meeting somebody new it is common to start by asking more closed questions and progressing to open questions as both parties relax.

Responses to questions

Given there are so many question types, there are equally many types of response. Theorists have tried to define the types of responses that people may have to questions, the main and most important ones are:

> ***A direct and honest response*** *–what the questioner would usually want to achieve from asking their question.*
>
> ***A lie*** *– the respondent may lie in response to a question. The questioner may be able to pick up on a lie based on plausibility of the answer, but also on the non-verbal communication that was used immediately before, during and after the answer is given.*
>
> ***Out of context*** *– The respondent's answer may be totally unconnected or irrelevant to the question or they may attempt to change the topic. It may be appropriate to reword a question in these cases.*
>
> ***Partially Answering*** *– Respondents may be selective about which questions or parts of questions they wish to answer. Think about politicians!*
>
> ***Avoiding the answer*** *– Politicians are also well known for this trait. When asked a 'difficult question' which probably has an answer that would not be good for them or their political party, avoidance can be a useful tact. Answering a question with a question or responding to some positive aspect of the topic are methods of avoidance.*
>
> ***Stalling*** *– Although similar to avoidance, stalling can be used when more time is needed to think of an acceptable answer. One way to do this is to answer the question with another question.*
>
> ***Distortion*** *– People can give answers to questions based on their perceptions of social norms, stereotypes and other forms of bias. This results in a response which is distorted form the truth, but is different from lying. Respondents may not realise their*

answers are influenced by bias or they exaggerate in some way to come across as more 'normal' or successful. People often exaggerate about their salaries.

Refusal – *The respondent may simply refuse to answer, either by remaining silent or by saying, 'I am not answering'.*

Maintaining Learning Momentum

Momentum in learning delivery can be difficult to maintain when the session is heavily theory based or the session is nearing its conclusion. Hunger, fatigue, tiredness, heat or cold can all constrain learner attention and focus meaning that tutors find themselves talking to a row of cabbages rather than a group of ardent learners who are anxious and keen to learn!

All sessions of delivery should be punctuated with engaging activities such as group work, watching a video, completing a quiz, playing games, etc. This not only provides a break from the direct learning process, but it can also help underpin the learning which has been experienced.

Try to include activities which engage the learners in the learning outcome or objective which is being worked upon.

Try to anticipate the questions which learners may ask. A tutor will be expected to answer any questions thrown at them. By thinking ahead about the questions which are likely to be asked, responses can be prepared and supporting examples which may underpin or further explain can be prepared.

When a question is asked which may distract from the learning being delivered, urban myths are often used to challenge the learning being presented, do not attempt to answer the question at that time, but rather defer it until the next break when you can speak to the learner on a one-to-one basis and address the issue they have raised directly.

There may also be a situation when a question is asked and the answer is unknown. There is an inclination to try and answer the question, however, the response may well be unconvincing for the learner and they may choose to come back with further questions, This effectively undermines the tutor and leaves others questioning the validity of the response. It is often better to be open and honest and say the correct answer is unknown but that research will be undertaken and findings reported back. This allows the tutor to find an answer which provides a comprehensive response which can then be sent, subsequently, to all members of the session along with any justifications or critique.

As each learning objective is addressed, the learning based on that objective should be reinforced by recapping what has been discussed and likewise, when completing a learning outcome, the key point relating to that outcome should be reiterated and reinforced before learners are invited to ask any further questions before moving on to the next outcome.

Assessing Learning

Assessment should be built into the design of the session

Learning should be checked at every stage in the delivery process, this is known as formative assessment and there is usually a need for summative assessment at the end of the session.

Types of assessment

	Formative Assessment	Summative Assessment
Informal	*Questioning* *Feedback* *Peer assessment* *Self-assessment*	*Essays in uncontrolled conditions* *Portfolios* *Coursework* *Tutor assessment*
Formal	*Further analysis or tests, exams, essays* *Target setting*	*Tests* *Exams* *Essay in controlled conditions*

A significant factor in adult learning compared to the way children learn, is that the adults desire to achieve, is a key motivational factor in their learning and that they will actively seek to fill the gaps in their knowledge. It is important to encourage them to identify those gaps and act upon them.

There are typically five stages in the assessment process.

> ***Questioning*** – *enables the learner, with the support of the tutor, to identify the level they are at*
> ***Feedback*** – *The tutor provides feedback to the learner has to how they can improve their learning*
> ***Recognition*** – *learners recognise what successful work looks like for each task they are doing*
> ***Formative Assessment*** – *Learners become more independent and use self-assessment and peer assessment*
> ***Summative assessment*** – *Examination papers or portfolios are used to help them improve.*

The apprenticeship programme is based on assessment – throughout the period of study learners will be subject to a variety of formal and informal assessment activities which may be formative or summative as detailed in the table above. Any of these assessments and the information they generate can be used to assess learner performance which can then be used to adapt teaching and learning outcomes, which in turn leads to an improvement in learner outcomes.

A group of learners who undertake a quick quiz at the end of a session all score reasonably well, but a significant proportion of them get question 7 wrong. By gathering and analysing this information, the tutor is immediately aware that the learning which took place around the subject of question 7 was inadequate and needs remediation. There is a clear gap in the learners knowledge which may well prevent them from understanding the next learning outcome if they are related.

Formal examinations are sometimes required in order to progress from one qualification to another. Given that these are summative assessments (at the conclusion of the programme) the feedback they generate can be used to develop programmes but this is only delivered in the longer term and for the learner who failed the examination it is too late.

This is why formative assessment is beneficial as it is current and live, but integrating summative assessment at the end of teaching session or a training day can also provide immediate feedback which can be worked upon and weaknesses corrected at the next session.

The greatest value from any form of assessment is the feedback it creates. The important thing to remember is that the learner needs to receive, understand and act upon the feedback they receive. When they submit work for assessment, they are only interested in the grade they receive – not the feedback that grade is accompanied by. It is for this reason that the grading of learner work is no longer a common practice.

It is important to encourage learners to reflect on the feedback they receive. It highlights not how well or badly they have performed, but rather what they need to do to improve further. If a learner scores 6/10 on a quiz – it is not the questions they got right which matter, but rather the ones they got wrong. They must be encouraged to ask themselves why they got the question wrong. The tutor knows their answer is wrong, but they don't know why the learner got it wrong!! Only the learner knows the why and until they share that information with the tutor, they will not get it right!

Feedback

Feedback is a two-way street. It is common for tutors to provide feedback to learners when assessing or marking work and it is now commonplace for training providers to issue "happy sheets" to learners for them to feedback about the learning experience they have encountered.

There can be no improvement without feedback.

Delivering feedback

It is often the case that a few notes at the end of piece of work submitted by a learner is deemed sufficient to constitute feedback, yet this could not be further from the truth. If feedback is not carefully considered, it could be considered as being criticism and result in the negative connotations it invokes.

Feedback is being "streamed" to learners continuously during every interaction. It is being delivered by the interaction which exists between the learner and the tutor, whether verbal, written or non-verbal. A dismissive response to a question delivers negative feedback. A critical comment at the end of a marked essay delivers negative feedback and making fun of an incorrect response can humiliate a learner, breeding negativity.

This does not mean that feedback cannot be critical or have a tendency towards negativity if the quality of work is inadequate. The feedback should be in context, collaborative and constructive.

It is vital when giving feedback to learners to make it so that it is useful to them. Delivering constructive feedback is an important element of effective communication.

There are a number of feedback models which can help ensure that the feedback delivered is constructive and effective.

STAR feedback model

An effective model is known as the STAR model. The purpose of this model is to help visualise a pattern of giving good positive feedback and encouraging individuals to take initiative and complete their tasks efficiently.

If you visualise a star, much like the one in the image, you can divide that star into three sections. the top point of the star, the left two-star points, and the right two-star points. The top point represents the situation or task at hand. the left two points refer to the action that was taken, and the right two points stand for the result of that action.

ST – The Situation or Task

The first part of being able to interpret and use feedback given is to understand the situation or task. What happened that means you need to deliver feedback? In order to be able to determine the sort of feedback that is appropriate, take a minute to think about what happened and what the consequence may be. By defining the situation or task that occurred, it pinpoints exactly what it is that needs to be addressed with the individual to whom you are providing feedback. For example, a situation might involve a learner who has not answered a question correctly. It is easy for a tutor to become frustrated if the learner still does not understand the subject after considerable effort. The key is to consider why they don't understand it.

A – The Action

What action was taken? Was that action good or bad? What action should have been taken? It is important to identify the action involved with the situation. When the outcome you are reviewing was positive, note that it was positive. When the outcome was negative, explain first what should have happened. In this example, ask the learner why they answered the way they did. Having established the reason it then becomes clear how to address the problem and this can be explained to the learner.

R – The Results
After the questioning and explanation reassess the situation by asking further questions around the same subject to ensure the learner has truly grasped the concept.

When providing a learner with feedback using the STAR model, put everything together and deliver the feedback. For example, the following might be said when giving feedback using this model:

> *You answered the questions about the new process incorrectly. When asked why that was the case you explained that you did understand the relationship between the two processes. I explained them to you and when I asked further questions you answered them all correctly and it is now clear that you have a good understanding of the process*

By acknowledging the situation, identifying the action, and praising the results, it is likely that in future the learner will think about their response carefully before they answer and ask questions inn areas where they are unsure.

CORBS feedback model

The principles of CORBS feedback model are as follows:

- ***Clear statement*** – *give clear and concise information.*
- ***Owned by the person speaking*** – *your own perception, not the ultimate truth. How it made you feel. Use terms such as "I find" or "I felt" and not "You are".*
- ***Regular*** – *give immediately or as close to the event as possible. NEVER delay*
- ***Balanced*** – *balance negative and positive feedback. DO NOT overload with negative feedback.*
- ***Specific*** – *base your feedback on observable behaviour. Behaviours that the recipient can change.*

CORBS

- Clear
- Owned
- Regular
- Balanced
- Specific

Situation, Behaviour, Impact Model

The Situation – Behaviour – Impact (SBI) Feedback tool helps deliver more effective feedback. It focuses the feedback on specific situations and behaviours, and then considers the impact that these behaviours have on others.

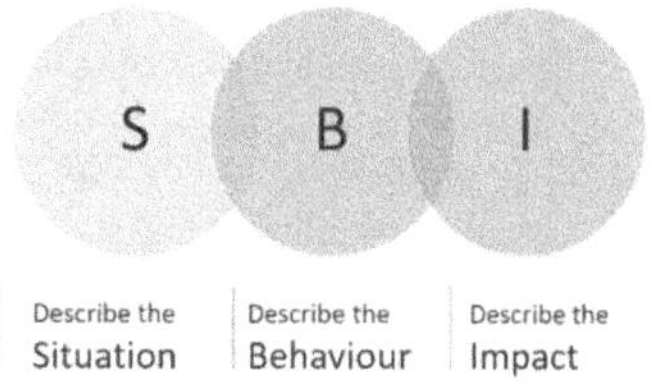

S B I

Describe the Situation | Describe the Behaviour | Describe the Impact

The SBI Feedback Tool outlines a simple structure that can be used to give feedback:

1. ***Situation.***
2. ***Behaviour.***
3. ***Impact.***

When feedback is structured this way, learners will understand precisely what is being commented on, and why. By outline the impact of what they have done, they are being given a chance to reflect on their actions and think about what they need to change. The tool also helps to avoid making assumptions that could upset the other person and damage your relationship with them.

Applying the Tool

1. Situation

When giving feedback, first define the where and when of the situation being referred to. This puts the feedback into context and gives the other person a specific setting as a reference.

2. Behaviour

The next step is to describe the specific behaviours being dealt with. This is the most challenging part of the process because only the observed behaviours should be considered – do not make assumptions.

Any assumptions could be wrong and this will undermine the feedback.

For example, if a learner could not complete a task, do not assume that they had not prepared thoroughly. Simply comment that they have made mistakes – and, ideally, note what the mistakes were.

Do not rely on hearsay or gossip, as this may contain other people's judgments and/or assumptions. Again, this could undermine the feedback and jeopardise the relationship.

Aim to use measurable information in the description of the behaviour. This helps to ensure that comments are unbiassed.

3. Impact

The last step is to use "I" statements to describe how the other person's action has affected themselves or others.

For example:

- *"In the group session all your research was correct, and each of the assessors questions were answered. I am proud that you did such an excellent job preparing and putting yourself in a good light. Keep up the great work!"*

Next Steps

Once you have delivered your feedback, encourage the other person to think about the situation and to understand the impact of their behaviour. Allow the other person time to absorb what you have said, and then go over specific actions that will help them to improve.

Pendleton's Model of feedback

Pendleton's Rules are structured in such a way that the positives are highlighted first, in order to create a safe environment. Therefore, the learner identifies the positives first.

This is followed by the tutor reinforcing these positives and discussing skills to achieve them.

"What could be done differently?" is then suggested, first by the learner and then by the tutor giving feedback.

The advantage of this method is that the learner's strengths are discussed first. Avoiding a discussion of weaknesses right at the beginning prevents defensiveness and allows reflective behaviour by the learner.

There are some deficiencies in the rules. They create artificiality and rigidity by forcing a discussion of the learner's strengths first. Therefore, an opportunity for an interactive discussion of topics that might be relevant to the learner is lost.

There is also inefficient use of time because the same topic is discussed twice in its entirety: first to discuss the strengths and then the weaknesses.

Phase	*Tutor*	*Learner*
Positive Aspects		Tells what went well
	Complements on what went well	
Areas for Improvement		Tells what went wrong and what could be done better
	Complements on what could be done better	
Action Plan for Improvement		Tells action plan
	Approves action plan with modifications	
Summary		Summarises the key points
	Complements if necessary	

When someone is expecting negative feedback, the discussion of strengths may appear patronising, which makes the feedback more stressful to accept and, perversely, a disproportionate amount of time may be spent discussing strengths to soften the impact of the negatives.

A judgemental tone may also creep into the feedback when "What was done correctly and what was incorrect?" is discussed, which goes against the non-evaluative and formative nature of feedback.

The Value of Constructive Feedback

For feedback to be useful, it needs to be constructive, not destructive. If there are problems and weaknesses that need to be addressed, learners need to be advised of these tactfully and shown how to improve.

Learners can see feedback as criticism and may react negatively. They can become defensive, make excuses, choose not to hear or take the feedback seriously. Destructive or negative feedback that is handled poorly can leave people feeling bad, hopeless and worthless. They can feel they are left without any useful information or ideas on which they can build.

However, learners often respond positively to constructive feedback because it concentrates on, for example:

- ***the individual's needs and abilities*** – *increasing self-awareness and offering them what they need to develop to succeed*
- ***positive messages*** – *providing useful information about performance and how to develop*

- ***being supportive*** – *offering encouragement and developing working relationships and trust*
- ***behaviours and actions rather than the person*** – *making the issues less personal*
- ***helping people to feel valued, respected and engaged in the workplace processes*** **–** *to aid team building and motivation*

Delivering Negative Feedback

Negative feedback does not need to be avoided; it just needs to be handled well. If a tutor only gives positive feedback, people will distrust their judgement after a while, as nobody is perfect and there must be some things that need correction and development. When giving negative feedback, it is useful to use a sandwich technique. For example:

give some positive comments about something that has gone well
deliver the negative feedback tactfully, maybe following the CORBS model
finish with some positive feedback and comments, maybe about the future

This enables the learner to be given the negative comments and end the conversation with an uplifting, positive comment that makes them feel valued and committed to the development.

Gathering Feedback

Feedback on tutor performance is critical if improvements are to be made. Learners should be invited to feedback their thoughts and feelings on how they found the session, the delivery, the resources, etc. These should be provided in confidence. Anonymity is key to the feedback being open and honest. Learners will not respond honestly if they fear that they may be judged on the comments they make, especially if the tutor is required to undertake any form of assessment of their performance.

The feedback received will typically offer a diverse range of opinion and experience. Some feedback will influenced by the learners reaction to events outside the training room, the

content of the session and whether there is a rapport between them and the tutor. Some responses may also be very critical and these may well be unjustified.

It is therefore important to consider the feedback collectively. If 5% of learners claim it was a boring session but 7% claimed it was excellent – it is fair to assume that the extremes should be discounted and most common responses accepted. Conversely if a few people thought the PowerPoint presentation was good, but more felt it was inadequate – it suggests that the presentation requires urgent review.

At the end of the day, the learner may not have any choice over what it is delivered but they should have influence over how it is delivered.

Everyone likes to feel valued and that their opinions matter. People cannot be forced to give feedback, although every effort should be made to follow the organisation's policies and procedures for giving and receiving feedback. As tutors in an ongoing process of developing self-awareness, feedback can be sought from a variety of sources that will help inform performance.

Understanding different feedback mechanisms helps to give insight into:

- *how to maximise the effectiveness of feedback we receive*
- *how to give effective feedback to others – particularly team members*

When giving feedback it is important to consider the person receiving the feedback. If the feedback is positive, it is a good opportunity to give praise and encouragement. This empowers and motivates the team member to continue doing well and not lose focus. They feel valued and respected and will benefit from feeling appreciated and recognised.

When asked to give feedback about someone else, it can be a good idea to only say things that one would say to that person's face. This helps keep comment's objective, fair, valid and useful.

When delivered tactfully, constructive criticism and genuine praise are both valuable and welcome.

There are many different mechanisms for giving feedback, including, for example:

Formal reviews

These provide valuable, organised and focused opportunities for a tutor to have detailed conversations with a line manager. Formal reviews usually start with a performance appraisal form that shows objectives, comments and maybe a rating system.

Informal feedback during work activities

Informal feedback can be given at any time – e.g., at the end of a planned programme, at the end of a short development session, or when something good or bad happens.

Opportunities to give informal feedback are usually unplanned and can just be a quick chat, a passing comment, or a spontaneous note or email.

Feedback from peers

Tutors can ask their peers to observe a session and give feedback. It can be useful to have feedback from people who perform a similar task and who can, for example:

- *understand the work environment and requirements*
- *understand how to do the tasks being discussed*
- *give valuable and appropriate information that can be used to make future improvements*

The feedback needs to be given carefully and tactfully and can be formal or informal.

Formal feedback from learners or other stakeholders

This can occur when learners, their line managers or employers are asked to give feedback. The information is usually collected on questionnaires, forms or in surveys.

Informal feedback from learners or other stakeholders

Learners or other stakeholders can decide to give spontaneous, informal feedback, verbally or in writing. This could be praise from a learner, or a complaints from a line manager about the lack of improvement in performance.

It is important to look at the feedback in detail and be objective about the comments. Some feedback will be reliable, useful and easily interpreted. Good-quality feedback is likely to be based on good knowledge about:

the individual
the workplace
observation of performance
the desired standards and expectations

This means that the results can be interpreted as being valid and truthful. This gives an honest review of performance and the recipient can be:

be positive about the feedback – *positive feedback is great for confidence and morale, and negative feedback is useful*
learn from the issues that need to be improved – *and appreciate the opportunity to learn something about their performance they might not have seen before*
enjoy and accept praise

take confidence from positive comments *– they are a guide that things are going well and need to continue to the same high standard*

Remember:

Some feedback is not reliable, however, due to the inexperience of some of those taking part. There may be emotional and over-critical comments from some people due to personal reasons, which may not be honest, valid or useful. For example, customers sometimes leave feedback that is biased, emotional and subjective. When this happens, it is important to interpret the feedback in context, check facts very carefully and look for useful and valid information that can be used as a guide for improving performance.

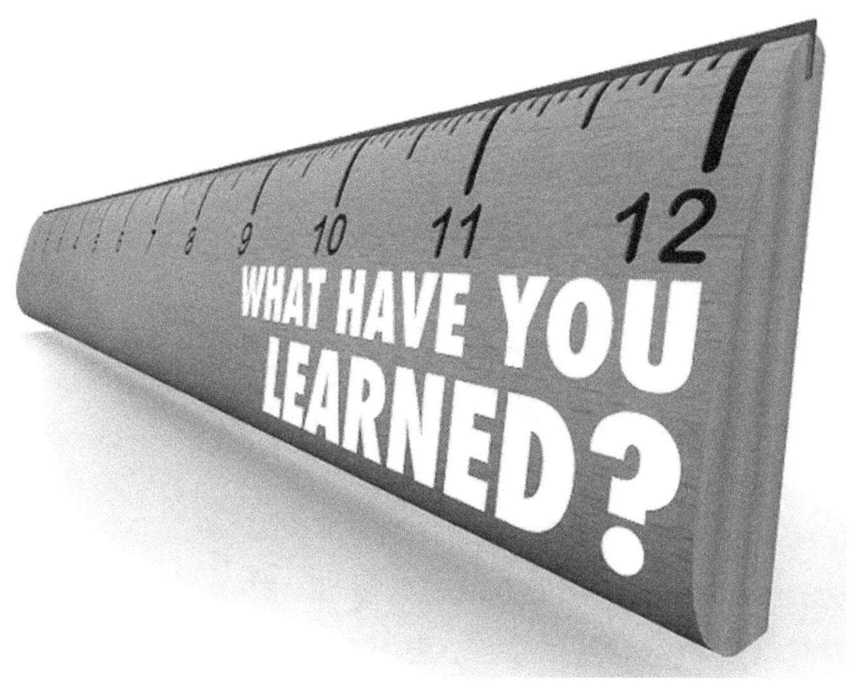

Chapter 9: Assessing Learning

Assessment of Learning

The assessment of learning takes place at the end of the learning cycle and although there is only one step dealing with evaluation, this actually represents a two-stage process. There is the assessment of learning and the evaluation of training. The latter will be dealt with in the next chapter.

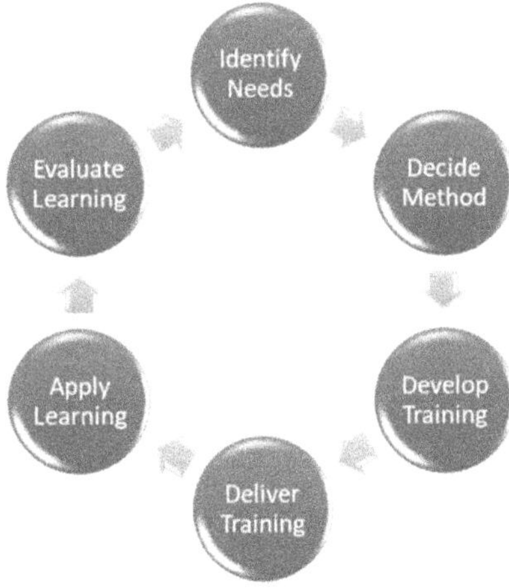

The assessment of learning actually takes place throughout the development process but in different forms and for different reasons.

Assessment of learning is simply another tool in the practitioner's toolbox.

Assessment is used to measure the knowledge which a learner has gained. The successful completion of an assessment suggest that a learner is ready to move on to the next module or level of learning. Assessment also provides learners with an opportunity to recognise the progress they have made and what they have learnt so far.

If you don't plan for and carry out any assessment with your learners, you will not know how well, or what they have learnt.

Assessment *is of the learners whilst* Evaluation *is of the programme.*

Principles of Assessment

The term "Principles of assessment" refers to how the assessment process should be implemented. There are two key principles which must be applied to every assessment. These are known by their acronyms, VARCS and SMART. VARCS should not be confused with the learning style known as VARK!

When Planning assessment activities the SMART technique should be applied to the assessment design in the same way it is applied when setting objectives. This will ensure all the required learning objectives included in the assessment will be met, providing the learner has achieved the required level of knowledge, skills and behaviours at the time of assessment.

- ***Specific*** – *the activity relates only to the objectives being assessed and is clearly defined.*
- ***Measurable*** – *the assessment activity can be measured against the defined requirements of the assessment, allowing any gaps to be readily identified.*
- ***Achievable*** – *the activity is appropriate and is set at the right level.*
- ***Relevant*** – *the activity is fit for purpose, is realistic and relates directly to what is being assessed and will deliver consistent results.*
- ***Time bound*** – *assignment and submission dates are clearly defined.*

VARCS is used to ensure the integrity of the assessment. Applying VARCS to each assessment will ensure the integrity of the assessment and ensure the process and assessment outcome is correct and valid.

The **VARCS** acronym stands for:

- ***Valid*** – *the work submitted is relevant to the objectives if the assessment and is at the correct level.*
- ***Authentic*** – *the work submitted is solely the product of the learner.*
- ***Reliable*** – *the work submitted is consistent over a period of time.*
- ***Current*** – *the work is relevant and appropriate at the time of assessment.*
- ***Sufficient*** – *the work covers all of the requirements defined in the assessment.*

These five questions should be asked of every assessment which is undertaken.

The assessment process should always be:

- ***ethical:*** *the methods used should be appropriate, right and proper for what is being assessed and also the context of assessment. The learner's welfare, health, safety and security must not be compromised by the assessment.*

- ***safe:*** *the authenticity of the learner's submission must be confirmed using VARCS. Plagiarism should be checked for and the confidentiality of information it contains should be considered. The assessment process should not be compromised in any way, nor the learner's potential to achieve. Safe in this context does not relate to health and safety, but rather, to whether the assessment is robust enough to make a reliable decision.*
- ***fair:*** *the methods of assessment used are appropriate for all learners and are set at the right level and consider any particular needs. Every learner should have an equal chance of a fair and accurate assessment decision.*

Assessment Methods

When planning the development activity, great care was taken to break down the development into Learning Aims, Learning Outcomes and Learning Objectives. The learning aims are the goals which the development seeks to achieve, whilst the learning outcomes break the learning down into workable sized elements and the objectives define what the delivery must cover. The evaluation of learning will measure the achievement of the learning aims and will be dealt with in the next chapter. The assessment of learning will measure whether the learning outcomes and learning objectives have been met.

There are four key stages in the assessment process and it is important to know and recognise the importance of each stage. These are:

- *Diagnostic*
- *Formative*
- *Interim*
- *Summative*

Without assessment, it is not possible to establish whether learning is necessary, whether it has taken place and how much knowledge has been gained.

Diagnostic assessment

A diagnostic assessment is used at the start of the any development activity to establish the knowledge the learner already has. You will recall the way adults learn is to build on past knowledge and experiences to create new, wider and deeper understanding of the subject. Rather than being referred to as assessment **of** learning, this might be better considered as assessment **for** learning as it precedes the development activity.

A builder cannot lay the next brick in a wall if the one below it is insecure – the same applies to learning.

Common assessment methods at this stage include:

- *Pre-tests*
- *Survey*
- *Checklist*
- *Observation*
- *Self-evaluation*
- *Interview*

Formative assessment

A formative assessment is used during the delivery of learning to establish that the defined learning objectives are being met. The use of formative assessments provides feedback to practitioners on the progress being made by each learner and allows support to provided quickly and effectively to those who need it, to ensure they continue to progress in live with the rest of the group. More importantly when teaching adults, it helps learners to identify their strengths and weaknesses and target the areas which need development themselves.

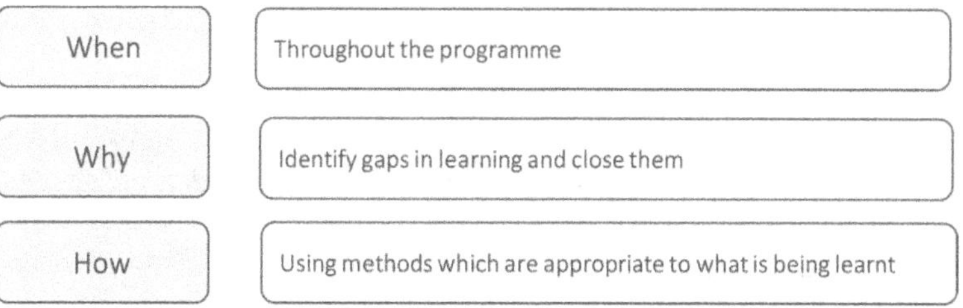

Typically, formative assessment will be used to measure whether the learner has learned and understood the knowledge defined by the learning objectives. The learning which has taken place in a session which is designed to achieve four linked learning objectives could be measured using formative assessment in the form of a test, Q&A with a tutor, discussion with peers, etc.

Formative assessment might be tutor led, peer led or by self-assessment. These types of assessment are rarely given a grade as they apply only to a small number of learning objectives and the award of a mark could be counter-productive in terms of learner engagement.

To engage leaners in formative assessment, it is important to:

- ***Explain the rationale behind the assessment.***
- ***Emphasise the importance of gaining experience at this level***
- ***Design formative assessment to contribute to the summative assessment***

- *Explain the link between the formative and summative assessment*
- *Increase the number of formative assessments and reduce the number of summative assessments*

Common assessment methods at this stage include:

- *Group activity*
- *Practice*
- *Reflection*
- *Question and Answer*
- *Peer-Evaluation*
- *Tutor feedback*
- *Self-evaluation*
- *Quizzes*
- *Polls*
- *Observation*
- *Worksheets*

Good practice in Formative assessment

- *Define what constitutes good performance*
- *Encourage learners to reflect*
- *Provide detailed, constructive, actionable feedback*
- *Encourage tutor and peer dialogue*
- *Encourage positivity*
- *Provides the opportunity to close the gap between current and desired performance*
- *Analyse assessment to develop learning delivery*

Interim assessment

Interim assessments are used to assess the progress of an entire cohort of learners to identify the gap between the highest and lowest achievement levels and can facilitate the delivery of remedial or repeated development to bring the weaker learners to the same level as others before the continuing the progression for all. Interim assessment is seldom used outside a formal learning environment as it can be time consuming and place a heavy demand on time.

Summative assessment

Summative assessment is used at the end of the development program or at the end of a module within it. This is used to ensure learning has been completed and knowledge consolidated before moving on to a new subject area. Because the assessment focusses holistically on the subject of study, the feedback provided to the learner is limited, unless the tutor provides additional, constructive feedback.

Assessing Learning

Given that the achievement of the learning objectives will have been assessed by the formative assessments the learning outcomes will be assessed by the summative assessment. Summative assessment is designed to measure if the learner is able to apply the knowledge thy have learnt and apply it to problems, situations, tasks, etc. According to Bloom, are they able to synthesise their own evaluation and solution to the problem they face.

When	At the end of the programme
Why	Gather evidence of learner's Knowledge, Skills and Behaviours
How	Examination, end point assessment, cumulative assessment

Common assessment methods at this stage include:

- ***Tests / Examinations*** – *useful for evaluating learning in terms of knowledge retention and application it application to ideas, concepts and scenarios. Less effective in assessing the ability to analyse, evaluate or create things which relate to learning*
- ***Assignment*** – *useful for assessing knowledge retention and encourages the application of knowledge to suggested concepts and scenarios. Allows the freedom for learners to express thoughts and ideas and demonstrate understanding.*
- ***Presentation*** – *allows the learner to present the results of their work by speaking and presenting to the tutor, peers and others. An effective tool for assessing the learners ability to critically analyse a topic*
- ***Work product*** – *allows the learner to demonstrate their skills and competences in a specific technique or techniques.*
- ***Portfolio*** – *Completed over a period of time, portfolios are particularly useful for assessing how student's learning, attitudes and beliefs have developed over the programme*
- ***KPI metrics*** – *learner performance against pre-defined metrics can also be used as a summative assessment tool. These can be used to measure performance prior to development with the results achieved after development. Effective in assessing the changes in the application of skills and the impact on behaviours*

Good practice in Summative assessment

- ***Create a marking scheme or rubric***
- ***Ensure questions are clear, effective and unambiguous***
- ***Check coverage of learning aims and objectives***
- ***Define the parameters of assessment*** – *word count, number of examples, etc*

Summary of Assessment Methods

Formative (informal) assessment tools	*Summative (formal) assessment tools*
• *Case studies*	• *Assignments*
• *Crosswords*	• *Dissertation*
• *Discussions*	• *Essays*
• *Journals/Diaries*	• *Examinations*
• *Peer assessment*	• *Learner Presentations*
• *Puzzles*	• *Showcase portfolio*
• *Practical Activities*	• *Multiple choice questions*
• *Projects*	• *Observations*
• *Quizzes*	• *Professional discussions*
• *Role play*	• *Review or evidence*
• *Self-assessment*	• *Tests*
• *Simulation*	• *Witness testimony*
• *Word search*	• *Written questions*
• *Worksheets*	• *Written statements*

Online Assessment Methods

The range and scope of assessment is virtually limitless; however, the suitability of assessment is the key. Skills development cannot be realistically assessed by a leaner writing an essay – they need to be able to demonstrate the skill. Similarly, knowledge cannot be truly assessed by using a practical activity as a single activity will not encompass and evidence all of the knowledge needed. Furthermore, whilst there is still the need for formal examinations and assessments to take place, there are an increasing number of online tools which can be used to conduct assessment which are much more readily accepted by learners today. These include:

- ***Mentimeter***
- ***Socrative***
- ***ASSISTments***
- ***Moodle***
- ***Flip***
- ***Edutastic***
- ***Formative***
- ***Quizlet***

Assessment for Learning (AfL)

A more recent development in the assessment of learning has been the concept of Assessment for Learning.

AfL helps learners understand what excellence looks like and how they can develop their own performance to achieve it.

It is proven that feedback is implicit in learner success. Learners have been shown to learn at twice the rate of their peers when AfL is applied.

When considering the theory of learning, consideration was given to metacognition or "thinking about thinking". The theory asserts that learners need to reflect on their own learning in order to identify how they learn best and to interpret new knowledge and skills and then conceptualise the understanding they have gained, the use of feedback stimulates that thinking process.

Not only does AfL improve learner outcomes, it also helps build confidence. By providing feedback, which is specific to the learning objective, the learners general capability is not question, but rather their knowledge or understanding of the specific objective. By sharing their understanding and ideas around a learning objective or aim, the learner can reinforce their learning by explaining their perception to their peers who may often respond better the their peers explanation than that of the tutor.

AfL also increases learner independence. . They will undertake self-assessment and as a consequence, will take responsibility for the development of their own learning which often translates into a commitment to life-long learning.

In the Seven Myths of Education (2014) it's author – Daisy Christodoulou state the need for tutors to be thermostats rather than thermometers. This implies that tutors should not just take a measurement of learner performance, but make changes depending on where they need to be based on what they achieved. The concept brings together assessment and feedback as a combined tool to increase achievement.

The model asks three questions which are cyclical in nature and design

Where is the learner now?

Where are the learners in terms of the learning aims? By regularly checking where they are up to it becomes straightforward to identify where they are being successful and where support may be needed. Ask the learner to reflect on their own progress and what support they feel they may need. This practice will lead to enhanced reflective skills through their own self-assessment

How can the learner get to where they want to be?

Think how the session could be adapted in order to bring them closer int line with the learning aims. Being responsive to the needs of learners will lead to more effective activities being chosen and the feedback they create will be even more constructive.

Where is the learner going?

This question identifies the goal or target of the session. It is important that the intentions of the session and the criteria for success, are shared with the learners to ensure they have a clear understanding of what they are expected to achieve and what success will look like. The use of jargon should be avoided here as this may hinder their perception of the task.

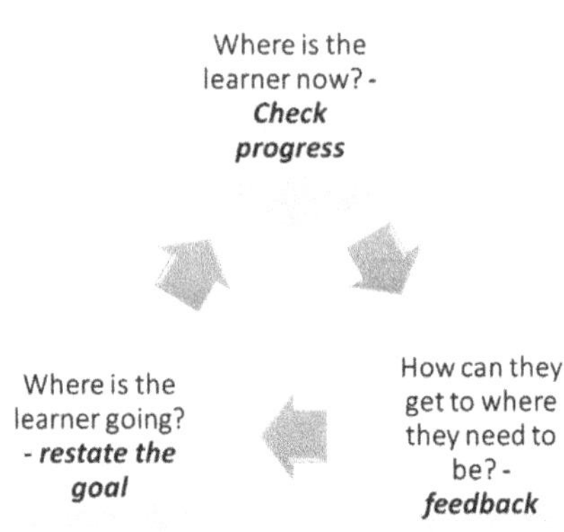

As a teaching approach AfL generates feedback which learners can then use to develop their performance. One of the biggest benefits is that the results are often immediate and the delivery can be changed to make it more effective.

As a result, AfL provides learners with greater control over their learning, helps build motivation and improve performance in summative assessment. The tutor also gain a deeper insight in the level of understanding held by the learner of the particular concept or subject, thereby enabling them to better support the learner.

AfL not only supports feedback – feedback is vital for success. It has been proven that the use of AfL is twice as effective on learner achievement than any other method.

The feedback must be focussed explicitly on the task and should be specific, timely, unbiased and clear for the learner to understand. More important still, the feedback should comprise useable information which the learner can use to improve their performance in order to reach their goal.

Embedding AfL into a session

Embedding AfL is not difficult. A session will start in the normal manner, but after the first learning objective has been covered, there will be an AfL assessment. The tutor will then measure the learning which has taken place and use the results of that assessment reconfigure teaching as necessary to ensure that progress has been made. There will then be a further AfL assessment and the review of delivery will once again take place. This cyclical process will gone on throughout the session, after each AfL the tutor will restate the goal before beginning the next cycle.

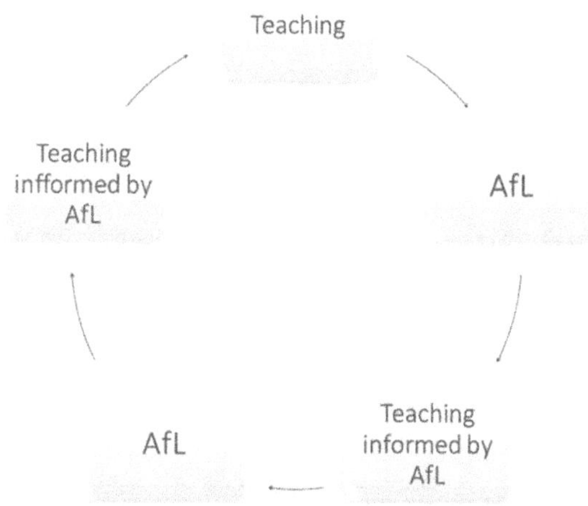

Conducting AfL

AfL does not have to be complex or challenging, in fact, the simpler and more straightforward it is, the clearer the feedback on progress will be.

Questioning

Ask questions which are directly related to the learning objectives. This could be asked of individuals or the entire group. Allow them to discuss the answer amongst themselves whilst listening to the arguments, incorrect answers or misconceptions can then be rectified immediately. By splitting the cohort into groups the tutor can spend time with each group and provide immediate feedback. This is also helpful when supporting retiring learners who are reluctant to speak in front of the whole cohort.

Hinge questions

These are questions which have a right or wrong answer relating to the learning objective. These can be asked of the whole group. These questions can be increased in difficulty until it is clear that not all learners are aware of the correct answer. At this point discussion between the two groups can be used to develop understanding and resolve any misconception until all learners are aligned. Further questions can then be asked to both consolidate and further check for learning.

Two stage tests

This technique requires learners to undertake a test on their own and they can mark their own test using responses from the tutor or from a mark scheme. The learners should then be put into groups and asked to complete the same test, but this time with only one piece of paper, so they must agree their collective answers, promoting peer learning.

Relationship between AfL and Formative and Summative assessment

AfL has always been closely associated with formative assessment because the use of questioning and providing feedback help to form learner knowledge and understanding.

A report published by the National
Foundation for Educational Research (NFER 2007) breaks down both formative and summative assessment into formal and informal methods.

	Formative Assessment	*Summative Assessment*
Informal	Questioning Feedback Peer Assessment Self-Assessment	Essays in uncontrolled conditions Portfolios Coursework Teacher assessment
Formal	Further analysis, tests, examinations Target setting	Tests Exams Essays in controlled conditions

It is clear that the informal formative assessment box is a key part of AfL, however, it could be argued that all of the listed assessment strategies in the table support AfL, given their designated purpose is to help develop learner progress.

Providing feedback on assessment

Feedback is an integral part of the assessment process. Without feedback, assessment has no value. The result of the feedback simply quantifies performance and identifies that development is necessary, however, it does not inform what development is necessary to improve performance. Feedback delivers that information. It allows the learner to understand the scale and scope of the gap between what they have demonstrated they know and understand and that which is expected. It is this explanation which allows the learners to put in place pro-active steps to close the gap and develop their knowledge understanding, skills and behaviours.

Formative feedback

Any feedback which is given to a learner should be meaningful and constructive, whether the feedback is good or bad. Formative feedback is the basis for improvement and must clearly identify how improvements can be made.

Do:

- *Select only the main points for comment – nothing more*
- *Focus the feedback on the learning objectives*
- *Ensure there is balance between the good and the bad*
- *Return the assessment as quickly as possible*
- *Provide immediate response to any questions*
- *Correct any misconceptions immediately*
- *Always record feedback in writing*
- *Provide verbal feedback for SEND learners*
- *Ensure the feedback is specific to the individual*
- *Only provide group feedback if it applies to all*
- *Comment on the strengths and weaknesses of performance*
- *Detail how the assessment could be improved*
- *Avoid personal comments*
- *Assess the work against a standard*
- *Be positive*

Do NOT

- *Correct every error*
- *Write a long list of feedback comments*
- *Write long feedback on poor work and short feedback on good work – the good work could still be better!*
- *Hold onto work after submission*
- *Ignore mistakes of misconceptions*

- *Do not provide feedback if delivery of the subject matter has completed – they cannot correct it*
- *Provide verbal feedback only*
- *Use the same comments for all or similar work standards*
- *Never give individual feedback – too time consuming*
- *Make the feedback impersonal*
- *Criticise without explaining how to improve*
- *Make personal comments*
- *Post reports which allow learners to compare self against others*
- *Give feedback of a general nature*
- *State that work is good or bad*
- *Grade work is for formative use*
- *Punish learners for poor performance*

Summative feedback

Whilst summative assessment is used far less frequently that formative, the feedback provided must be just as valuable as that provided for the formative assessments.

Summative assessment should be used to deliver a rounded summation of learning and should be linked to the formative assessment feedback provided earlier.

Summative feedback should reflect the final learning outcome and how this aligns with the Learning Aims defined in the programme.

The assessment tools used to inform the summative feedback can include, essays, examination, projects, portfolios, etc. These should be very carefully designed to ensure that all necessary objectives and aims are covered by the assessment and that each is examined at the appropriate level and depth. The use of portfolios as an assessment tool combines the use of formative assessment and feedback as the portfolio is built up from evidence and assessments gathered across the duration of the programme.

The results of summative assessment can then be used to evaluate whether changes or development are necessary to the content and structure of the programme or whether the standard of teaching practice is in need of review.

Feed Forward

Feedback has long been a part of the assessment process, however, more recent thinking has started to focus on Feed Forward.

Whilst feedback focusses on what has been achieved, or has not been achieved, what was unsatisfactory and where the learner evidenced weakness it focusses on the past and things which cannot be easily changed.

Feed Forward uses the benefits of hindsight and past experience to encourage forward planning by the learner to avoid the mistakes which have been experienced previously and put in place a plan to eliminate them and be proactive in the preparation for the next assessment.

This could constitute planning for assessment earlier, widening and deepening the level of research which will be undertaken and applying time management techniques to the planning process.

Feed Forward provides valuable guidance to learners how to avoid past mistakes and effectively prepare for the next assessment.

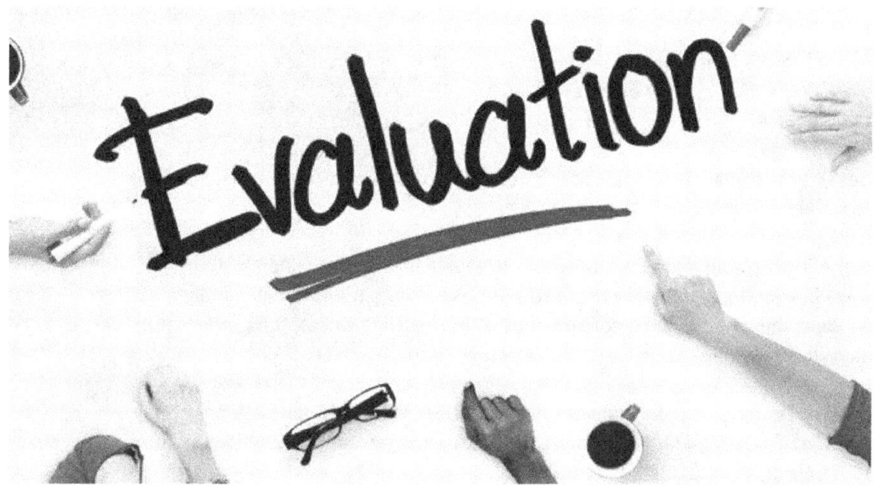

Chapter 10: Evaluating Learning and Development

Evaluation of Learning and Development

The evaluation of learning and development is quite different to the evaluation of learning.

The evaluation of Learning and Development enables organisations to assess whether the development activities they offer, actually meet the needs which prompted there creation in the first place.

The result of the evaluation are used to develop programmes or terminate them if they prove to be ineffective.

The benefits of training are considerable. It enables the review of programmes to identify any gaps in knowledge delivery the result of post activity quizzes may highlight gaps in knowledge which needs to be corrected by either revising the existing programme or developing a new one.

Effective development programmes save a business significant amounts of money, however, poorly designed programmes can cost an organisation a significant amount without delivering any tangible benefits.

Without evaluating a programme, its true value will not be known. It will be unclear whether the true potential of the programme is being realised or whether it is failing in its planned use.

It has been stated many times in this publication, that the delivery of development without an identified need is a complete waste of money and a futile exercise.

Think back to the earlier chapters and you will recall that the Learning and Development Needs analysis was based on the needs of the business and what development was necessary to achieve those Learning Aims.

The learning outcomes and learning objectives were related to the learner and have been assessed at the conclusion of the training. It is now time to assess Whether the learning aims have been met by evaluating the impact of the learning and development which has been provided.

The first question being asked is how did the development affect the business? This, of course, is the principal reason for undertaking the training in the first place.

The evaluation of training provides invaluable feedback on the value of the development activity and its effectivity in supporting the achievement of the business goals. It will also allow the analysis of any additional or remedial training which may be required to further close and remaining skills gaps.

Additionally it will also allow the assessment of:

- *issues and improve the overall processes of training programs*
- *analyse the effectivity of training materials and delivery methods*

- *identify the need for further development*
- *assess the overall impact of the development on the business*

When should evaluation take place?

The evaluation of development is dependent on a variety of factors including the duration of the activity, the scale and scope of the activity and the degree of importance to the organisation.

Evaluation does not has to be a single stage in a process. Evaluation can take place during the activity, at its conclusion, as short time after or via the organisational appraisal system.

The level of evaluation which also vary depending on the nature of the programme. An activity which is being run for the first time may undergo evaluation form many perspectives and can result in changes to the delivery method, resources used, etc. As a result, further re-evaluation will be needed to ensure that not only the activity, but also the changes will be necessary to assess success. Once a programme has been tried and is known to be effective, the need for evaluation will diminish and may be less far reaching and detailed.

There are a number of tools which can be used to evaluate the development and one of the key models is Kirkpatrick's.

Kirkpatrick's Taxonomy

Kirkpatrick's Taxonomy is widely used across all business sectors as it helps to evaluate the return on the investment made in the development activity and helps to ensure that development activities are both cost effective and time efficient. It was developed by Don Kirkpatrick in the 1950s'

The taxonomy itself has four levels which are as follows. The first two of which are covered at the assessment of learning stage:

> ***Level 1 – Reaction*** – *assesses the learners response to the development – typically measured using a survey form at the conclusion of the activity*
> ***Level 2 – Learning*** – *Measures what the participants have learnt and can be measured using quizzes, test or end of activity assessment.*
> ***Level 3 – Behaviour*** – *Has there been the desired change in behaviour? – This can be measured by observation in the workplace comparing current behaviour compared to past behaviour*
> ***Level 4 – Results*** – *These step evaluates the effects on the participant. The metrics for measuring this will have been defined in the training needs analysis and can be measured through changes in productivity, morale, quality, sales, efficiency and customer satisfaction. This is known as the Return on Expectations (ROE).*

Limitations of the Kirkpatrick Taxonomy

There are two challenges with this model – the first is that people are aware of it, but do not follow the full process. The second is that people agree with its content but fail to apply it correctly.

Whilst the taxonomy is often referred to as a model or theory, it is actually neither as there is no scientific basis within it. Unless it is applied with vigour, it does not tend to create much data which can be used effectively to change the development activity.

There is no evidence that if level one is achieved in full that it will subsequently impact on levels two, three and four. There is no causal link between the first two levels, even though the presentation as a taxonomy suggests there should be.

A common criticism of Kirkpatrick is not the model itself, but rather how it's applied in practice. Organisations generally have processes for evaluating at Levels 1 and 2, but then either don't get around to, or aren't able to, evaluate Levels 3 and 4.

Finally, most organisations are less concerned about the return on expectation (ROE) but are much more interested in the return on Investment (ROI) – in other words – was there a financial benefit gained from undertaking the development activity.

Kaufman's Five Levels of Evaluation

This model builds from Kirkpatrick's model. Kaufman's split the first level in Kirkpatrick models in two grouped levels 2 and 3 together and added a fifth!

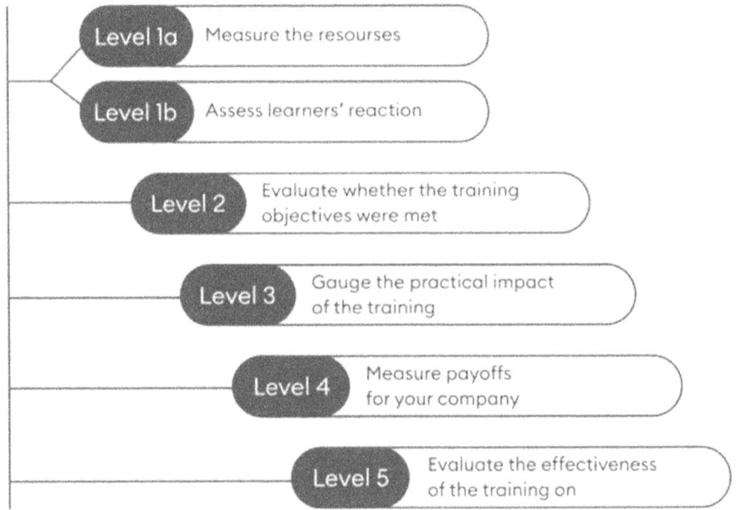

Level 1a Measure the amount of time and money invested in the development activity
Level 1b Assess the participants reaction to the development activity

Level 2 Identify whether the learning objectives were met and therefore asks the question has the new knowledge or skill been achieved?

Level 3 Assess how well the participant applies the new knowledge or skills

Level 4 Measures the benefits for the organisation

Level 5 Measures the benefits to be derived by the wider audience such as clients or society

He further classifies these levels using descriptor for each level.

Kaufman's Levels	*Kirkpatrick Equivalent*	*Kaufman Level's Explanation*
Input	**1a**	*Resource availability and quality. These are training materials, digital resources, etc., used to support the learning experience.*
Process	**2b**	*Process acceptability and efficiency. This is the actual delivery of the learning experience.*
Micro	**2 and 3**	*Individual and small group benefits. This is the result for the "micro-level client" (normally the learner). Did the learner "acquire" the learning? Did he or she apply it on the job?*
Macro	**4**	*Organisational benefits. This is the result for the "macro-level client," the organisation, and includes evaluation of performance improvement and cost benefit/cost consequence analysis.*
Mega	**n/a**	*Societal contributions. This is the result for the "mega-level client," either society as a whole or a company's clientele.*

Clearly, the model is not directly applicable to real life! Measuring the impact training has had on the wider society would be hugely expensive and probably not produce any valuable information. However, this may be beneficial when the development impact activity is delivered to one department and the impact on other departments can be measured.

The CIRO Model

The CIRO model was developed by Warr, Bird and Rackham in 1970. It tends to be more effective when evaluating management training. Like the other models it is hierarchical in structure meaning that each stage must be progressed through in order.

CIRO is an acronym and stands for:

- *Context*
- *Input*
- *Reaction*
- *Output*

It focusses on the measurements taken before and after the development activity.

Stage 1: Context – This uses the results of the Learning and Development Needs Analysis to identify the areas where development is necessary. Once the needs are identified they are prioritised into three levels

- ***The Ultimate objective*** *– defines the identified operational deficiency – such as poor efficiency, low customer satisfaction or poor quality.*
- ***The Intermediate objective*** *– defines the desired change in behaviour necessary to achieve the Ultimate Objective*
- ***The Immediate objective*** *– defines the new skills and knowledge required to deliver the desired change in behaviour*

Stage 2: Input – *Practitioners analyse the available resources to identify the optimum delivery solution to achieve the identified objectives*

Stage 3: Reaction *– Feedback is gathered from participants and analysed to facilitate further improvement / development of the development activity*

Stage 4: Outcome – *Evaluates the development activity at four distinct levels:*

- ***The Learner level***
- ***The Workplace level***
- ***The Team or Department Level***
- ***The Business Level***

A criticism of this model is that it does not consider behaviour. As a consequence it is considered as being more appropriate for management training evaluation rather than those who operate at lower levels in the organisation where behaviour may be more important.

Phillips ROI Model

The author of this theory was Jack Phillips who published in 1980. He set out to address the shortcomings of the Kirkpatrick theory. This model seeks to quantify the return on the investment (ROI) made in the development activity. The model mirrors the Kirkpatrick Model to a degree, but adds a fifth stage which addresses the shortcoming by dealing with the Return on Investment.

> ***Level 1 – Reaction*** *– assesses the learners reaction and satisfaction to the development*
> ***Level 2 – Learning*** *– Measures the Knowledge and Skills participants have gained*
> ***Level 3 – Application*** *– Has there been the desired change in behaviour? Identifies the need for remedial or further development*
> ***Level 4 – Impact*** *– These step evaluates the effects of the development on the organisation. It also seeks to identify if other factors were complicit in the change*
> ***Level 5 – Return on Investment*** *– The uses a cost benefit analysis to compare the cost of the development activity with the quantified benefits to the organisation*

Data is gathered before, during and after the activity and quantifiable factors are identified. Some of these will have been identified as part of the Learning and Development Needs analysis. By identifying these, a comparison can then be made in a Cost Benefit Analysis which will identify the financial impact of the development activity on the organisation.

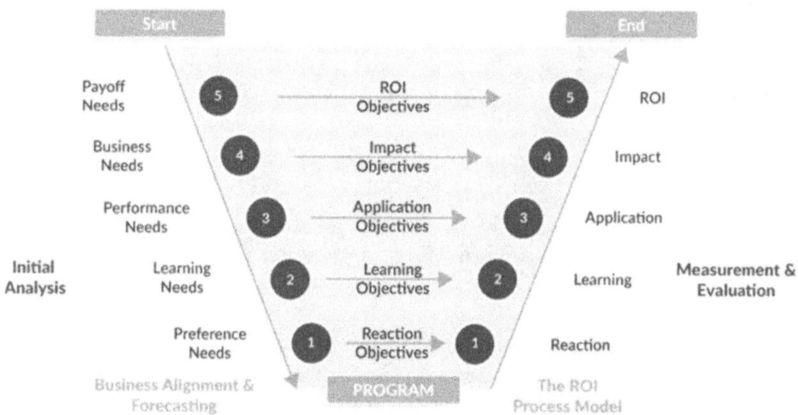

CIPP Model

Developed by Daniel Shufflebeam in the 1960s', it is often also referred to as the Shufflebeam Model. The model is not dissimilar to the CIRO Model.

The acronym stands for:

- *Context*
- *Input*
- *Process*
- *Product*

CIPP is used to evaluate the value of the programme. Kirkpatrick and Phillips tend to evaluate what has been done whilst CIPP focusses on improving what you are doing. This suggest sit may be more beneficial for businesses than others.

The model was later expanded to include:

- *Sustainability*
- *Effectivity*
- *Transportability*

The model aims to link the evaluation to the decision making that is applied in the delivery of the development activity.

Each of the four stages of evaluation above are used to provide an analytical basis for decisions made regarding the programme. These can be grouped into five key areas:

- *Planning*
- *Structuring*
- *Implementing*
- *Reviewing*
- *Revising*

These five criteria create a logical framework for making decisions by asking four questions:

- ***What do we need to do?*** *– Considers the needs, attitudes and perceptions of the business. By gathering and analysing data , it enables the most urgent development needs to be identified*
- ***How should the development be approached?*** *– Prompts research into the best solution to the identified need. Who will deliver it? Where will it be delivered? etc.*
- ***Is the development on track?*** *– Constantly monitors the development activity during its delivery and fine tuning as necessary. Anticipates and identifies problems allowing corrections to be made.*

- ***How successful was the development?*** *– This stage deals with both revising and reviewing. It measure the outcome of the training and helps to determine whether to continue, revise or discontinue the development activity.*

These four questions can be applied at each stage in the CIPP Model and helps to improve the quality of development and identify the best approach to its delivery.

Factors which determine the effectivity of development

From the Learning and Development Needs analysis – it was defined what the root cause of the problem was and also what the resolved situation would be like. The learning aims were developed form this analysis. It is this which can be used to set the metrics for evaluating the development which has taken place and might include:

- *New Skills and Knowledge*
- *The Learning experience*
- *Employee satisfaction*
- *Cultural impact#*
- *Impact on efficiency*
- *Financial impact*

Gathering Data for Evaluation

The Learning and Development Needs Analysis will define what data needs to be gathered at the conclusion of the development activity – the key decision her is how to gather it. There are many ways of gathering feedback but some of the more common ones are listed below.

Questionnaires - *used to gather statistical evidence via a series of questions. Often use at the conclusion of the development activity*
Interviews *– Allows deeper questioning of participants after the activity has completed and therefore provides more detailed information. May be conducted face to face or online.*
Focus Groups *– the is a facilitated discussion among participants . Helps to understand the participants view of the activity and how the activity could be developed in future.*
Observation *– Used to measure behavioural change by observing the participants as they engage with the processes and activities which were covered in the development activity.*

Analysing the Data

The final step in the process is to analyse the data which has been collected and document the findings. The document will then be used as a point of referral in any further development activity where there is overlap between the subject of this activity and any future planned activity.

Alternative Methods for Evaluation

It is clear from the models discussed above, that some are more effective than others and some are better suited to particular environments than others. As a result a number of alternative ways to evaluate development activities have evolved which can be used strategically as and when necessary.

Measure the increase in Knowledge.

The fact that a participant in a development programme has satisfactorily reached the end of the programme does not, in itself, provide any evidence that a change in the level of Knowledge has changed.

The only way to measure this is through a post programme assessment. A quiz could be designed to assess knowledge of the defined learning objectives. Online learning materials will allow ongoing and progressive assessment of knowledge development across the programme.

It is important that participants have the opportunity to discuss their thoughts and concepts with others during the programme to help consolidate their learning and build new knowledge.

Align development with need

The development delivery will only be effective if it meets the needs of the participant and the organisation. It is important to ensure that the knowledge of the participants is established at the start of the programme to avoid wasting time and money. A participant who has a sound knowledge in the subject will not benefit from any development until the level of the activity is equal to their level of knowledge. This means they are wasting time, effort and money, attending a programme which is not relevant to their needs. Likewise, a participant with a very basic level of knowledge may not be able to grasp the initial concept if their knowledge is too low, meaning they are unlikely to gain any new knowledge whilst on the programme because it is above their level of basic understanding. Once again, this will wate time, effort and money.

It may be prudent to offer a tiered level of delivery where the true beginners participate in a basic programme before being joined by others at an intermediate stage with those holding an advanced level of knowledge joining at towards the end of the programme.

Prioritise Satisfaction

Employees are more productive when they are happy. Motivation levels ae higher and loyalty to the organisation is greater. Development is becoming an increasingly common way of enabling employees to achieve more and become more effective in the workplace.

Only employees really know the development they need. Unless there is an explicit need for specific development of employees, all development should be based on the needs of the individual. By being able to select the development activity, employees will gain more form the activity than when they are "sent" on a development activity. The uptake of development activities by employees provides a clear view of what is needed and a programme of developmental activity can be planned from this.

Ensure Currency of Resources

In a fast-changing world, legislation, approved practices and procedures can all change very quickly and where such changes are taking place, development will inevitably be required to ensure that employees are operating at operational standards.

It is therefore important to ensure that every resource is checked to ensure accuracy and currency, both routinely and ahead of programme delivery. A development activity which expounds inaccurate or out of date practices or processes is of no value to the participants and results in the unnecessary waste of money, time and resources.

Return on Investment

It is clear for the models detailed above that the return on investment is a key metric in evaluating the performance of development activity.

It is rare that an activity which is delivered does not impact on the business financially. Whether it is the cost of employees attending the programme, the loss of production during delivery, the cost of developing the programme, the cost of the practitioner delivering it, the costs of hospitality during the delivery and the cost of evaluation can very quickly become a significant sum of money.

It is clear that there must be a financial benefit to the organisation after making the investment in the development. This is known as the Return on Investment (ROI). It is important that the benefits are calculated as accurately as the costs, however, the ways in which the return is measured is often qualitative rather than quantitative. It is therefore more challenging to work out what the benefits are.

When the development need was identified I was a s a result of the identification of the cause of a problem. This is the point where the metrics can be identified.

Suppose an organisation has received a significant number of complaints about the performance of a product it produces. There will be a cost to the business of replacing the faulty item, shipping the faulty item and the loss of both the profit on the item and the cost of the components. This can all be calculated quite readily and fairly easily. What is not so easy to quantify is the level of customer satisfaction. Will the fact that they have purchased an item which proved to be faulty prevent them from buying another one – even though it was replaced? This is where estimation comes int effect. If we anticipate that a person buys four of these items a year and that 50% of the people who purchased a faulty item will not buy the same brand again – we can begin to quantify the effect on future sales as well as the direct costs.

If the development activity were to reduce the failure of the item by 80%, not only would there be a significant reduction in costs, but also a marked increase in sales, because those would buy another brand will remain with this brand because the number of faulty items have been significantly reduced.

The calculation used to calculate the return on Investment is shown below:

$$\text{ROI \%} = \frac{\text{£ Benefit of Development - £ Cost of Training}}{\text{£ Cost of Training}} \text{ X } 100$$

www.ingramcontent.com/pod-product-compliance
Lightning Source LLC
LaVergne TN
LVHW010535100826
845148LV00001B/191

9781789633917